This book details the policy subsystems – links among members of Congress, interest groups, program beneficiaries, and federal and subnational government agencies – that blanket the American political landscape. Robert Stein and Kenneth Bickers have constructed a new data base detailing federal outlays to congressional districts for each federal program, and use it to examine four myths about the impact of policy subsystems on American government and democratic practice. These include the myth that policy subsystems are a major contributor to the federal deficit; that, once created, federal programs grow inexorably and rarely die; that, to garner support for their programs, subsystem actors seek to universalize the geographic scope of program benefits; and that the flow of program benefits to constituencies in congressional districts ensures the reelection of legislators. The authors conclude with an appraisal of proposals for reforming the American political system, including a balanced budget amendment, a presidential line-item veto, term limitations, campaign finance reform, and the reorganization of congressional committees.

PERPETUATING THE PORK BARREL

PERPETUATING THE PORK BARREL

Policy subsystems and American democracy

ROBERT M. STEIN
Rice University

KENNETH N. BICKERS
Indiana University

CAMBRIDGE
UNIVERSITY PRESS

Published by the Press Syndicate of the University of Cambridge
The Pitt Building, Trumpington Street, Cambridge CB2 1RP
40 West 20th Street, New York, NY 10011-4211, USA
10 Stamford Road, Oakleigh, Melbourne 3166, Australia

First published 1995

Printed in the United States of America

Library of Congress Cataloging-in-Publication Data
Stein, Robert M.
Perpetuating the pork barrel : policy subsystems and American
democracy / Robert M. Stein, Kenneth N. Bickers
p. cm.
Includes bibliographical references (p.   ).
ISBN 0-521-48298-4
1. Grants-in-aid – United States. 2. Economic assistance,
Domestic – United States. 3. Budget deficits – United States.
4. Campaign funds – United States. 5. Item veto – United States.
6. United States. Congress – Reform. 7. Democracy – United States.
I. Bickers, Kenneth N., 1960–   . II. Title
HJ275.S728   1995
336.3'9'0973 – dc20   95-858
                                                          CIP

A catalog record for this book is available from the British Library.

ISBN 0-521-48298-4 Hardback

For
Edward Stein, 1912–1994,
and
Thomas and Nancy Bickers

Contents

Tables and figures   *page* ix
Acknowledgments   xiii

PART I

1   Policy subsystems and the pork barrel   3

PART II

2   The programmatic expansion of U.S. domestic spending   15

3   The geographic scope of domestic spending: A test of the universalism thesis   30

PART III

4   A portfolio theory of policy subsystems   47

5   Policy subsystem adaptability and resilience in the Reagan period   70

6   PAC contributions and the distribution of domestic assistance programs   90

7   Congressional elections and the pork barrel   118

PART IV

8   Policy subsystems in practice and democratic theory   139

APPENDIXES

1   Descriptive data base of domestic assistance programs   153
2   Geographical data base of domestic assistance awards   157
3   Programs by agency and policy type   161

Contents

4 Departments and their distributive policy agencies   187
5 Federal agencies in four cabinet departments: Budgetary
   changes proposed by the Reagan administration for
   FY1983   190
6 Financial assistance programs by public law bundle   193
7 PACs whose parent interest groups testified in hearings,
   grouped by public law and PAC coalition   196
8 Roll call votes in the U.S. House of Representatives on
   nine public laws   201
9 Probit results for House roll call votes on nine public laws   208
10 Concepts and measures   212

Notes   215
Bibliography   219
Index   227

Tables and figures

TABLES

2.1 U.S. domestic programs, 1971–90: Policy function, number, and average size   *page* 23

3.1 Regression estimates for number of congressional districts receiving assistance from distributive programs: 98th–101st Congress   40

3.2 Regression estimates for number of congressional districts receiving assistance from subsystem portfolios for distributive programs: 98th–101st Congress   42

4.1 Regression estimates for the average change in district coverage of program portfolios: 98th–101st Congress   65

4.2 Regression estimates for the average change in recurrence of district benefits: 98th–101st Congress   66

4.3 Regression estimates for the average change in diversity of program recipients: 98th–101st Congress   67

4.4 Regression estimates for the average change in program portfolio appropriations: 98th–101st Congress   68

5.1 Threatened and nonthreatened agencies during the early Reagan administration: Effect on number of programs, district coverage, recipient diversity, and budget outlays   79

5.2 Regression estimates for change in the number of programs in portfolio   80

5.3 Regression estimates for change in district coverage   82

5.4 Regression estimates for change in recipient diversity of programs in portfolio   84

ix

Tables and figures

5.5 Regression estimates for change in annual portfolio
obligations (millions of constant 1982 dollars)   86
6.1 Expected strategies of PAC coalitions   96
6.2 Public law categorization   100
6.3 PAC coalitions and contributions to House members,
by subsystem environment and breadth of
particularized benefit distribution   102
6.4 Summary of probit results for impact of PAC
contributions on voting behavior of House members   104
7.1 Distributive grant awards by congressional district,
99th and 100th Congresses   128
7.2 OLS regression estimates for electoral margins of
House incumbents in 1988   130
7.3 OLS regression estimates for change in the percentage
of new to total grant awards from the 99th to the
100th Congress   131
7.4 Probit estimates for voter awareness of new projects
in the district   132
7.5 OLS estimates for incumbent thermometer rating   133
7.6 Probit estimates of individual votes for incumbent
congressional candidates   134

FIGURES

2.1 Total appropriations for U.S. federal domestic
spending programs: Redistributive and distributive
programs, 1971–90   19
2.2 Number of U.S. federal domestic spending programs:
Redistributive and distributive programs, 1971–90   21
2.3 Appropriations for agencies with redistributive
program portfolios, 1983–90   26
2.4 Appropriations for agencies with distributive
program portfolios, 1983–90   26
3.1 Number of congressional districts receiving assistance
from distributive programs: Medians, first and third
quartile distances by Congress and administration in
which program originated   38
3.2 Number of congressional districts receiving assistance
from subsystem program portfolios for distributive
programs: Medians, first and third quartile distances
by Congress and administration in which agency
originated   41
4.1 A typology of domestic assistance programs   56

4.2 Hypothetical probability frequency distribution for
four types of program structures based on likelihood
that programs will provide assistance in a
congressional district   57

8.1 Inflation-adjusted per capita outlays for three
entitlement programs and all other domestic financial
assistance programs, 1983–90   140

Acknowledgments

We have received generous assistance and support from many individuals and institutions in completing this book. Many current and former students have worked long and cheerfully on the data sets used in this volume. In particular, we wish to thank Amy Barton, Anthony Carmona, KaLyn Davis, Merrill Davis, Heather Fenstermaker, Ellen Forman, Tom Kirsch, Sharon Koch, Tamara Louzecky, Edward Stewart, and Jodi Suhr. Special gratitude is owed to LaVonna Blair and Valerie Heitshusen, the graduate student assistants who were responsible for managing many of the day-to-day activities of the project. We are particularly grateful to Margaret Anderson, Patty Hale, Bonnie Cleary, Joyce Collins, and Carolyn Zerda for their assistance and patience.

We owe many debts of gratitude to our colleagues at Rice University, Indiana University, and elsewhere for their encouragement and advice on this project. For their careful reading of our work, we would like to thank Ted Anagnoson, Thomas Anton, David Brady, Peter Eisinger, Joseph Cooper, Keith Hamm, Don Kettl, Keith Kreihbel, David Lowery, Tony Matejczyk, Kenneth Meier, Peter Mieszkowski, Mike Rich, Barry Rundquist, Mark Schneider, Rick Wilson, and John Witte. Especially useful was the exchange with Barry Weingast that appears in the *Political Research Quarterly* 47 (June 1994).

We are grateful to a number of institutions that have been instrumental in supporting our research. In the early stages of the project, Rice University provided Kenneth Bickers with a Faculty Research Grant to undertake the preliminary stages of the data collection effort. The Robert M. LaFollette Institute for Public Affairs at the University of Wisconsin–Madison provided Kenneth Bickers with a year of support and permitted him to discuss many of the issues involved in this volume in a stimulating intellectual environment. The Rice University Center for the Study of Institutions and Values provided additional funding to the authors to purchase government data tapes. The National Science Foundation (grant number SES-8921109) provided major funding for the project. We would like to thank Robert Brown, staff director for the Catalog of Federal Domestic Assistance, and David Kellerman, director of the Government Division of the U.S. Census Bureau, for their suggestions and assistance in the use of federal data on programmatic expenditures. Finally we would like to thank Alex Holzman and Brian MacDonald of Cambridge University Press, along with the reviewers of the manuscript.

Some of our analysis draws on material appearing in earlier articles: Bickers and Stein, "A Portfolio Theory of Policy Subsystems," *Administration and Society* 26 (August 1994): 158–84; Stein and Bickers, "Congressional Elections and the Pork Barrel," *Journal of Politics* 56 (May 1994): 377–99; Bickers, "The Programmatic Expansion of the U.S. Government," *Western Political Quarterly* 45 (December 1991): 891–914; Stein and Bickers, "Universalism and the Electoral Connection: A Test and Some Doubts," *Political Research Quarterly* 47 (June 1994): 295–318.

Marty, Nora, and Annie Stein deserve special thanks for their patience, support, and helpful suggestions in the preparation of this book. Laura Bickers also deserves thanks for her patience and good humor, as do Steven and Kevin Bickers, who are too little to care about books without pictures.

As always, responsibility for remaining errors and oversights is ours.

PART I

1

Policy subsystems and the pork barrel

On November 3, 1992, Mike Andrews, Democrat from Houston, Texas, was reelected to his sixth term in the U.S. House of Representatives. Andrews received only 54.5 percent of the vote in defeating Dolly McKenna Madison, a candidate who had never run for elective office. Previously, Congressman Andrews had breezed through his reelection bids. In 1986 he was unopposed; in 1988 he won with 71 percent of the vote; and in 1990 he received 65 percent of the vote. His 1992 reelection bid demonstrated that he had become vulnerable. Something needed to be done to shore up his support in the district. A week later his administrative assistant approached him about shifting staff resources to his district office in Houston. The plan that he and his staff devised was to focus their efforts on bringing more federal spending into his district. They would aggressively seek federal grant awards for his constituents. The idea was to link the congressman to good things that were coming into the district. Grant awards would make him more familiar and valuable to his constituents. Not coincidentally, new grant awards would also provide him with the opportunity to garner positive media coverage. The efficacy of this strategy was not tested by Congressman Andrews, however, as he gave up his House seat in 1994 for a primary bid for a seat in the U.S. Senate. Whether the procurement of new grant awards would have bought Congressman Andrews a larger electoral margin is a moot question, but it is a time-honored strategy among his colleagues in the U.S. Congress.[1]

During the debate over President Clinton's first budget proposal, Phil Boyer, president of the Aircraft Owners and Pilots Association (AOPA), sent a letter to the 300,000 members of AOPA alerting them to the administration's proposed cutbacks in funding for the Federal Aviation Administration (FAA). Letters of this sort are common between interest groups and their members. What made this letter particularly interesting was that included with it was a copy of a supposedly confidential memorandum from Joseph Del Balzo, the head of the FAA, to the secretary of transportation. The memo outlined a number of options for how the FAA might meet the $600 million in cutbacks that the administration had instructed it to prune from its budget request for fiscal year 1995. In his memo, Del Balzo emphasized how each of the options would seriously compromise the operational services of the FAA, including air traffic control and weather information services provided to pilots and their passengers, as well as the construction and maintenance of airport and air traffic facilities. It is no accident that this memo was leaked to an interest group that would share the FAA's concerns and would be quick to mobilize its members to fend off the Clinton administration's budgetary proposal. In Boyer's words, the president's requirement that the FAA cut its budget was "way out of line. You and I know it. The FAA knows it. Now, we have to make sure Congress and the President know it."[2]

These two anecdotes illustrate basic features of American politics – the utilization of domestic spending programs to address the needs of specific constituency groups, legislators seeking to use domestic programs to bolster their electoral fortunes, interest groups working in concert with bureaucrats to influence elected officials, the demands on policy makers to support individual policy objectives despite the need to reduce federal spending in the aggregate. These anecdotes are suggestive of the myriad roles pork barrel spending plays in the day-to-day operation of policy subsystems within the American political system.

Policy subsystems are networks of relationships among different actors, all of whom have a stake in a policy arena. At the heart of most policy subsystems is a set of government programs. Our argument is that these programs are bundled together in nonrandom ways that are intended to address the heterogeneous preferences of the diverse actors in the subsystem. These bundles of programs, which we call program portfolios, provide opportunities for subsystem actors to pursue their own interests but, at the same time, force them to engage in some degree of cooperative behavior with one another. Around each portfolio is a distinct set of actors who use the portfolio to promote their individual and organizational goals.

Policy subsystems have a curious status in studies of U.S. politics. When viewed as iron triangles, they are both despised and dismissed. They are despised for their insularity from accountability and democratic control. They are dismissed as being no longer able to resist the pressures of myriad interest claimants and irrelevant to an understanding of the modern policy process. When viewed as issue networks, policy subsystems are both applauded for their openness and derided for the ease with which special interests are able to press their agendas on policy makers.

This book examines policy subsystems as they have developed and

4

operated over the past two decades, and particularly during the decade of the 1980s. The thesis of this book is that to appreciate the purposive actions of legislators, interest groups, agencies, and others actors in the American political process, we must understand the ways in which policy subsystems are created and maintained. What we conclude is that both the strengths and the dangers associated with policy subsystems have in large measure been misspecified. This book offers a framework for understanding the operation and performance of policy subsystems within the larger process of American democracy.

POLICY SUBSYSTEMS

The central quandary for students of politics in democratic societies is the problem of how consensus is built in the face of the diverse interests and values of societal groups. The diversity of interests in American society is reflected in the wide array of policy subsystems and the domestic programs that constitute their program portfolios. The composition of actors with a stake in a portfolio will vary as a function of the substantive character of the programs in a specific portfolio and the preferences of the interested actors. We are not the first to notice the large number of narrow purpose domestic programs or the fact that they are clustered in particular policy areas. Arnold (1979, 1990), Baumgartner and Jones (1993), Ferejohn (1974), and Mayhew (1974) have written about domestic programs. Our contribution is to draw attention to the ways in which domestic programs constitute not merely an end product of the policy process, but also serve as a means for diverse actors to pursue their political objectives.

There are at least three groups of actors that will be involved in each policy subsystem. One is legislators, grouped into the committees or subcommittees with jurisdictional responsibility for the programs in the portfolio. Second is the agency charged with the day-to-day administration of the program portfolio. Third are the organized groups with a stake in the implementation of programs in the portfolio. Such subsystems may occasionally take the form of old-style iron triangles (Lowi, 1969; McConnell, 1966; Freeman, 1965; Cater, 1964; Truman, 1951). Subsystems, however, need not, and today typically do not, take such a form. They are more likely to be relatively permeable (Heclo, 1978; Berry, 1989). There may be several of each type of actor involved in a portfolio; and, indeed, the actors may bring to the portfolio conflicting preferences. The degree of insularity and permeability will depend in large measure on the strategies that these actors adopt. Our argument is that the various actors in the subsystem jointly play a role in the management of the portfolio. What they get from the portfolio is more than programmatic benefits. They obtain the resources to pursue their individual goals.

5

The story we tell is about the policy subsystems that blanket the American political landscape. These subsystems encompass the thousand or so relatively small programs that make up the bulk of the programmatic activities of federal agencies. We argue that policy subsystems play a crucial role in undergirding and structuring the electoral opportunities of members of Congress, the behaviors of officials within agencies, the organizational strategies of interest groups, and the incentives of diverse groups of program recipients to form organizations to pursue their own interests. What we attempt to describe is a logic underlying the creation of subsystems and how subsystems, once created, serve the interests of the political actors that have a stake in the policy area. This book is therefore about the policy process. It is not, however, another restatement of the four, five, or eight steps of policy making as presented in any introductory text on the policy process. What we describe is a messier, less linear process.

THE MODEL IN BRIEF

In this section we present in abbreviated form the model of the policy process that is developed and tested in this volume. Central to this model is the premise that each actor in the policy subsystem attempts to pursue his or her goals, but requires the cooperation of other actors in the subsystem. The functional relationship between legislators, agencies, interest groups, and program recipients is symbiotic. Each actor in the subsystem relies on other actors in the policy subsystem. Legislators depend on interest groups to provide them with campaign funds and other types of electoral resources. Interest groups depend on agencies to provide federal moneys and other forms of assistance to their members. Beneficiaries of programs depend on interest groups to voice their concerns both to the agency and to the legislators. And agencies depend on legislators to provide funding and programmatic authority. These circular flows of dependency and influence define the policy subsystems that populate the federal government.

When constituents and interest claimants make demands on legislators for help with their problems, legislators seek to find solutions through bureaucratic agencies and the aid programs that the agencies administer. Although Congress enacts and funds these programs, members of Congress are dependent on agencies to implement programmatic solutions to the needs and problems of their constituencies. Members of Congress need agencies to provide benefits to their constituencies, if these constituencies are to return the favor with electoral support. The problem for members of Congress is that these constituencies must be organized and

6

mobilized if they are to provide them with electoral support. Legislators are thus dependent on the actions of others in order to seek reelection.

Agencies thus have both the opportunity and motivation to be responsive to requests for help from legislators and their constituents. An agency is able to demonstrate directly its responsiveness to its legislative overseers. An agency's successful resolution of a problem does more than produce the gratitude of a particular legislator or a pensioner whose complaint of a late check brings a prompt and positive agency response. The agency is able to help constituencies become organized by working with the interest groups that represent such constituencies. Efficacy is the interest group's currency. By demonstrating its efficacy, a group is better positioned to increase its membership, secure dues, and mobilize its membership – in short, to solve its collective action problems. Concentrated benefits to a recipient increase the willingness of these individuals to share in the cost of the group's political activities. Organized interest groups are thus able to provide electoral resources to members of Congress. Agency problem solving, therefore, serves two sets of needs: the needs of interest groups and the needs of legislators.

This arrangement helps promote the self-interest of the agency. The agency's incentive to help interest groups overcome their collective action problems is that the group will be more capable and willing to support the agency's programs before Congress. Agencies need the support of members of Congress, but do not have the votes or campaign resources to be much of a direct factor in any reelection campaign. By helping interest groups reduce their collective action problems, agencies indirectly help deliver campaign resources and votes to members of Congress. In so doing agencies make themselves indispensable to the electoral fortunes of members of Congress. Over the long run, the payoff for the agency is legislative support for its programs.

ALTERNATIVE MODELS

Situating the creation and management of program portfolios within policy subsystems allows us to explain important features of American politics that otherwise are difficult to explain. One consequence of this approach is that it forces us to examine some of the "stylized facts" that have come to be accepted about pork barrel politics. Our findings demonstrate that many journalists, politicians, and political scientists have made assumptions about the way the federal aid system looks and works that, in some cases, are simply false.

A prominent explanation among political scientists for the proliferation of programs is that they are created to enhance the reelection of incumbents. Beginning with Buchanan and Tullock (1962) and reflected in later works by Barry (1965), Mayhew (1974), Fiorina (1977), Shepsle and Weingast (1981), and others, a school of thought developed that held that legislators pursuing reelection engaged in logrolling to produce particularistic programs benefiting their individual districts. In the simple model developed by Buchanan and Tullock, bare majorities of legislators pass programs providing particularistic benefits only to the districts of the winning-coalition members. Beginning with Barry, complexities were added to the legislative model, with the result that the predicted outcome was not minimum-winning coalitions, but rather oversized or universal coalitions. Because legislators tend to be risk-aversive about being on the losing side of a coalition bestowing particularistic benefits (since this might handicap them when running for reelection), they accept more modest benefits for their districts in return for the guarantee that they will be included in the winning coalition. Cementing the coalition are exchanges of votes for the programs of interest to each legislator's district (say, education, transportation, agricultural subsidies), with the result that particularistic benefits of one type or another flow to every legislative district.

In various papers, Shepsle and Weingast have argued that this process leads to at least three unintended, and negative, consequences. First, the costs of providing particularistic benefits to all districts will exceed the "true" level of demand for government expenditures. This inefficiency, they argue, is the inevitable product of a legislature organized along the lines of the U.S. Congress. Second, the types of programs that are created tend to be highly particularized in order to limit positive externalities of projects from spilling into other districts. Such spillovers represent wasted political investments, since residents of other districts cannot vote for the legislator who sought the program benefits for his or her district. Third, the expenditures tend to be organized into many different types of programs that begin small, but grow with time as support for them broadens to encompass increasingly large groups of legislators. Underlying this explanation is the assumption that electoral margins are positively related to the moneys from domestic assistance programs flowing into the member's district.

An alternative explanation found in the work of scholars such as Kelman (1987) and Goodsell (1983) is that public policy reflects the efforts of policy makers who divine policy problems and who devise programs to solve these problems. Central to this argument is the belief that people who seek public service usually choose to do so in order to promote public goals rather than their own private ambitions. Kelman writes:

My own view is that this account [the "public choice" school] of the operation of the political process is a terrible caricature of reality. It ignores the ability of ideas to defeat interests, and the role public spirit plays in motivating the behavior of participants in the political process. By "public spirit," a somewhat old-fashioned term which I consciously choose to use, I mean behavior motivated by the desire to choose good public policy. (Kelman, 1987:81)

For scholars such as Kelman, the large number of programs reflects the large number of policy problems identified by public servants. The number of programs is not a function of how policy makers respond to diverse private ambitions, but rather the triumph of an ethos of public spiritedness. Although Kelman and Goodsell recognize that the political process is sometimes messy, their view is that the individuals working in public institutions generally succeed at serving the public interest.

A third explanation for the large number of relatively small programs can be found in Lowi's *The End of Liberalism*. Lowi's argument is that, beginning with the New Deal and culminating in the 1960s, a new view of public authority emerged in the United States. During this period, Lowi argues, organized interests emerged in every sector of society and the role of government became one of "insuring access to the most effectively organized, and of ratifying the agreements and adjustments worked out among competing leaders" (Lowi, 1979:51). Public law as a formal legislative product degenerated and was replaced by interest group bargaining. This condition endures with time and new administrations. According to Lowi, political parties do not operate as a countervailing force against the influence of interest groups. Attendant with this process is the colonization of the public purse by organized interest groups that seek programs to advance their private goals and use the programs to underwrite their permanent existence.

It is noteworthy that the foregoing explanations emphasize a different set of actors as being central in the creation of domestic programs. One emphasizes the electoral motivation of legislators; the second, the efforts of policy makers within the executive branch to identify and solve public problems; and the third, the role played by interest groups in the formulation and implementation of public policy. Our own perspective integrates elements from each explanation. Where previous explanations have emphasized the interests and motivations of one type of actor, we show how the relationships among actors in policy subsystems generate program portfolios that serve the interests of the different actors.

For example, what do we make of the fact that three-quarters of all domestic programs provide benefits to fewer than a third of all house districts? Likewise, how do we account for the inability of researchers to detect a causal relationship from a district's receipt of domestic assistance to increased electoral margins for the incumbent representing the district? How can we explain the difficulty that researchers have had in establishing empirically a link between PAC contributions and legislative voting? Why, despite Gramm–Rudman and successive Republican administrations, did the number of discretionary federal assistance programs grow by 50 percent during the 1980s? Why did many of the agencies targeted for cuts by the Reagan administration experience growth during the 1980s? These questions, and others, which we will explore in the chapters that follow, are not readily answered by extant theories. We believe, however, that our policy subsystem thesis can provide the answers to these questions.

BOOK OUTLINE

Part I of this book consists of this introductory chapter. In Part II, comprising Chapters 2 and 3, we examine some of the stylized facts that have come to be accepted about American politics. It is commonly thought that federal programs once created exist in perpetuity, growing inexorably over time. In Chapter 2 we examine this characterization and find it to be a half-truth that masks important differences in the growth of different types of programs. This characterization is more or less true for redistributive programs. Not only is it not true for distributive programs, it misses the relevant political importance of distributive policies for actors in policy subsystems who have a stake in the programs. We show that a handful of redistributive programs account for the lion's share of growth of the federal budget. Distributive programs, however, while large in number are fiscally modest and during the 1980s have exhibited a schizophrenic growth pattern. While funding for these programs, on average, fell sharply, the number of such programs grew dramatically. We also find evidence that the number of policy subsystems grew commensurate with the number of distributive programs. But like individual programs, total funding available to policy subsystem portfolios declined during the 1980s.

Chapter 3 addresses a second characterization of federal programs. In this chapter we examine the thesis that domestic programs provide benefits that are universalized across all congressional districts. This outcome is thought to result from the logrolling behavior of legislators who are assumed to have their reelection enhanced if their district receives a program benefit. We test this hypothesis in two ways. First, we test to see if oversized majorities of legislative districts receive benefits from individual programs. Next we examine the extent to which the benefits from program portfolios are received by oversized majorities of districts. Our findings fail to confirm that benefits from most individual programs or most program bundles are distributed to even a simple majority of congressional districts, although we do find some movement in this direction over time. Legislative support for programs cannot be explained solely by reference to how many members of the legislature receive benefits from the programs. Some additional factor or group of factors must be at work.

In Part III, comprising Chapters 4 through 7, we develop and empirically examine our subsystem model. Underlying this model is a premise that the stylized characterization of federal programs examined in Part II misconstrues what is politically important about domestic programs to subsystem actors. This misconstrual, we argue, stems from the failure to take seriously the role of policy subsystems in the American political system. Chapter 4 lays out the logic of the program portfolio thesis. Here we explain how agencies in concert with interest groups and legislators fashion portfolios of domestic programs. Specific strategies are identified for building and maintaining program portfolios that provide political resources required by all the different actors with a stake in the portfolio.

Chapter 5 looks at how program portfolios responded to the efforts of the Reagan administration to cut agency budgets. What we find is that the Reagan proposals had an effect, but the opposite of the one that was intended. Actors in the subsystems rallied. Most agencies that were slated to be eliminated survived and, in some cases, grew. Most agencies whose budgets were pared back managed to recover with time. Our argument is that the unintended consequence of the administration's budgetary proposals stimulated actors in the policy subsystems, helping them to overcome their organizational and collective action problems in order to save their program portfolios.

Chapter 6 focuses on the role played by interest groups in promoting program portfolios. The argument is that PAC contributions can be treated as the electoral equivalent of program benefits. Absent the receipt of particularized benefits in their district, campaign contributions from interest groups give legislators an electoral motivation for supporting a set of programs. The underlying thesis is that legislative support for program portfolios is not solely based on the distribution of particularized program benefits. Interest groups and their campaign contributions provide an alternative vehicle for achieving legislative support.

In Chapter 7 we examine the relationship between program benefits and the electoral margins of House members. Others have examined the impact of federal spending in the district on electoral margins but have not found a significant relationship. We argue that this approach has been flawed for two reasons. First, if legislators are trying to maximize their vote margin, they may be best served by bringing a large number of new awards into their district, regardless of the size of the awards. The announcement of awards provides opportunities for credit taking by legislators. A focus on dollars, rather than numbers of new awards, may miss this politically relevant behavior. Second, the causal connection between program awards and electoral margins has been miscast. Not all legislators need to focus their energies on bringing more awards into their districts. Our contention is that vulnerable incumbents will be most in need of the political capital that results from shepherding grant awards into the district. Moreover, the political capital that they seek to accumulate may not involve all their constituents. Rather the target audience of the credit-taking activities of legislators may be primarily the constituents in their districts that are political activists and the interest group members that have a stake in the federal awards. The electoral connection, we argue, is both mediated and conditional.

In Part IV, comprising the concluding chapter, we reflect on what our findings suggest about the way the American policy process works. We argue that policy subsystems do not pose the problem for American politics that most people think they do. We discuss the implications of our argument and empirical findings for four myths that have developed about the impact of policy subsystems on American government and democratic practice. One is the myth that policy subsystems are a major contributor to the federal deficit. A second, and related, myth is that, once created, federal programs grow inexorably and rarely die due to the power of subsystem actors in the policy process. A third is that to garner support for their programs, subsystem actors seek to universalize the geographic scope of program benefits. A fourth myth is that the flow of program benefits to constituencies in congressional districts ensures the reelection of legislative incumbents. These myths, though often repeated, have not been systematically scrutinized for their empirical veracity. We argue that the main problems posed by policy subsystems are rooted in their impact on the practice of democratic theory in America. Our discussion centers on three issues: (1) To whom are policy subsystems accountable? (2) Whose interests do they serve? (3) How is the connection between the public and its elected representatives distorted by policy subsystems? We conclude the volume with an appraisal of proposals for reforming the American political system, including a balanced budget amendment, a presidential line-item veto, term limitations, campaign finance reform, and the reorganization of congressional committees.

PART II

trivial in cost. As a result, overall expenditures for distributive policies are a poor indicator of policy achievement.

We follow, here, Rose's injunction that "we must consider *what* government does as well as *why* it grows" (1984:1). On his view, size is only one issue, and not necessarily the most important one: "To measure the totality of government by one undifferentiated observation reduces everything to a denominator so common that it tells us nothing in particular" (1984:5). Rose proposes a programmatic approach as a way of analyzing the mix of qualitatively different activities in which governments can be engaged. Such a focus permits a wider and richer range of comparisons than a focus only on aggregate measures of government size.

There is another and potentially more important reason for focusing on programmatic activities. The politics that surround distributive programs may not be dependent on the size of the expenditure. The political importance that accrues from distributive programs may have as much to do with the existence of the program as with any specific amount of money that is expended by the program. Our thesis is that opportunities for political advantage from distributive programs are the result of how the programs are managed by actors in policy subsystems.

In this chapter we shift attention away from a single-minded focus on dollars, toward an examination of change in the programmatic activities of the federal government. Our argument is that a program portfolio approach offers a potentially fruitful avenue for rethinking the dynamics that contribute to the operation of the American political system. After introducing a program-level data base covering U.S. federal domestic programs for the period from 1971 through 1990, we present empirical data on the pattern of programmatic expansion over this period. We show that spending during the 1980s grew steadily for redistributive programs, though most of the spending for redistributive purposes was confined to a small number of fiscally large programs. In the aggregate there was growth in the appropriations for distributive programs over most of the period. Distributive programs experienced two episodes in which substantial numbers of programs were cut. Growth in the number of distributive programs, however, reemerged after both episodes. Individually distributive programs were fiscally modest throughout the entire period but, as the number of distributive programs has grown, their size has declined. Then, we turn to an examination of the program portfolios that were at the heart of domestic policy subsystems during the 1980s. Agencies with redistributive program portfolios grew in number only slightly. We find significant growth in the number of agencies with distributive program portfolios, as well as growth in the number of programs among the largest distributive agencies. These findings indicate the emergence of new policy subsystems and the resilience of old policy subsystems.

16

PART II

2

The programmatic expansion of U.S. domestic spending

A common myth is that federal programs, once created, exist forever, growing unabated over time. This characterization may be more or less true for redistributive programs, but is not at all true for distributive programs. Yet distributive programs play a role in the political process independent of their size in dollars. Indeed, our argument is that there is little correlation between spending on distributive programs and their value measured in political terms. As we argue in later chapters, distributive programs are a key source of political capital for actors in policy subsystems that have a stake in the programs.

Too much of the research on the federal government has been preoccupied with expenditures. Yet not all dollars are equal. A dollar for a new bridge or dam buys something quite different than a dollar of educational assistance. A dollar of regulatory activity implies something much different than a dollar of redistribution. The point is that government does not merely spend dollars. It uses dollars to do things, to make things, and to engage in a host of disparate activities. Not all activities are well measured by counting the dollars spent.[1]

For redistributive policies, dollars are everything. How much money and how it is allocated determine whether redistribution occurs. The zero-sum quality of redistributive policies drives analysts to focus on expenditure measures. In regulatory policies there probably is some sort of correlation between program expenditures and regulatory enforcement, though the strength of this relationship doubtless is more attenuated than for redistributive policies. Additional resources devoted to regulation may not produce an equal increase in regulatory compliance. By contrast, there is great diversity of distributive projects in which the government can be involved, some of which may be quite expensive and others relatively

15

trivial in cost. As a result, overall expenditures for distributive policies are a poor indicator of policy achievement.

We follow, here, Rose's injunction that "we must consider *what* government does as well as *why* it grows" (1984:1). On his view, size is only one issue, and not necessarily the most important one: "To measure the totality of government by one undifferentiated observation reduces everything to a denominator so common that it tells us nothing in particular" (1984:5). Rose proposes a programmatic approach as a way of analyzing the mix of qualitatively different activities in which governments can be engaged. Such a focus permits a wider and richer range of comparisons than a focus only on aggregate measures of government size.

There is another and potentially more important reason for focusing on programmatic activities. The politics that surround distributive programs may not be dependent on the size of the expenditure. The political importance that accrues from distributive programs may have as much to do with the existence of the program as with any specific amount of money that is expended by the program. Our thesis is that opportunities for political advantage from distributive programs are the result of how the programs are managed by actors in policy subsystems.

In this chapter we shift attention away from a single-minded focus on dollars, toward an examination of change in the programmatic activities of the federal government. Our argument is that a program portfolio approach offers a potentially fruitful avenue for rethinking the dynamics that contribute to the operation of the American political system. After introducing a program-level data base covering U.S. federal domestic programs for the period from 1971 through 1990, we present empirical data on the pattern of programmatic expansion over this period. We show that spending during the 1980s grew steadily for redistributive programs, though most of the spending for redistributive purposes was confined to a small number of fiscally large programs. In the aggregate there was growth in the appropriations for distributive programs over most of the period. Distributive programs experienced two episodes in which substantial numbers of programs were cut. Growth in the number of distributive programs, however, reemerged after both episodes. Individually distributive programs were fiscally modest throughout the entire period but, as the number of distributive programs has grown, their size has declined. Then, we turn to an examination of the program portfolios that were at the heart of domestic policy subsystems during the 1980s. Agencies with redistributive program portfolios grew in number only slightly. We find significant growth in the number of agencies with distributive program portfolios, as well as growth in the number of programs among the largest distributive agencies. These findings indicate the emergence of new policy subsystems and the resilience of old policy subsystems.

16

FEDERAL DOMESTIC PROGRAMS

In general, distributive programs allocate direct or indirect subsidies to a recipient in a manner that does not make one recipient's allocation dependent on what another recipient receives (Ferejohn, 1974; Shepsle and Weingast, 1981). According to Ripley and Franklin (1991:20), "Distributive decisions, both within a specific substantive field and across different fields, are made individually, without consideration for their interrelation or overall impact. They are decentralized and uncoordinated." The allocation of distributive benefits creates the appearance that there are only winners and never any losers. Redistributive programs dispense expenditures in a manner that is designed to redress differences in society. These "programs are intended to manipulate the allocation of wealth, property, political or civil rights, or some other valued item among social classes or racial groups" (Ripley and Franklin, 1991:21). Here, one recipient's allocation is very much dependent on another's allotment. The distribution of redistributive program awards is zero sum, with some groups clearly perceived as winning at the expense of other groups. Regulatory policies and programs are designed to compel some actors to abide by rules of behavior that protect other actors from dangerous, harmful, or undesirable consequences. These programs are intended "to protect the public by setting the conditions under which various private activities can occur" (Ripley and Franklin, 1991:21). The policy output of a regulatory program need not be a direct or indirect expenditure, but rather is typically an authoritative action intended to obtain compliant behavior.

How to define and identify a program is not a simple task. The functions, responsibilities, and activities of government can be disaggregated and grouped together in an almost infinite number of ways. Although no definition is likely to be fully satisfactory, the approach taken here is to define a program in terms of the set of official activities designed to accomplish a specific public purpose. Linking programs to purposes places the analytic focus on the array of things that governments do. Such a definition has an intuitive appeal. In ordinary usage, we tend to think of programs in terms of the goals for which tax revenues are collected and spent, the assignments to which government employees devote their energies, and the benefits enjoyed by the recipients of government aid.

Operationally, of course, differentiating between individual programs is sometimes problematic. The purposes to which government resources are mobilized may be partially overlapping, or be so broad or ill-defined as to defy clear delineation. Some resources (e.g., staff, government office buildings) may be devoted to multiple purposes more or less simultaneously. As a result, some degree of ambiguity will always exist when trying empirically to establish boundaries between programs.

17

The difficulty of differentiating between distributive, regulatory, and redistributive programs is reflected in the literature (Lowi, 1964, 1972; Froman, 1968; Hayes, 1978; Salisbury, 1968; Ripley and Franklin, 1991). In our research on the properties of these policy categories, we have adopted multiple operationalizations to define the boundaries between redistributive and distributive programs. Regulatory programs are not included in the data base for reasons discussed earlier.

We have constructed a data base that encompasses the population of government programs over a substantial period of time. This data base includes information on the domestic programs of the U.S. government from 1971 through 1990 (see also Bickers, 1991). The primary source for this data base is the *Catalog of Federal Domestic Assistance*, which was first published in 1965 and has been issued and updated annually from 1969 to the present. The operational definition of a domestic assistance program used in the catalog provides a reasonable approximation to our formal definition of a program. It defines a program as an activity or function of an agency that provides assistance or benefits to a category of recipients to accomplish a specific purpose. The data base used in this chapter includes information on all of the programs listed in the catalog from 1971 through 1990. The average number of programs in each year has been 1,048, resulting in a data base of more than 21,000 program observations over the twenty-year period. An extended discussion of this data base, which is also employed in later chapters, is included in Appendix 1.

U.S. PROGRAMMATIC CHANGE, 1971–90

This section presents descriptive data on the population of domestic programs over the period from 1971 to 1990. Figure 2.1 reports the total amount of spending for redistributive and distributive programs. The operational criterion used to distinguish between redistributive and distributive programs is a variable that identifies whether the program included income level or unemployment status in the eligibility requirements for the selection of program participants. This identifies programs that deliver benefits, at least in part, on the basis of income levels or employment status. This decision rule is designed to identify programs whose purpose is to allocate resources in a compensatory manner. All budgetary figures for distributive and redistributive programs are shown in constant 1982 dollars.

What Figure 2.1 unambiguously shows is that spending on both redistributive and distributive programs has grown steadily during the 1970s and 1980s, consuming an ever increasing amount of budgetary resources. This finding conflicts with the conventional wisdom about the

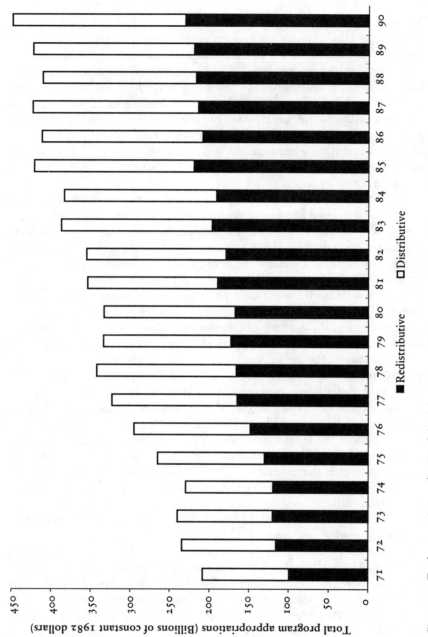

Figure 2.1. Total appropriations for U.S. federal domestic spending programs: Redistributive and distributive programs, 1971–90.

■ Redistributive   □ Distributive

Total program appropriations (Billions of constant 1982 dollars)

Reagan period. Many people, confusing rhetoric with reality, have lamented the cuts imposed on redistributive programs during the Reagan period (see, e.g., Schwarz, 1988). This was not the case. Although Republican administrations, especially the Reagan administration, have attempted to cut redistributive spending and much Republican rhetoric has been devoted to this goal, redistributive spending continued to grow throughout the two decades. As a hypothetical issue, it is possible that, had there been Democratic administrations through these years, the rate of growth might have been greater. But the fact is that Republican administrations presided over increasing budgetary commitments for redistributive programs.

Underlying this conventional wisdom is a sense that Republican administrations have been successful at eliminating domestic programs. Figure 2.2 shows that there is a basis in fact for thinking that programs were eliminated early in the Reagan administration as well as in Nixon's presidency. The basis for this view, however, rests on a limited examination of the facts. The reduction in the number of programs was limited almost entirely to distributive programs. The number of redistributive programs remained virtually constant throughout the 1970s and 1980s. Moreover, the reduction in the number of distributive programs that occurred after Nixon's reelection and after Reagan's election was only temporary. In both administrations, the initial cutbacks in the number of programs constituted merely an interruption in the overall pattern of growth in the number of distributive programs. In 1973, the Nixon administration, through consolidations of categorical programs into block grants (Conlan, 1988) and the use of presidential impoundments, eliminated almost 100 programs from the federal government's repertoire of domestic spending programs. Most of these programs were soon restored. The interesting point, however, is that after this short episode, the number of distributive programs once again began to grow, increasing by 24 percent by the time Carter took office. A similar pattern is observed for the Reagan administration. In 1981, when Ronald Reagan was inaugurated, there were 768 domestic spending programs listed in the *Catalog of Federal Domestic Assistance* that we categorize as distributive. After two years of cuts, this number had been slashed to fewer than 600. In every year after 1983, there was a net increase in the number of distributive programs. When Reagan left office in 1988, there were 765 distributive programs on the books, only three less than when he assumed office. By the second year of the Bush administration, there were 845 such programs, an all time high in the number of distributive programs. What these data suggest is that the political dynamic that underlies the creation of new programs asserted itself throughout the twenty-year period, regardless of administration. Reductions in the number of programs were, at best, fleeting.

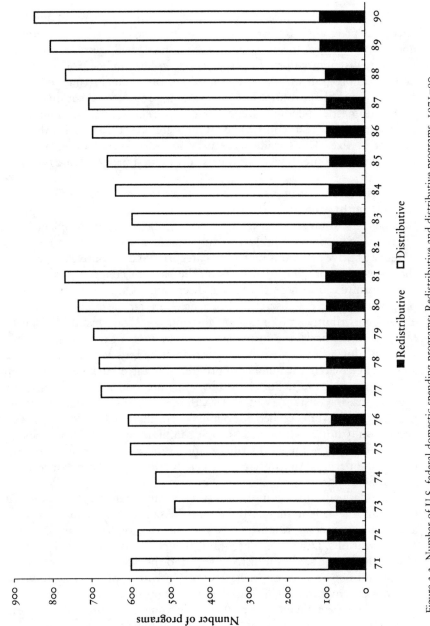

Figure 2.2. Number of U.S. federal domestic spending programs: Redistributive and distributive programs, 1971–90.

■ Redistributive   □ Distributive

A comparison of Figures 2.1 and 2.2 reveals an asymmetry in domestic spending programs. Redistributive programs, which typically number about 100, account for approximately one-half of all appropriations. By contrast, distributive programs, which range in number from a low of about 400 programs in 1973 to almost 750 programs in 1990, consume the other half of appropriations for spending programs. What this means is that domestic spending is composed of a relatively small number of programs that are large in size and a large number of programs that are modest in size. The fiscally large programs are almost exclusively re-distributive in content, whereas the fiscally modest programs are typically distributive.

A closer examination of programs reveals that most of the changes in the number of programs are driven by the class of distributive programs that delegate to agencies discretion over the selection of recipients and distribution of moneys. Table 2.1 compares the number and average sizes of redistributive programs with both categories of distributive programs – that is, those that allocate moneys on the basis of congressionally mandated formula and those that lodge discretion in agencies. Distributive programs that afford discretion to agencies are far more numerous than either redistributive programs or distributive programs that allocate moneys on the basis of a formula. Moreover, most of the programs that were cut during the two episodes just described, as well as the largest source of growth in the number of programs, involved these discretionary distributive programs. But these programs are typically quite small in fiscal terms. In constant 1982 dollars, the average discretionary distributive program never exceeded $100 million during the twenty-year period, and typically hovered around $65 to $70 million. By contrast, appropriations for nondiscretionary distributive programs averaged over $1 billion during the period. Appropriations for redistributive programs averaged almost $2 billion.

These data suggest a complex set of political dynamics. Redistributive programs are fairly immune from political assaults and are able to garner additional budgetary resources even in the face of hostile presidential administrations. Distributive programs – in particular, those which lodge discretion for the selection of recipients and the allocation of moneys in the hands of bureaucratic agencies – experience more of the vicissitudes of the political environment. These programs, while they may be temporarily cut in number, are nonetheless resilient. They tend to absorb relatively few budgetary resources and are able to grow in number most of the time. We argue in subsequent chapters that these programs play a special function in the political process because of their value to actors in policy sub-systems. They help fulfill the needs of key subsystem actors, including legislators, interest groups, and agencies.

Table 2.1. *U.S. domestic programs, 1971-90: Policy function, number, and average size*

Year	Redistributive programs		Nondiscretionary distributive programs		Discretionary distributive programs	
	Number	Approp.[a]	Number	Approp.[a]	Number	Approp.[a]
71	93	1.07	114	0.744	393	0.061336
72	96	1.21	98	0.911	388	0.076137
73	73	1.65	97	0.956	319	0.085789
74	74	1.62	98	0.793	365	0.088674
75	90	1.45	104	0.958	407	0.085690
76	85	1.74	111	0.989	411	0.090416
77	96	1.72	119	0.999	460	0.085358
78	97	1.71	113	1.164	470	0.094993
79	96	1.80	119	1.041	479	0.076986
80	97	1.73	128	1.014	508	0.069783
81	99	1.92	141	1.021	528	0.037776
82	82	2.18	123	1.235	399	0.059613
83	83	2.37	125	1.324	388	0.063428
84	90	2.12	130	1.275	417	0.062604
85	88	2.49	142	1.221	428	0.065675
86	96	2.17	149	1.196	451	0.055390
87	96	2.23	152	1.215	457	0.053677
88	99	2.19	170	0.986	496	0.053060
89	113	1.94	170	1.044	521	0.049441
90	114	2.02	168	1.136	563	0.048392

[a] Average appropriations in billions of constant 1982 dollars.

PROGRAMMATIC CHANGE AND POLICY SUBSYSTEMS

Policy subsystems generally revolve around groups of programs rather than individual programs. Programs are not organized randomly. They are administered by agencies and lie at the heart of policy subsystems. The composition of program portfolios significantly influences the operation of policy subsystems and, thus, the degree to which subsystem actors are able to achieve their objectives. Consequently, to study the politics of programmatic change, it is necessary to focus on the evolution of the portfolio of programs that lies at the center of each subsystem. A subsystem perspective requires us to examine the dense set of relationships among actors within the subsystem as they attempt to utilize programs in the portfolio. To do this type of analysis, we need to identify the set of programs that constitute the program portfolios of each subsystem.

One of the key empirical challenges that arises from this approach is to identify the boundaries of policy subsystems. Although it is sometimes assumed that congressional subcommittees demarcate the boundaries of policy subsystems, this view tends to oversimplify the number and scope of committees involved in a policy area. With subcommittees often sharing overlapping policy jurisdiction within a legislative body, along with duplicative committee responsibilities in the House and Senate, there are always multiple subcommittees involved with the same programs. These conditions of congressional organization make it particularly difficult, in practice, to demarcate the boundaries of a policy subsystem with reference to a committee. The strategy we have adopted is to operationalize policy subsystems by focusing on the programs under the jurisdiction of a single administrative agency, typically the specific bureaucratic unit with responsibility for implementation of a set of programs. It is generally the case that multiple programs from an agency are reviewed simultaneously by the same committee. Operationally, we have identified portfolios based on the lowest-level or most discrete bureaucratic unit listed in the *Catalog of Federal Domestic Assistance* that has administrative responsibility over a set of programs. This measure of subsystems should be a relatively good approximation but may not coincide perfectly, with the true, though unobservable, boundaries of subsystems.

One limitation of this method of identifying the boundaries of subsystems is that it is premised on the presence of domestic assistance programs. Some agencies may be actors within policy subsystems but be engaged in activities that do not involve the allocation of moneys to groups of recipients. Specifically, what we miss with this approach is any subsystem where the participating agency is involved solely in regulatory activities. It is important to note, however, that this operationalization does not eliminate all, or even most, regulatory agencies. This is because regulatory agencies often have responsibility for distributive assistance programs. Such programs provide regulatory agencies with the opportunity to build legislative support for their agency by maintaining a positive presence in a member's district. As an example, the Maritime Administration, which is responsible for regulating the commercial shipping industry, is involved in a host of controversial decisions effecting the livelihood of thousands of constituents in a large number of coastal congressional districts. Nevertheless, between 1982 and 1988 the Maritime Administration was responsible for fourteen distributive aid programs that allocated assistance and moneys to private citizens, companies, and communities for activities including shipbuilding, training of merchant seamen, insuring sea vessels, and compensating losses resulting from unfair foreign shipping competition.

We do, however, distinguish between agencies with redistributive and

24

distributive program portfolios. Agencies with redistributive program portfolios were identified as those in which 50 percent or more of the appropriations were for programs that imposed an income or unemployment criterion in the selection of applicants and/or beneficiaries. Distributive agencies were identified as those in which less than 50 percent of appropriations were for programs that imposed an income or unemployment criterion. Most agencies fall at one end or the other of the spectrum: their appropriations were either for redistributive or distributive programs almost exclusively. Agencies are also fairly stable over time on this dimension: they were either redistributive or distributive throughout the time period that we examined.

We have limited our analysis of policy subsystems to the period of 1983 through 1990. This was done because of difficulties in tracking agencies through presidential administrations. Reorganizations, splits, consolidations, and transfers of agency responsibilities make it difficult, and sometimes impossible, to know if one is looking at the same subsystem across long periods of time. Although we can locate programs within agencies, we had little confidence in the comparability of tracking subsystems over long time periods.

Figures 2.3 and 2.4 report appropriations for redistributive and distributive program portfolios, respectively. This presentation allows us to examine how appropriations are distributed across portfolios. The four agencies with the largest portfolio appropriations are reported along with the appropriations for all remaining agencies. The appropriations for the remaining agencies are reported together. Figure 2.3 shows that for agencies with redistributive program portfolios, one agency, the Social Security Administration, accounts for the overwhelming majority of appropriations. The other three large agencies, while dwarfed by the Social Security Administration, account for an additional 15 to 20 percent of the total appropriations of redistributive portfolios. This means that all the other redistributive portfolios account for less than 10 percent of the appropriations. A similar finding is observed in Figure 2.4 for agencies with distributive program portfolios. One agency, the Agricultural Stabilization and Conservation Service, dominates the appropriations for these agencies, accounting for 44 percent of the appropriations in 1983, increasing to 57 percent by 1990. Three other agencies – the Federal Highway Administration, the Health Care Financing Administration, and the Veterans Benefit Administration – accounted for 29 percent of appropriations for distributive portfolios in 1983, declining to 18 percent in 1990.[2] The remaining 100-plus agencies with distributive program portfolios were responsible for approximately a quarter of the appropriations.

Responsibility for programs is more evenly parceled out among agencies than are dollars. This is true for agencies with redistributive as well as

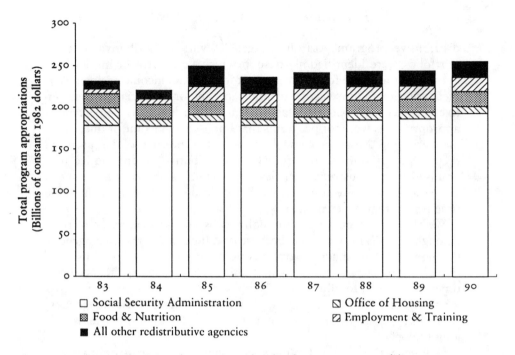

Figure 2.3. Appropriations for agencies with redistributive program portfolios, 1983–90.

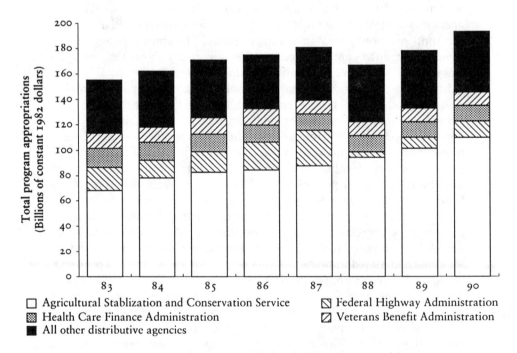

Figure 2.4. Appropriations for agencies with distributive program portfolios, 1983–90.

distributive program portfolios. Given its huge fiscal size, the Social Security Administration has a relatively small number of programs, ranging from 11 programs in 1983 to 7 through the later years of the 1980s.[3] HUD's Office of Housing had, on average, 9 programs; Food and Nutrition Service had, on average, 15 programs; and Employment and Training Administration had, on average, 10 programs throughout the period. The remaining redistributive agencies had, on average, 5.5 programs throughout the period. Although the four redistributive agencies with the greatest appropriations have a larger number of programs, they do not overshadow the other redistributive agencies in terms of programmatic responsibilities.

Among agencies with distributive program portfolios, there were two notable trends during the 1980s. First, a small percentage of the existing agencies experienced increases in the size of their program portfolios. This growth was located within those agencies which already had large program portfolios. In 1983, there were 95 distributive agencies, of which 84 continued to exist through 1990. The 16 distributive agencies with the largest number of programs in their portfolios in 1983 garned the lion's share of programs that were created from 1983 through 1990. These 16 agencies accounted for a net increase of 103 programs between 1983 and 1990, which represents almost half of all programs added to distributive agencies during this period. The remaining 68 distributive agencies that existed through the period received 17 of the 214 programs added to distributive agencies between 1983 and 1990. The 16 agencies with the most programs received, on average, over 6 additional programs during the eight-year period. This compares to an average increase of only one-quarter of a program added to the remaining 68 distributive agencies that existed throughout the period. This increase in the largest agencies is suggestive of the success of subsystem actors in protecting and enhancing their interests. An increase in the number of programs is a mark of this success. The smaller agencies spent much of the 1980s maintaining their portfolios rather than expanding them. As we show in Chapter 5, protecting program portfolios and surviving through the 1980s was characteristic of a majority of policy subsystems.

The second trend was a significant growth in the number of agencies with distributive program portfolios. During this period there was a net increase of 18 agencies. Only in three cases – the National Archives and Records Administration, the Commission on the Bicentennial of the U.S. Constitution, and the United States Institute of Peace – were the new agencies created as "stand alone" entities outside existing departments or bureaucratic units. In every other instance, the agencies were the offspring of existing agencies. The process through which these new agencies were created resembles a biological process of cell division in which specialized activities within an agency were subdivided and assigned to a newly created bureaucratic office. These new distributive agencies were almost always endowed with a small number of programs and limited budgetary resources. These agencies on average, had 1.6 programs in their portfolios. The median number of programs in these agencies was 1 program. This is in contrast to a median across all continuing distributive agencies of 3 programs. These new distributive agencies also had markedly lower budgetary appropriations. The median appropriation (in constant 1982 dollars) for the new agencies was a mere $4.6 million. This contrasts with a median of $94.6 million for continuing agencies with distributive program portfolios.

Newly created agencies with distributive program portfolios do not represent a major claim on the federal budget. Neither do they represent a dramatic expansion in the programmatic responsibilities of the federal government. These agencies do, however, signify the development of new policy subsystems. The new agencies mark a process of colonization – a process described by Theodore Lowi (1979) as delegation. The delegation of programs to new agencies, according to Lowi, is a response to the demands of organized interest groups. Organized interest groups do not compete with one another for scarce resources. Instead, spending and programmatic coverage expands to accommodate the plethora of interest group demands.

The specialization of programs within an agency reinforces the role of interest groups in the policy-making process. Lowi's focus is on interest groups. Our argument is that these newly created agencies offer opportunities for a wide array of actors, including, but not limited to, interest groups, to pursue their interests. Policy subsystems develop around the portfolio of programs in newly created agencies. The agencies and their programs provide a venue for actors with distinct goals to engage in cooperative behavior that is mutually beneficial.

CONCLUSION

During the 1970s and 1980s, there has been substantial growth in federal domestic spending. This growth, however, has been lumpy. Among both redistributive and distributive programs, a small number of programs account for most of the growth in spending. Within the redistributive policy area, programs in the Social Security Administration account for the vast majority of the growth, as well as the spending. Within the distributive policy area, agricultural support payments, highway construction, and health care benefits account for virtually all of the spending growth.

In spite of the concentration of spending growth in a handful of agencies, other agencies benefited from the addition of new programs. Two types of agencies were the primary beneficiaries of new programs. The first were agencies that had distributive portfolios with large numbers of programs. The second were new distributive agencies that were spun off of existing agencies. These agencies signal the evolution of new policy subsystems. This finding points to the value of distributive programs, which, we argue in later chapters, has little to do with their dollar size. Distributive programs provide opportunities to the actors in policy subsystems to advance their interests. What has happened with regard to distributive programs is more complex than with redistributive programs and is, from a political perspective, more interesting.

3

The geographic scope of domestic spending: A test of the universalism thesis

In Chapter 2, we showed that the growth in the number of distributive programs coincided with a decline in their average size. These programs were evidently attractive despite the absence of additional funding. Indeed, we argued that the attractiveness of the programs is independent of their size. A widely held thesis in the political science literature offers a possible reason for why this might be the case: the tendency for legislators to form oversized coalitions that bestow distributive projects on virtually every district represented in the legislature. The budgetary size of the projects is typically considered to be irrelevant to their desirability.

This thesis, in brief, is as follows. Formal models of legislative voting behavior have shown that legislators, when considering programs that involve geographically concentrated benefits and diffuse costs, have an incentive to form legislative coalitions far larger than simple majorities. This tendency was first characterized by Mayhew (1974) as universalism, which, he suggests, serves the desire of legislators to win reelection. Weingast (1979), Shepsle and Weingast (1981), and Weingast, Shepsle, and Johnsen (1981) identify uncertainty as to whether a legislator will be included in the final winning coalition, and thus will obtain valuable assistance in his or her reelection bid, as the primary impetus driving universalism. They argue that by ensuring every district receives some amount of federal spending, supporters of spending programs eliminate the uncertainty about the inclusion of each member of the legislature in the winning coalition. Niou and Ordeshook (1985), by contrast, find that universalism is sensitive to the nature of the legislative bargaining process. They link universalism to constituent preferences for district-specific representation. Nevertheless, whether because of the reduction in uncertainty or because of constituent preferences for district-specific programs, the empirical expectation generated by most formal models is one of unanimous or near unanimous (cf. Baron, 1989) legislative coalitions forming

30

to support programs that distribute benefits to virtually all legislative districts.

According to a reviewer of the formal literature on universalism, empirical investigations of these models of legislative voting behavior generally have a poor record in testing the main hypotheses. Collie (1988a:449) argues that "the traditional methods of investigating distributive policy empirically are not suitable for testing the predictions developed in the formal models . . . they fail to investigate the geographic distribution of benefits on a program-by-program basis." Although Collie may be overly harsh in this judgment, she is correct in arguing that there is an important need for more clearly specified and executed empirical tests of the models. In particular, there is a crucial lack of clarity about whether the expectation of universalism extends only to how large a proportion of the legislative body is included in winning vote coalitions, extends to how large a proportion of legislative districts receives benefits from a particular program, or extends to how large a proportion of districts receives benefits from a group of programs in a legislative package.

Underlying this literature is the assumption that electoral advantage is derived from the provision of programmatic benefits to a legislator's district. Collie's work (1988b) demonstrates that the incidence of voting coalitions of oversized majorities of legislators has increased in recent decades. What has not been shown is that program-by-program benefits are universalized to all (or almost all) districts. Indeed, there remains ambiguity about what is universalized: individual programs or benefits from bundles of programs. In this chapter we show that the evidence on the extent to which benefits from distributive programs are universalized is virtually nonexistent. We offer two tests. First, we examine the distributional expectation of the universalism thesis under the assumption that separate logrolls occur over the distribution of benefits for individual programs. Second, we test the thesis under the assumption that logrolls occur over portfolios of programs organized by policy subsystems.

Our argument, however, is that the universalism thesis, though widely presumed to be true, misconstrues the relationship between distributive programs and the electoral advantage that derives from the allocation of distributive benefits. The reason for this misconstrual is that the universalism hypothesis is premised on a singular political relationship. The picture of the political process that implicitly underlies the universalism hypothesis is one in which the political world is composed only of legislators and voters. In this abstracted world, legislators procure projects for their districts and grateful voters acknowledge this fact and respond by casting their votes for the incumbent at the next election date. Our thesis is that this is not likely to be the most fruitful strategy for incumbents to enhance their reelection prospects.

31

One reason that this is unlikely to be a fruitful strategy is that it assumes that constituents in the district are aware of the benefits flowing to their district. For most constituents, this assumption is unrealistic. Few individuals have the incentive to bear the cost of monitoring the flow of moneys into the district. Most programs do not provide benefits directly to individual voters, but rather distribute benefits to institutions such as universities, hospitals, nonprofit organizations, government agencies, and school districts. Many of the awards that flow to individuals stem from entitlement programs, such as Medicare, Social Security, and other pension programs, rather than from distributive programs. Also, most awards are not the subject of daily newspaper accounts or featured prominently on the evening television news, making it difficult for even the most informed voters to know what types of benefits flow to their district.

For legislators, the electoral impact of obtaining benefits for the district will be muted to the extent that voters are unaware of the benefits and do not credit the legislator for securing them. It would be inappropriate, however, to conclude that there is no connection between the benefits to a district and the electoral fortunes of its representative. When the role of subsystems is considered, it becomes obvious that the linkage can exist via other actors in the subsystem. Specifically, we argue that this connection is supplied by interest groups, which can often overcome the problems faced by individual voters in trying to monitor the activities of legislators and the flow of moneys to districts. Interest groups are positioned to play a vital role in aggregating constituent preferences and linking these preferences to the policy-making activities of the legislature, in general, and to members of the relevant committees, in particular. With group members present in many districts, the organized interest group may have special clout in lobbying for programs. Interest groups can serve as the eyes and ears of individual voters.

Legislators receive electoral resources from interest groups that have a stake in the program portfolios that lie at the center of policy subsystems. Indeed, resources provided by interest groups may be more effective than program benefits in enhancing a legislator's reelection prospects. Unlike programmatic benefits to the district, campaign contributions are fungible and bankable. They can be used in ways and at times that the legislator deems likely to have the greatest positive impact on his or her reelection bid. Interest groups are thus positioned to mediate the relationship between legislators and voters. Consequently universalization of program benefits need not occur. Rather, what must occur is the cooperation between legislators and interest groups in seeking program portfolios that are responsive to the concerns of the interest groups. Policy subsystems may thus permit legislators to acquire electoral resources more effectively than in the abstracted world depicted in the universalism hypothesis.

PROGRAM UNIVERSALISM

The first test of the universalism thesis focuses on the possibility that supporters of distributive programs attempt to build separate legislative coalitions for each individual program. Shepsle and Weingast (1981) argue that, while the process of building a separate logroll for each program might pose a high barrier for new or controversial programs, legislative coalitions tend to become universalized as programs age:

> The distributive tendency in many of the recent social policies is such that, while the initial authorization and/or outlay establishing a program may be controversial (and hence associated with a barely winning support coalition and a large opposing coalition), after a time legislative support grows for subsequent authorizations and more and more districts become beneficiaries of the program. (96)

Although it is not implausible to assume that program benefits will become increasingly universalized as programs age, there are two reasons why fully universalized distributions for most programs may not be achieved.

The first limiting factor is that every program imposes opportunity costs. Legislators evaluate proposals, at least in part, in light of the competing policy or political objectives that they would like to pursue (Arnold, 1990). This calculus is likely to be political as well as economic. Not all programs, even those that provide forms of assistance, are equally desirable to constituents. Programs are evaluated not only by how much money they provide but also by the structural characteristics built into the program, including the severity of matching costs or maintenance-of-effort requirements (Stein, 1984) and the decision rules utilized in the preapplication and application approval processes (Anagnoson, 1983). Such costs lower the likelihood that a member of Congress will want to join a support coalition on behalf of a program. Even during the very best of economic conditions, legislators are faced with a broader array of proposed policies than they can fund.

The second, and no doubt more important, factor is related to the diversity of constituent needs and preferences across congressional districts. If a key reason for legislators to support a program is that it brings them electoral benefits, then programs must actually be needed and desired by at least some of their constituents. A program that targets the needs of particular types of constituents (e.g., mine health and safety, Indian child welfare, hematology research) will effectively exclude a number of districts since the districts contain few, if any, constituents that might plausibly benefit from the program. Due to the differences between legislative districts, this lumpiness of potential recipients into a small number of districts is likely to be relatively common. This is especially likely given the fact that most federal domestic assistance programs are small project grants (Bickers, 1991), which typically provide benefits to a small range of narrowly defined recipients (Gramlich, 1977). To be sure, some programs address problems or needs that exist in every district, but, as we will show, this appears to be the exception rather than the rule.

For many programs, though doubtless not for all of them, these two factors will be sufficiently severe as to render a support coalition too small to ensure passage of the program's authorizing legislation and budgetary appropriations. The fact that most programs rarely provide benefits broadly, but instead are usually small and narrowly drawn, runs counter to an argument that is premised on the incentives of legislators to form universal coalitions on behalf of individual spending programs. Although few programs are likely to have an immutable upper boundary on the scope of their geographic coverage, the basic problem is difficult to fix. The functional specificity that is often built into programs limits the range of congressional districts that contain potential recipients. The creation and expansion of programs is never entirely free of opportunity costs. Joining a legislative coalition to support a program may thus be unattractive for many legislators, even if their district stands to benefit from the program, to the extent that some other program is likely to provide higher benefits and lower costs.

The second test of the universalism thesis focuses on the possibility that legislative coalitions form around a portfolio of programs. Here, the assumption is that every member of the legislature has an incentive to join the support coalition, even though every district does not receive benefits from every program. The potential size of a support coalition is therefore not limited by the substantive character of any individual program. In principle, the potential for combining programs into portfolios is infinite. The literature on Congress, however, would suggest that the most common venue for bundling distributive policy initiatives is likely to be committees and the policy subsystems that form around committees (cf. Clubb and Traugott, 1988; Brady, Cooper, and Hurley, 1979; Cooper and Brady, 1981; Jones, 1981; Sinclair, 1981; Bullock and Loomis, 1985; Deering and Smith, 1985; and Hammond, 1991). Ripley and Franklin (1984), for example, indicate that relationships between congressional committees, executive branch agencies, and organized interest groups in distributive policy areas, in contrast to regulatory and redistributive policy areas, tend to be consensual and close.

The empirical literature on distributive policies is replete with studies that attempt to demonstrate efforts by bureaucratic administrators and legislative sponsors of programs to distribute benefits as broad as geographically possible. Most of these studies focus on individual policy areas (an exception is Owens and Wade, 1984): for example, tariffs (Schattschneider, 1935), rivers and harbors projects (Maass, 1951; Ferejohn,

34

1974; Wilson, 1986), urban renewal (Plott, 1968), tax preferences (Manley, 1970; Witte, 1985), military procurement (Rundquist, 1973), grants-in-aid (Mayhew, 1974), and grants for the arts and humanities (Carlton, Russell, and Winters, 1980).

Weingast et al. argue that logrolling over bundles of programs within policy subsystems is a common pattern in the U.S. Congress:

> In those policy areas characterized by a project-by-project orientation, the geographic concentration of benefits, and the diffusion of costs, there is abundant evidence that universalism and reciprocity are prevailing decision rules in the U.S. Congress. The former practice assures any interested district a project; the latter, in recognition of the fact that district differences translate into different policy priorities, facilitates a process of mutual support and logrolling. These two practices combine to permit packages of distinct projects earmarked for interested districts to obtain the support even of those without a stake in the package in exchange for reciprocal treatment. (1981:651)

Bundling programs into portfolios may help mitigate the constraints on universalism faced by individual programs. It does nothing to resolve the opportunity costs for individual legislators. It does, however, help reduce the constraint imposed by the functional specificity present in most programs. Recipients with different needs can be provided benefits from different programs within a portfolio. Nonetheless, the degree to which dissimilar recipients can be grouped together is likely to be limited by demands for administrative coherence. Programs with widely disparate goals may be difficult to administer through the same agency.

RESEARCH DESIGN, DATA BASE, AND OPERATIONAL MEASURES

In this chapter we examine two different conceptions of how legislators form coalitions for the distribution of program benefits. First, we analyze the number of congressional districts receiving outlays from each individual federal domestic spending program. Because a key question is whether program benefits are initially universalized or become so over time, we focus on two related questions. From a static point of view, do individual program benefits go to all or almost all congressional districts? From a dynamic point of view, do individual program benefits begin at a bare majority of congressional districts and approach a universal distribution with time? Second, we analyze the number of congressional districts receiving outlays from the bundles of programs contained within policy subsystems. As with the analysis of individual programs, we are interested in both the static and dynamic properties of the subsystem program portfolios. Do program portfolios begin with universalized (or nearly universalized) benefit distributions? Or do they begin well below universalism but trend toward universalized geographic coverage with time?

Data for this chapter come from two sources. Information on the distribution of outlays is drawn from the *Federal Assistance Awards Data System* (FAADS). Available quarterly in machine readable form since 1982 from the U.S. Bureau of the Census, FAADS reports awards to the recipients of financial assistance from each domestic spending program of the federal government. For a detailed discussion of coding rules and caveats that should be noted in interpreting these data, see Appendix 2, as well as the introduction and appendixes in Bickers and Stein (1991). Our second data source, which is used to identify administering agencies, is the U.S. Government's *Catalog of Federal Domestic Assistance* (CFDA). The CFDA data set was introduced in the previous chapter and is described in Appendix 1.

To test the proposition that legislators engage in separate logrolls over individual distributive programs, we have compiled data on direct outlays to congressional districts from each federal domestic program over the period 1983 through 1990.[1] The list of these programs is contained in Appendix 3. Because congressional decision making on domestic assistance programs occurs within the two-year congressional cycle, the observations are aggregated into four sets of two-year periods corresponding to the 98th, 99th, 100th, and 101st Congresses. Districts that received outlays of more than zero dollars are coded as benefiting; districts that received zero or, in a handful of cases, less than zero dollars (e.g., due to deobligations from unspent federal awards) are coded as not benefiting. For each program and program portfolio, the sum of all benefiting districts serves as our measure of the extent that benefits are universalized.

Most of the programs in our sample were in existence prior to 1983, the first year of FAADS data on program awards to congressional districts. Because programs have evolved over varying lengths of time, the opportunity for expansion of program benefits has been much greater for older programs. To control for this possibility, we have coded a variable indicating the administration in which each program was created, grouped into five periods: pre-Nixon (1968 and earlier), Nixon/Ford (1969–76), Carter (1977–80), and Reagan (1981–9). Information on the year of program creation is taken from the historical profile of programs contained in the U.S. government's 1990 *Catalog of Federal Domestic Assistance*. This measure is based on the year a program was first added to the CFDA, and assumes a one-year lag between the creation of a program and its inclusion in the catalog.[2]

We have employed the same decision rule to differentiate distributive from redistributive programs as used in Chapter 2. Recall this operationalization identified programs as redistributive if they applied an income or unemployment test as one criterion in the selection of recipients or beneficiaries. Our operationalization defines the population of distributive programs as any program that does not include income level or unemployment status in the eligibility requirement. There are 1,543 programs that meet this criterion.

To test the proposition that legislative logrolls are organized by portfolios, we have grouped program outlays by federal agency. Although an agency may have responsibility for distributive, regulatory, and redistributive programs, we have limited our analysis to only an agency's distributive programs. Appendix 3 also indicates the agencies that have responsibility for implementing one or more distributive programs. There are seventy-one agencies that contain one or more distributive programs throughout the entire 1983–90 period. Regulatory agencies, as discussed earlier, often have responsibility for distributive programs. This occurrence is readily explained given the contentious nature of many regulatory activities. The regulation of private behaviors often places agencies in situations where they may be vulnerable to congressional reprisals for unpopular decisions (cf. Pertschuk, 1982). Our analysis includes the distributive programs of regulatory agencies.

Districts are coded as benefiting if they received a positive sum from at least one of the programs in the portfolio that each agency administers. The extent of universalism for program portfolios is measured as the total number of districts receiving outlays from any one or more of an agency's programs. Only agencies that contained at least one distributive domestic financial assistance program in each Congress between the 98th and 101st Congresses were included in the analysis.

Because program portfolios may have been in existence for different lengths of time, we identified the administration in which each agency originated. In most cases this information was obtained from the *U.S. Government Manual* (Office of the President, 1980). In some instances it was necessary to consult the enabling legislation for the agency's programs to identify the year in which the administrative agency was created. In a handful of cases we were unable to identify the agency's year of creation. These agencies were excluded from the analysis.

ANALYSIS AND FINDINGS

Figure 3.1 reports the median and first and third quartile values for the number of congressional districts receiving outlays from all individual programs except those with regulatory or redistributional intent. The programs are grouped by the administrations in which they were created, and displayed by Congress. The most striking finding is the narrowness of

37

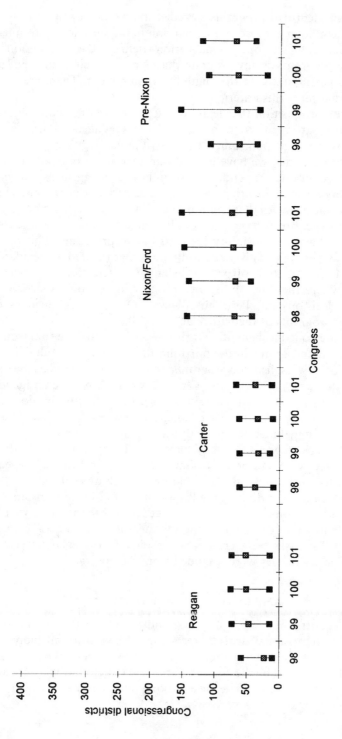

Figure 3.1. Number of congressional districts receiving assistance from distributive programs: Medians, first and third quartile distances by Congress and administration in which program originated.

district coverage for most programs. The median number of congressional districts receiving outlays never exceeds half the total number of districts in any Congress. Indeed, the median does not ever exceed seventy-five districts. The smallest 25 percent of programs from each administration never provide coverage to more than fifty districts. The narrowest 75 percent fail to provide outlays to even a simple majority of districts.

There is no support for an argument that assumes that the distribution of individual program benefits will move from minimum winning coalition size to universal coalition size as programs age. Programs created in earlier administrations do have slightly broader benefit distributions, but even the oldest cohorts of programs do not distribute benefits to anywhere near a simple majority of congressional districts. The only upward trend line visible occurs among programs created during the Reagan administration, which also begin with the narrowest level of benefit distributions.

A regression analysis confirms the lack of support for the universalism hypothesis for district coverage by individual programs. Table 3.1 reports the regression estimates for the number of congressional districts benefited by individual distributive programs. The independent variables include three dummy variables indicating the administration in which a program was created (the excluded category references programs created prior to the Nixon administration), a counter for the Congress in which we observe each program's benefit distribution, and a variable measuring each program's annual outlays. This last variable is included as a control to avoid incorrectly attributing district coverage to differences in the level of outlays across programs.

The parameter estimate and t-value for the Congress counter do not support the idea that programs undergo evolutionary increases in district coverage. The most important predictor of district coverage is the amount of money available to be spent on the program. The coefficient for this independent variable is statistically significant and positive. There is also evidence that the extent of district coverage varies by the administration in which a program was created. Controlling for the other variables in the model, the average district coverage is 76 districts for distributive programs created prior to the Nixon administration, 94 during the Nixon and Nixon/Ford presidencies, 65 during the Carter presidency, and only 54 during the Reagan presidency. The estimates for the administration dummy variables show that by the 1980s programs created prior to the Carter administration had attained somewhat broader distributions than those created during and after the Carter administration. In sum, individual programs, on average, exhibit no evidence of universalism or movement in that direction. If the objective of legislators in joining a logroll is, at least in part, to obtain benefits for the member's district, then most

Table 3.1. *Regression estimates for number of congressional districts receiving assistance from distributive programs: 98th-101st Congress*

	Distributive programs	
	Coefficient	T-value
Constant	76.78	12.59[*]
Congress	-0.263	-0.142
Program outlays	0.658	11.31[*]
Nixon/Ford	17.14	2.74[*]
Carter	-23.48	-3.43[*]
Reagan	-25.46	-3.84[*]
N	1,543	
R square	0.162	

Notes: Outlays measured in billions of dollars.

Nixon/Ford, Carter, and Reagan are dummy variables coded 1 if the program was created in the administration and coded 0 otherwise. Estimates for the constant reflect the excluded possibility of programs created prior to the Nixon administration. Congress is coded 98, 99, 100, and 101.

Programs that are primarily designed with a regulatory purpose have been excluded (e.g., IRS subsidies to states for setting up tax models for auditing purposes; EEOC compliance and litigation grants). Also excluded are assistance programs that do not involve forms of direct monetary assistance such as technical assistance, insurance, loan guarantees, direct loans, and tax expenditures.

[*]$p < 0.05$

individual programs are too limited in scope to sustain a winning legislative support coalition of any size, minimum or otherwise.

When we turn to the proposition that legislative logrolls are organized around portfolios, we continue to find no evidence of universalism. Figure 3.2 reports the median and first- and third-quartile values for the number of congressional districts receiving outlays from portfolios composed of distributive programs. District coverage is reported for agencies grouped by the administration in which the agency was created and displayed for each Congress. Older agencies tend to have broader coverage, but in every instance the median district coverage does not approach a simple majority of congressional districts. The median district coverage is at its broadest, 172 districts, in the 101st Congress for agencies created in the Nixon and Ford administrations. District coverage for agencies at the third-quartile level exceeds, though only marginally, a simple majority for those created during the Carter administration and prior to the Nixon administration.

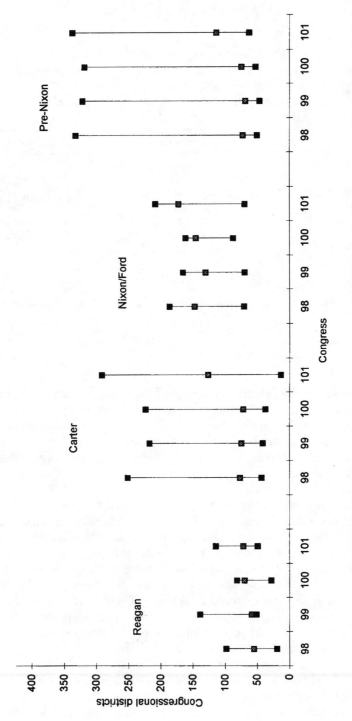

Figure 3.2. Number of congressional districts receiving assistance from subsystem program portfolios for distributive programs: Medians, first and third quartile distances by Congress and administration in which agency originated.

Table 3.2 *Regression estimates for number of congressional districts receiving assistance from subsystem portfolios for distributive programs: 98th-101st Congress*

	Distributive programs	
	Coefficient	T-value
Constant	109.1	7.35*
Congress	-1.02	-0.178
Program outlays	12.0	4.75*
Number	7.95	7.71*
Nixon/Ford	-22.98	-1.12
Carter	-7.81	-0.50
Reagan	-45.15	-2.27*
N	274	
R square	0.408	

Notes: See Table 3.1
*$p < 0.05$

The slope for median district coverage of portfolios does not exhibit a clear upward trend line. Though not increasing monotonically, median district coverage among agencies created in the Reagan administration increases from 55 districts in the 98th Congress to 71 in the 101st Congress. For agencies created before the Nixon administration, median district coverage grew from 72 districts in the 98th Congress to 113 districts in the 101st Congress.

Table 3.2 reports estimates for a regression of district coverage by subsystem portfolios on the same set of independent variables included in Table 3.1, plus a control variable for the number of programs in the portfolio. The regression analysis of portfolio coverage confirms what is visible in Figure 3.2. The estimate for the trend variable (i.e., the Congress counter) is statistically insignificant in the model. Substantively this indicates no change in district coverage over time. There are, however, significant differences in coverage for older cohorts of portfolios. Portfolios in agencies created in earlier administrations exhibit broader district coverage than portfolios in agencies created more recently. During the 1980s, average coverage was 169 districts for portfolios in agencies created during the Nixon and Ford presidencies and was only 106 districts for those created during the Reagan administration.

The strongest determinants of district coverage by agencies are the number of programs in the portfolio and the amount of money available to spend on program outlays. The addition of a new program to a portfolio increases coverage by twelve congressional districts. A $1 billion increase in outlays is associated with an increase in coverage of eight districts. Greater coverage by a portfolio is associated with three conditions: older agencies, large numbers of programs, and high levels of outlays. Most portfolios do not possess these traits. The regression reported in Table 3.2 shows that most portfolios have modest district coverage, not approaching a simple majority of congressional districts.

The general conclusion that emerges from these data is that universalism is rare both at the program and portfolio levels. There is only modest evidence to support the idea that benefits move in the direction of universalism over time. Programs and agencies created in earlier administrations exhibit somewhat broader district coverage than those created more recently. The measure that directly captures the effect of time on coverage (i.e., the Congress counter) is not statistically significant in either regression. These findings provide little or no support for either of the variants of the universalism hypothesis as it pertains to the distribution of benefits to congressional districts.

DISCUSSION

In the universalism hypothesis, the motivation for legislators to seek distributive benefits for their districts is the presumed electoral connection between benefits and votes. We do not find evidence that either individual programs or portfolios of programs are universalized. Nor do we find evidence of much movement toward universalism. Most individual programs provide benefits to relatively small minorities of Congressional districts and never approach even a simple majority of districts over time. Likewise most program portfolios provide benefits to fewer than half of all legislative districts. Only approximately a third of the program portfolios provide benefits to more than half the districts. Even so, very few individual programs or bundles ever approach anything close to a universalized distribution of benefits.

The absence of universalized distributions that we have observed does not preclude a connection between how program benefits are distributed and the electoral fortunes of legislators. It does mean, however, that there is not a simple unmediated connection between legislators and voters that is cemented by the provision of particularized benefits. The problem is that the universalism hypothesis depicts an overly simplified political process. The universalism hypothesis ignores the role of other political actors in establishing an electoral connection. Our policy subsystem thesis provides a richer set of relationships through which legislators can reap elec-

43

toral advantage. In the next chapter we lay out this argument. In subsequent chapters we show how relationships between legislators, interest groups, agencies, attentive publics, and voters promote an electoral connection between legislators and voters. These relationships serve the political needs of the actors in policy subsystems.

PART III

4

A portfolio theory of policy subsystems

In this chapter we turn to the development of our subsystem thesis. The literature on policy subsystems has been undergoing something of a renaissance. In recent years, public policy research has begun portraying the relationships that frequently develop between agencies, interest organizations, and legislative committees in terms that suggest fluidity, dynamism, and openness to the larger political environment (see, e.g., Hamm, 1983; McCool, 1990; Jenkins-Smith, St. Clair, and Woods, 1991). Heclo (1978), for example, describes policy subsystems as loose issue networks (cf. Berry, 1989). Kingdon (1984) argues that we should think in terms of policy communities. Cohen (1986) describes systems of variable political control involving Congress, the president, the courts, and interest groups. Sabatier and Pelkey (1987) point to potentially competitive advocacy coalitions spanning multiple actors in a policy domain. Meier's (1985) synthesis of the regulatory literature treats subsystems as interconnected sets of dyadic linkages, which may be consensual or conflictual, between agencies, subnational units of government, legislative subcommittees, industry groups, interest advocacy groups, and assorted others. All of these views reject the classic depiction of policy subsystems as "iron triangles," composed of informal, but durable, linkages between executive agencies, legislative committees or subcommittees, and special interest groups (Lowi, 1969; McConnell, 1966; Freeman, 1965; Cater, 1964; Truman, 1951).

Taken together, this recent work suggests that the "iron triangle" literature was seriously deficient in not recognizing the conditions under which the insularity of subsystems could be breached from the outside by the rise of new interest claimants and issues or from the inside by shifting alliances and loss of consensus. Our thesis is that, under some circumstances, subsystems may be relatively insular and take the form of iron triangles (Lowi, 1969; McConnell, 1966; Freeman, 1965; Cater, 1964; Huntington, 1952; Truman, 1951). Under other circumstances, which are today

47

far more common than in earlier days, policy subsystems are likely to be more permeable and resemble issue networks (Heclo, 1978; Berry, 1989). The degree of insularity or permeability is dependent upon the strategies employed by subsystem actors and the constraints imposed by the larger political environment.

SUBSYSTEM ACTORS

Our subsystem model differs in a number of important respects from both iron triangles and issue networks. Indeed our subsystem model subsumes both of these perspectives and treats them as special cases on a continuum. Policy subsystems are populated by a combination of interest groups, legislators, agencies, attentive publics, program recipients, and journalists for specialized media. A subsystem is defined by the network of relationships among these actors (cf. Hamm, 1983). Our argument is that the various actors in the subsystem jointly play a role in the management of programs that lie at the center of a policy subsystem. What they get from this portfolio of programs is more than programmatic benefits. They obtain the resources to pursue their individual goals. Each set of actors has preferences that it pursues through the subsystem.

Legislators

Legislators value their reelection. Reelection may be a preference either for its own sake or because the pursuit of other legislative goals requires retaining office. The interests of most members of Congress center on the performance of legislative activities that, at least in part, help in securing reelection. On a daily basis members of Congress are presented with a host of problems that require their immediate attention. In an overwhelming majority of instances these problems are resolved through a routinized process referred to as constituent service (see Fiorina, 1989; Johannes, 1984; Parker, 1986). Congressional offices, both in Washington and the home district, are organized to process and resolve quickly particularistic constituent requests for assistance. In some instances the nature of the request goes beyond the scope of routinized constituent service. Requests from members of interest groups (e.g., school districts, counties) differ greatly from the more numerous particularized service requests made by individuals and are dealt with differently by congressional offices. Here the fix for a problem often involves securing programmatic resources (usually, but not always, moneys) from a federal agency.

The search for a solution in this instance has two possible paths: a review of existing programs or, in the absence of a suitable solution among current programs, introduction of new legislation. The likelihood that the

48

former path will be pursued is higher because the quest for assistance froman existing program is a low-cost activity for congressional offices.

Consider, for example, how easy it is for members of Congress to identify existing programmatic resources for their constituents. The Government Services Administration maintains the Federal Assistance Programs Retrieval Systems, (FAPRS), an on-line computer file of all federal domestic assistance programs. FAPRS enables congressional staff to identify, from among more than a thousand programs, one or more that closely match the needs of constituents. The data file includes information for each program on applicant eligibility, application procedures, program requirements, average funding for recipients in the three previous fiscal years, and specific contact persons in the administering agency. From FAPRS, congressional staff can identify the probability that a request for assistance will be fulfilled – without leaving the congressional office or making a single phone call.

Agencies

Agencies try to secure stable and increasing budgets, larger staffs, and additional resources. This is necessary if agency personnel are to pursue the policy goals to which they are ideologically attached as well as nonpolicy goals such as slack resources, career advancement, and greater prestige. The functional relationship between agencies and Congress is symbiotic. Congress seeks solutions to constituent problems through domestic aid programs administered by bureaucratic agencies. Although Congress enacts and funds these programs, members of Congress are dependent on agencies to implement programmatic solutions to the needs and problems of their constituencies. This in turn gives these constituencies an incentive to return the favor by providing electoral resources to members of Congress. The problem for members of Congress is that these constituencies must be organized and mobilized if they are to provide them with electoral resources.

This fact gives agencies an opportunity. How they administer their programs is instrumental in helping potential recipients of awards to achieve their individual objectives. It is doubtless a truism that potential recipients of federal program benefits want to receive generous government support that is structured in ways compatible with their interests and without burdensome or odious regulations. At the same time, however, how agencies administer their programs can help program recipients become better organized in formal interest groups, which in turn permits them to mobilize for the provision of electoral resources to members of Congress. Agency problem solving, therefore, serves not merely the needs of individual program recipients, but also the needs of interest groups with a stake in the policy subsystem.

Agencies have a powerful incentive to help interest groups overcome their collective action problems, because an interest group that can mobilize its membership is more capable of supporting the agency's programs before Congress. This is a primary means by which agencies try to secure stable and increasing budgets, larger staffs, and additional resources. Agencies need the support of members of Congress, but do not have the votes or campaign resources to be much of a factor in any reelection campaign. By helping interest groups solve their collective action problems, agencies indirectly help deliver campaign resources and votes to members of Congress. In so doing, agencies make themselves indispensable to the electoral fortunes of members of Congress. The payoff for the agencies is support for their programs.

Interest groups

Interest groups can be influential in persuading members of the legislature to support programs (see, e.g., Sabato, 1985; Denzau and Munger, 1986; Hall and Wayman, 1990). Interest groups may provide inducements in the form of electoral resources, evaluations or rankings of legislators in newsletters, and assistance on issues of more direct interest to the legislator. Interest groups may also attempt to persuade members to support programs by providing information in a different light than that provided by the administration. For example, interest groups may point to positive externalities generated by a program which may directly benefit a member's district either in the short or long run. Finally, interest groups, in extreme circumstances, may attempt to mobilize local support or opposition to a member of the legislature whose support or opposition is crucial to the group's interests. This can take a variety of forms, some more benign than others, from publishing letters in the local paper's editorial page, to placing advertisements in the local media, to setting up telephone banks to influence voters on election day, to encouraging local officials more sympathetic to the group's interests to run against the incumbent in the primary or general election.

Interest groups and their members have arrays of public policy goals. For interest groups to pursue these goals, they must maintain their organizational strength, which requires that they continually overcome collective action problems. In the management of programs, agencies assist interest groups in organizing and mobilizing grant recipients and other attentive publics to support the interest group. Concentrated benefits to a recipient increase the willingness of these individuals to share in the cost of the group's lobbying activities.

Legislators benefit from interest groups to the degree that the groups are able to mobilize to reward support for programs. In specific policy areas interest groups often can overcome the problems faced by individual voters in trying to monitor the activities of legislators and the flow of moneys to districts. Membership contributions to political action committees broaden the interest group's influence beyond those districts in which it may have modest membership. Although individual membership contributions may be relatively small, aggregated across the total membership they may comprise a significant purse (cf. Sabato, 1985). Targeted, these contributions can be effective in aiding legislators who are supportive of the subsystem. Electoral resources, such as PAC contributions or volunteering for campaign activities, can be provided if resources of group members can be mobilized. The problem all interest groups face is how to induce current and potential members to support the group's activities both financially and otherwise. Our thesis is that other actors in the policy subsystem will be important in determining how well interest groups are able to overcome their collective action problems and provide electoral resources to legislators. With the cooperation and assistance of other actors in the policy subsystem, the group is better positioned to increase its membership, secure dues, and mobilize its membership – in short, to solve its collective action problems.

Summary

Subsystem actors are linked by sets of dyadic relationships. These relationships collectively define the subsystem. As we will argue, no subsystem actor can pursue its own goals without the cooperative behavior of other actors in the subsystem. Legislators need interest groups and the resources they provide to fund their reelection bids. Agencies need legislators to support their program authorizations and budgetary appropriations. Potential grant recipients need agencies to engage in favorable funding decisions and sympathetic program implementation. Interest groups need program recipients and other attentive publics to provide resources to the group so it can be efficacious in the promotion of their interests. It is through these dyadic relationships that the preferences of each of the actors are facilitated.

SUBSYSTEM STRATEGIES

To understand the strategies available to policy subsystem actors to organize legislative coalitions, it is useful to conceptualize the policy subsystem's activities in terms of a portfolio of programs. As in a portfolio of stocks and bonds, which, by pooling low- and high-risk investments, provides an acceptable return while reducing the probability of catastrophic loss, the group of programs of concern to policy subsystem actors can likewise be managed in ways that promote the subsystem's goals while reducing the risk of loss. The broader the base of investors in the portfolio of programs, the more secure it is against downturns in the political environment.

Thinking in terms of portfolios shifts attention away from individual programs and their implementation. In most cases, individual programs are likely to be a rather slender reed for building a strong support coalition among legislators. The main reason for this stems from the diversity of constituent needs and preferences across congressional districts. A program that targets the needs of particular types of constituents (e.g., miners, Native Americans, medical researchers) will effectively exclude a number of districts because the districts contain few, if any, constituents that might plausibly benefit from the program. Moreover, differences among constituency groups often means that, even when there is consensus over broad policy objectives, there will be sharply different preferences over the content of policy proposals. Programs are evaluated not only by what they are supposed to do, but by the structural characteristics and decision rules that affect how they will be received by recipients and other interested parties (Stein, 1984; Anagnoson, 1983).

Due to differences across districts, the lumpiness of potential recipients into a small number of districts is likely to be relatively common. This is especially likely given the fact that most federal domestic assistance programs are small project grants (Bickers, 1991), which typically provide benefits to a small range of narrowly defined recipients (Gramlich, 1977). Among this type of program, only a few grow to the point that they eventually provide benefits to most districts (Hamman, 1993). As we demonstrated in Chapter 3, some programs provide funds to address problems or needs that exist in every district, but that is the exception rather than the rule. Although few programs are likely to have an immutable upper boundary on the size of their support coalition, the basic problem is that the functional specificity built into programs tends to limit the number of legislative districts that contain potential recipients. Hence portfolios of programs permit supporters of one program to combine forces with supporters of other programs to help build a coalition on behalf of the entire group of programs that they favor. Portfolios offer synergies. The limits represented by one program can be offset by the benefits of another.

Minimizing collective action problems

One line of attack that policy subsystems may pursue, either in isolation or in conjunction with other strategies, is the mobilization of interest group support on behalf of the policy subsystem's portfolio of programs. This strategy may be especially effective when a policy subsystem is threatened. In the formal literature on legislative behavior, the motivation for legislators to seek distributive benefits for their districts is the presumed electoral connection between benefits and votes. The implicit assumption is that individual constituents are more or less aware of benefits flowing to their district. Clearly, for most constituents, this assumption is unrealistic since few individuals have the incentive to bear the cost of monitoring their member's support of distributive programs or to track the actual flow of moneys into the district. In specific policy areas, however, interest groups often have the capacity and incentive to monitor the support or nonsupport of legislators for programs and the flow of moneys to beneficiaries.

Among the various issues that must be considered in building and managing program portfolios that lie at the center of policy subsystems, one concern that is likely to be central to the political viability of the subsystem is the reduction of the collective action problems faced by interest groups. Committees and agencies can be instrumental in reducing these problems. One way they can help reduce collective action problems is to create programs with homogeneous recipient populations. This helps reduce the potential for conflict among recipients over the objectives and allocation rules built into a program. Other ways of reducing collective action problems may include giving a quasi-official role to interest groups in agency decision-making processes, providing information to the group about new recipients and potential members, and working with groups to help them appear efficacious in the eyes of their members. These things help ensure that program recipients can be represented, organized, and mobilized by an interest group. Most important, these help interest group leaders in soliciting and marshaling the resources of present and potential group members.

In creating and maintaining a homogeneous population of program recipients, diversity of recipient populations across programs may stay the same or even increase. What is crucial is the degree of homogeneity of recipients within programs. Within-program homogeneity of recipients helps ensure that the interests of the recipients of a given program will be similar and can be represented by an interest group. A homogeneous population of program recipients reduces conflict among recipients over the goals and purposes of the program. This makes it easier for an organized interest group to form and be active in support of the program. Incrementally redesigning the portfolio to create homogeneity in the midst of heterogeneity reduces the opportunity for recipients to fight with one another over each program's administration. It also allows different interest groups to specialize. Each group can organize and mobilize with respect to specific programs in the agency's portfolio. Theodore Lowi (1979) pointed to this phenomenon as an essential element in the functioning of interest group liberalism:

When a program is set up in a specialized agency, the number of organized interest groups surrounding it tends to be reduced, reduced precisely to those groups and factions to whom the specialization is most salient. That almost immediately transforms the situation from one of potential competition to one of potential oligopoly. (p. 58)

With recipient homogeneity, an interest group is better able to appeal to the recipients and marshal their resources to share in the costs of maintaining the group's activities. The enhanced viability that this gives to an interest group helps produce more effective lobbying by the interest group on behalf of the agency and its programs. This affords the interest group maximum opportunity to take credit for the benefits that a group member receives and to support future increases in the agency's budgetary appropriations. It also permits interest groups to finance the reelection campaigns of representatives that are sympathetic to the concerns of the group.

Viewed from this perspective, reducing collective action problems can be an effective substitute for the provision of distributive benefits to legislative districts. Universalization of benefits may be one way to help ensure the reelection of legislators. It is not the only way. Nor is it necessarily the most effective way. The symbiotic relationships among subsystem actors produce benefits for members of the legislature that may be more important in determining their electoral fortunes than the program benefits that may flow to their district. This offers an explanation for why universalization of benefits is absent in the findings of Chapter 3.

Agencies, in particular, have a strong motivation for trying to create homogeneous recipient groups. Recall that agencies are responsible for monitoring program implementation. If the composition of recipients within a program is heterogeneous, the agency may find that it needs to promulgate different types of rules and regulations to implement the program. This may create an impression that the agency is arbitrary and engages in favoritism toward some recipients. This condition is likely to undermine programmatic support.

Subsystems have varying degrees of latitude to shape the homogeneity of recipient populations. In many subsystems, the administering agency has substantial discretion over who receives program assistance, how much they receive, and how program moneys are to be spent by recipients. In such cases, the agency may be able to establish new programs without express congressional action. This can be done by splitting or consolidating existing programs or by establishing demonstration programs. In so

54

doing, the agency shifts moneys and recipients to new programs, increasing the homogeneity of each population of program recipients. In other subsystems, the administering agency may not have broad discretion to refashion the program portfolio. In these cases, it will be necessary for legislators working together with interest group supporters and the administering agency to seek legislation altering the program portfolio. If legislation is required, it may be more difficult to create a more homogeneous recipient population for each of the programs in the portfolio. Indeed, such an effort might expose the subsystem to long-dormant internal conflicts or unwanted interventions by outside influences.

Creating more homogeneous recipient populations is only one of the strategies that may be pursued to reduce collective action problems of interest groups. A second strategy is to structure the program so that an intermediary agent will be responsible for the direct implementation of the program. This strategy, which may be more difficult to execute since legislative action is likely to be required, may be attempted when a program's ultimate beneficiaries lack the resources or are unable to bear the collective action costs to support interest group activities. By shifting implementation to intermediary agents, a new stakeholder is created, which may be in a much stronger position to bear collective action costs. An example of such a situation is aid to poor families. Poor people are difficult to organize, lack resources to support interest groups, vote in disproportionately low numbers, and in general are politically inefficacious. In short, they are not an influential constituency group. Examples of programs with this characteristic include food stamps, Aid to Families with Dependent Children (AFDC), and Medicaid. These programs are structured with states and local governments as the intermediate agents for implementation. The advantage of such a structure is that these intermediate agents will have an ongoing stake in the program's growth and they are already organized, possess resources for interest group activities, and are politically well connected. The intermediate agents will be far more willing and capable of bearing the costs of collective action in support of the subsystem's program portfolio.

Maximizing political support

The minimization of the collective action problems of interest groups is only one subsystem goal. Another important goal is to create a broad political base of support in the Congress. This goal is achieved by maximizing the number of congressional districts that are benefited by the subsystem's program portfolio. As demonstrated in Chapter 3, except with a program portfolio that includes large redistributive programs, fully universalized program portfolios are not easily achieved. This is, however,

District Coverage

		Narrow	Broad
Functional specificity	**Non-recurring**	Problem: Limited political support Collective action obstacles Solution: Increase recipient homogeneity Broaden functional scope Bundle with recurring programs	Problem: Collective action obstacles Solution: Increase recipient homogeneity Bundle with recurring programs
	Recurring	Problem: Limited political support Solution: Bundle with other programs	Problem: Supporters free- ride (i.e., complacency) Solution: Agency lobbying of interest groups and Congress

Figure 4.1. A typology of domestic assistance programs.

a condition toward which the subsystem has an incentive to move, since this maximizes political support in the legislature.

One of the key constraints on the possibility of universalizing program portfolios is the functional specificity of programs in its portfolio. Some problems that programs are designed to solve are not present in every congressional district. For example, price support for cotton farmers is geographically limited to districts where cotton farmers live. In some instances, problems may be present in virtually every district. An example is income support for the elderly. The implication is that subsystems will be constrained in their ability to universalize their portfolios by the degree to which the programs in their portfolio address problems that are geographically concentrated or dispersed.

The functional specificity of a program can be characterized in terms of two dimensions as shown in Figure 4.1. The first is the degree to which the program addresses problems that recur over time in the same geographic area. A program designed to address an ongoing problem, such as price supports for an agricultural commodity, is likely to provide assistance on a recurring basis to the same geographic areas. Conversely, a program designed to address a one-time-only problem, such as the construction of a wastewater treatment facility, will not provide assistance on a recurring basis to a given area. The second dimension of functional specificity is how broadly or narrowly a problem is distributed across the country.

56

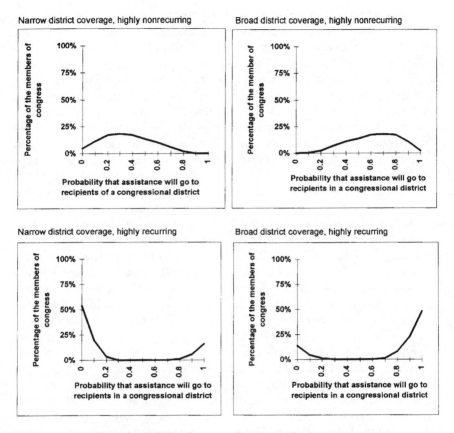

Figure 4.2. Hypothetical probability frequency distribution for four types of program structures based on likelihood that programs will provide assistance in a congressional district.

There are elderly people in every congressional district. There are not cotton farmers in every district. Where a problem falls on these two dimensions will determine the constraints the subsystem faces in universalizing its portfolio.

Programs with narrow and recurring district coverage pose a problem for subsystem actors. In programs that are recurring, the probability that any individual member of Congress will receive a benefit will be, for all practical purposes, one or zero. This type of program is illustrated in the lower left-hand frequency distribution in Figure 4.2. The narrower the breadth of such a program, the more the program will fall short of having enough members of Congress for whom the probability of receiving benefits is nonzero. Consequently, legislative adoption and subsequent reauthorization of these programs will be problematic in the absence of

57

logrolls between the members of Congress benefited by the programs. This produces a strong incentive to bundle these programs so that the union of district coverage across the portfolio of programs will be sufficient to secure a majority of votes.

There is anecdotal evidence that the strategy of bundling programs into portfolios is used to win approval for narrow, recurring programs. Price support programs for agricultural commodities exhibit the characteristics of recurring and narrow district coverage. It has long been the practice of the Department of Agriculture and the agriculture committees in Congress to bundle individual commodity price support programs together for legislative action. Rarely does the full committee or Congress vote on separate agricultural price support programs. Legislative support for each program can best be achieved through a voting coalition comprising the union of district representatives benefited by individual price support programs.

Subsystems whose program portfolios have broad and recurring district coverage would seem to be in an ideal situation. This type of program portfolio is illustrated in the lower right-hand frequency distribution in Figure 4.2. The potential problem with programs that are recurring and provide broad coverage is that complacency may arise among all interested parties. Interest group members come to believe that their receipt of program benefits is permanent and unchanging, reducing their incentive to support the interest group's efforts on behalf of the program. General Revenue Sharing (GRS) is an example of how complacency can undermine a broad, recurring program. Between 1972 and 1986 every city, county, and state received assistance under this program. There is evidence that after 1977 municipal governments relied on these moneys as a "permanent fixture of the federal system" (Stein, 1981). Yet when the program benefits were first cut in 1980 and then terminated in 1986, opposition was token and not "sufficient to save this endangered and unusual species of federal aid" (D. Wright, 1988:222). District and interest group coverage were so extensive that individual recipients behaved like free riders, believing other recipients would bear the costs of saving the program.

In contrast to programs with recurring coverage, for programs with nonrecurring coverage, the probability that an individual member's district will benefit is not constrained to probabilities near zero and one (see frequency distributions in the upper half of Figure 4.2). Nonrecurring district coverage removes this constraint and increases the opportunities for legislative support. These programs face a different type of problem. Because of their nonrecurring nature, it may be difficult for any group of legislators to justify bearing the costs involved in organizing a coalition to support the program. Lobbying by constituents from the home district may be infrequent, since the nonrecurring character of the program will prevent any group of constituents from having an expectation that they will benefit from the program in subsequent years. Consider the case of a program designed to help alleviate the damages of natural disasters. Everyone fears that there is some nonzero probability that a disaster might befall them, but few people expect a disaster every year. To remedy this problem, a subsystem may bundle nonrecurring programs with other programs that have a high incidence of recurrence. The advantage of this strategy is that it provides greater certainty that a district will receive a benefit from the portfolio of programs. This is, in fact, how disaster relief programs are organized. They are bundled with disaster prevention programs, which not surprisingly provide benefits to districts whether or not there has been or ever will be a disaster in the district (Anton, Cawley, and Kramer, 1980).

Nonrecurring programs may pose an additional problem, depending on the breadth of the portfolio's district coverage. In the case of narrow nonrecurring programs, there may be many districts for which the probability of receiving an award is virtually zero. This may be due to the functional specificity of the program, which limits its applicability to a small number of districts. An example would be a program that provides earthquake relief. Only a small number of districts have the (mis)fortune of being located on earthquake fault lines. Consequently building support for this program may be akin to the problems of building support for narrow, recurring programs. There are two potential remedies. One is to bundle the program with other programs. A second is to broaden the functional scope of the program. For example, the administering agency might lower the thresholds for inclusion in a program by lowering damage level requirements. The need to employ these strategies will be greatest for programs with narrow district coverage and least for those with broad district coverage.

Trade-offs between subsystem strategies

In sum, subsystem allies must pursue two basic goals. First, they seek to maximize the number of congressional districts serviced by the subsystem's entire portfolio of programs. The primary strategy for this goal is to distribute awards to recipients in as many Congressional districts as possible, through one or more of the programs in the portfolio. Second, they seek to minimize the collective action problem for supporting interest groups. One primary strategy for achieving this goal is to create homogeneous recipient populations within programs. These two goals are not always mutually exclusive. Under favorable economic and political conditions, subsystem actors should be able to effect both goals. When subsystem actors confront fiscal and/or political constraints, they may have to make a trade-off between district coverage and homogeneity of program recipients. Agencies and their congressional supporters may respond to tight or declining budgets by increasing program recipient homogeneity at the expense of district coverage. The latter may be difficult to attain when budgets are tight. Conversely, during periods of economic and political expansion, subsystem supporters might sacrifice some level of program homogeneity in order to preserve or even expand geographic coverage.

Subsystems with universalized and homogeneous program portfolios are expected to be in an advantageous position to resist budgetary cuts brought on by severe economic constraints or presidential hostility. Most subsystems, however, do not possess this happy coincidence of characteristics. During periods of budgetary constraint, we expect that subsystems whose program portfolios have narrow district coverage and a high level of recipient heterogeneity will be most anxious to restructure their portfolios. The problem for these subsystem actors is how to move the portfolio from a position of peril to a position of safety during a period in which the opportunities for change may be limited by the very political and economic conditions that make such change necessary. What strategies subsystem actors choose and whether or not the strategies succeed will depend in large measure on how the program portfolio is structured at the time that it is subjected to fiscal stress.

We have shown in Chapter 3 that there is little evidence of program universalism. Most programs are distributed to less than a majority of House districts. To a lesser degree the same is true of program bundles. This condition, however, does not preclude policy subsystems from successfully seeking broader legislative support for their programs. Recall that interest groups seek to maximize programmatic benefits for their membership and to solve their collective action problems. Legislators seek programmatic benefits to secure their reelection through credit-taking opportunities with their constituents. It is possible that interest groups can substitute campaign contributions (moneys and in-kind contributions) for district-level distributive benefits. Contributions from political action committees may serve as the functional equivalent of programmatic benefits in enhancing the electoral fortunes of legislators. We empirically examine this possibility in Chapter 5. In the remainder of this chapter we examine descriptive data on domestic program portfolios that existed during the 98th, 99th, 100th, and 101st Congresses, which corresponds to the 1983–90 period.

Our discussion of the strategies of policy subsystems treats subsystem actors as coparticipants in a set of mutually advantageous relationships. Agencies require the support of key members of Congress, as well as interest groups, to maximize legislative support and to reduce the collective action problems of supporting interest groups. Alteration of program requirements is likely to require express approval or the active acquiescence of the committees with jurisdiction over the agency. Similarly, increasing within-program homogeneity by shifting recipients into different programs within the portfolio is likely to be easier if key interest groups support such incremental changes. In short, achievement of these goals is dependent on the cooperation of actors across the subsystem.

HYPOTHESES, DATA, AND OPERATIONAL MEASURES

The maximization of political support is estimated with two dependent variables: district coverage and recurrence. Together, these two variables affect the likelihood that a member of Congress will have a direct, ex ante, predisposition to support a policy subsystem's program portfolio. District coverage directly measures the number of legislative districts receiving benefits. The extent of recurrence affects the probability estimates of legislators about the chances that their districts will receive benefits in the future. A high level of recurrence means that the districts not currently receiving benefits are unlikely to receive any in the future. Lower levels of recurrence indicate that a district, if it is not currently receiving a benefit, has a nonzero probability of receiving a benefit in the future.

Reductions in the collective action problems of recipients may be sacrificed in order to increase the geographic distribution of benefits. Change in district coverage is expected to be negatively related to change in the diversity of program recipients. That is, we expect there to be a trade-off between maximizing district coverage and increasing the homogeneity of recipients. The other factor that may lead to increasing district coverage is an increase in the number of programs contained in the portfolio. An increase in the number of programs should make it possible to distribute benefits to additional legislative districts. The model in which these relationships are examined also includes changes in appropriations for the program portfolio. This variable is included in order to control for the possibility that changes in district coverage is simply a function of available funds, rather than the pursuit of strategies designed to build political support for program portfolios.

Changing the extent to which benefits flow to the same districts over time may be a difficult task for subsystems due to the functional specificity of many distributive programs. To the extent that functional specificity of programs can be altered, subsystem actors may be able to reduce the rate at which benefits are recurrent to the same districts over time. Change in the recurrence rate is expected to be related to the change in the number of programs in a subsystem portfolio, and the change in the homogeneity of program recipients. Increases in the number of programs should make it possible for policy subsystems to broaden the functional specificity of their existing stock of programs, and thus move benefits to different districts from one year to the next. The new programs may permit the agency wider latitude so that it is not locked into providing benefits to recipients in the same districts over time. Changing the functional specificity of programs to afford the agency greater latitude in determining where benefits will be allocated may also mean that the agency must sacrifice recipient homogeneity. Thus, reducing the rate of recurrence may increase the collective action problems for interest groups in the subsystem. As district coverage exceeds a simple majority of legislative districts, recurrence is expected to decline.

Reducing collective action problems for interest groups in the subsystem is facilitated by increasing homogeneity of recipient populations within programs. Changes in the diversity of a recipient population is expected to be a function of the change in the number of programs in a subsystem portfolio and changes in the number of districts receiving program benefits. Additional programs may make it possible to rearrange recipients among programs so that recipient homogeneity within each program is maximized. As discussed already, there is likely to be a trade-off between reducing recipient diversity and maximizing district coverage. Therefore, we expect to observe a negative slope between increases in district coverage and increases in the homogeneity of recipient populations within programs.

Information on program portfolios has been compiled from the *Catalog of Federal Domestic Assistance* (CFDA) and the *Federal Assistance Awards Data System* (FAADS). As discussed in Chapter 2, information on program attributes, appropriations for programs, as well as the grouping of programs by agency, is obtained from CFDA (see Appendix 1). Information on awards to congressional districts and different types of recipients is derived from data provided in FAADS (see Appendix 2). In this chapter, these two data sources are combined to provide information about the strategies pursued by subsystems with distributive program portfolios.

The data set for this chapter is composed of biennial measurements on the 72 agencies with distributive program portfolios providing financial assistance awards in each two-year period corresponding to the 98th, 99th, 100th, and 101st Congresses. A list of these agencies is contained in Appendix 4. The portfolios included in this data set had at least one distributive program, though not necessarily the same program, under which awards were made in each of these Congresses. This decision rule was employed to remove the possibility that shifts in our measures over time might be due to agencies coming into and going out of operation, rather than changes within a fixed population of program portfolios. The potential for selection biases due to the entrance of new portfolios and premature exit of others led us to conclude that the safest and most conservative research design was to include in our sample only those portfolios that were providing financial assistance in the 98th Congress and continued to do so through the 101st Congress.

To tap the concept of program bundling by agencies, we measure the number of programs in an agency's portfolio. The measure is the number of financial and nonfinancial programs, including both direct assistance programs and indirect subsidy programs such as loans and loan guarantees, as well as programs providing nonfinancial assistance.

District coverage is measured as the number of congressional districts receiving benefits from at least one financial assistance program in the subsystem's program portfolio. This variable measures the total number of districts receiving awards during the two-year period corresponding to a Congress. The data source for this variable is FAADS, and thus the measure counts benefits only from programs that provide direct financial assistance (i.e., it excludes nonfinancial assistance, as well as subsidies from direct loans, loan guarantees, and insurance).

Recurring district coverage in a program is defined operationally as the proportion of districts that contained recipients of a program's assistance in the consecutive pair of years of a given Congress. Notice that no assumption is made as to whether the recipients in a recurring district are the same in consecutive years or are different recipients from one year to the next. The concept of recurrence used here applies only to the congressional district: does a district contain recipients of a program's assistance in a consecutive pair of years or not? This is measured as: RECUR = [N/D] *100, where N = number of districts receiving assistance in both years, and D = union of districts receiving assistance in either of two years.

We report the rate of recurrence of benefits to districts from all programs in an agency's portfolio. This measures the proportion of districts that received benefits in consecutive years from any program in the portfolio. As with the measure of district coverage, the data source for this variable is FAADS, and thus the measure taps recurrence of benefits only from programs that provide direct financial assistance. For some smaller agencies, no direct financial assistance awards were made in one of the two years during a particular Congress. This made it impossible to calculate a rate of recurrence for the agency's programs during the Congress. For this reason, analyses that include the recurrence measure are limited to sixty-two, rather than to seventy-two, program portfolios.

Our measure of program recipient diversity is calculated by summing across the number of different categories of recipients that receive at least one award from a program. FAADS classifies recipients into twelve categories including states and state-supported universities, cities and towns, counties, special districts, independent school districts, Indian tribes, nonprofit agencies, private universities, for-profit organizations, small businesses, individuals, and a residual category for all other types of recipients. Our measure of diversity ranges between 1 and 12, since a program could provide assistance to recipients in as few as 1 and in as many as 12 categories. The shortcoming of this measure is that it does not pick up differences across recipients within categories. For example, a program may allocate awards entirely to cities, and thus would be coded as a 1 on the diversity measure, despite nontrivial differences across cities. Differences between, say, Chicago, Illinois, and Dime Box, Texas, are important and involve very real diversity among recipients. Yet, as a practical matter, it is impossible to find an operational measure that could do justice to the differences of recipients within each recipient category. It is also true, however, that differences across categories, say between the city of Chicago and the University of Illinois or between Dime Box and an elementary school, constitute real, and enduring, sources of diversity across recipients. Our measure picks up this latter type of diversity.

Budgetary resources of subsystems are measured in terms of the total appropriations across the programs administered by an agency. This figure is taken from the CFDA and represents authority to spend money, which may not precisely equal the actual amount of money that an agency may have spent on outlays to specific recipients in a particular time frame. Appropriations are reported in constant 1982 dollars and reflect the average total appropriation level for the programs in the portfolio across the two years of each Congress.

The hypotheses that we examine are inherently diachronic in operation. Subsystem actors are expected to manipulate their portfolios, over time, in ways that compensate for deficiencies in the structure of their portfolios. All five variables – numbers of programs in portfolios, district coverage, recurrence, recipient diversity, and appropriations – are therefore measured in terms of the average change across the four Congresses. For each variable, the average change in each adjacent pair of Congresses is used to operationalize the change over time in the dependent and independent variables.

FINDINGS

Table 4.1 reports the regression estimates for the average change in district coverage. As hypothesized, increases in district coverage are positively related to the changes in the number of programs contained in a subsystem portfolio. An increase in the number of programs included in a portfolio has a modest effect on district coverage. For every new program added to a portfolio, district coverage increases two districts. Given a median portfolio size of three programs, it would be difficult for any subsystem to augment significantly its district coverage through a strategy designed to increase the number of programs in its portfolio.

Table 4.1. *Regression estimates for the average change in district coverage of program portfolios: 98th-101st Congress*

Variable	Coefficient	Standard error	T-value
Constant	4.53	1.83	2.47**
Change in			
Program recipient diversity	3.51	1.39	2.51**
Number of programs in portfolio	1.81	0.68	2.65**
Total appropriations	0.126	0.613	0.201
N	72		
R square	0.140		

*$p < 0.05$ **$p < 0.01$

The addition of programs to a portfolio, however, may provide another source of political support for the policy subsystem. Interest groups that are benefited by program additions are likely to lobby legislators on behalf of new programs that might be added to the portfolio. Organized beneficiaries of a subsystem's program portfolio may be better positioned than other subsystem actors (i.e., legislators or agency personnel) to garner legislative support for the subsystem's portfolio. In part, this is because organized groups can substitute campaign contributions for district-level distributive benefits. Because campaign funds are more fungible for the purposes of reelection than program benefits, this type of political support may be more coveted by legislators than program benefits. Interest groups can often be effective in lobbying legislators in whose districts subsystem program benefits are not distributed.

Table 4.1 also indicates that there is a significant trade-off between district coverage and reductions in the collective action problems of recipients. On average, the addition of one recipient category per program increases district coverage nearly four districts. The coefficient for change in program diversity is significant and in the negative direction. This means that expanding district coverage comes at the expense of recipient homogeneity. The change in appropriations for program portfolios does not have a significant effect on the changes in district coverage. Contrary to conventional thinking, additional funding per program does not enhance district coverage. This finding indicates that the pursuit of growth in district coverage is not simply a matter of subsystem actors harvesting greater fiscal resources for their program portfolios. Building political support for policy subsystems is considerably more complex, requiring

Table 4.2. *Regression estimates for the average change in recurrence of district benefits: 98th-101st Congress*

Variable	Coefficient	Standard error	T-value
Constant	0.039	0.009	4.12**
Change in			
Program recipient diversity	0.0004	0.0008	0.543
Number of programs in portfolio	-0.034	0.004	-1.03
District coverage	-0.000576	0.000595	-0.967
N	62		
R square	0.040		

*p < 0.05 **p < 0.01

subsystem actors to strike a balance between district coverage and reducing collective action costs.

Table 4.2 reports the regression estimates for the average change in the recurrence of district coverage. The change in the number of districts containing program recipients in pairs of consecutive years is not significantly related to the change in the number of programs, recipient diversity, or district coverage. The weak performance of the recurrence model is due in large part to the lack of variation in our measure of recurrence. The median change in the number of districts containing program recipients in adjacent years is 2 percent. This shows that very little change occurs over time in the set of congressional districts where program recipients are located.

Our sense is that the rate at which benefits are recurrent to the same districts over time is highly constrained by the functional specificity of programs. Radically altering the functional content of a subsystem portfolio is difficult, and likely to require a gestation period longer than the two-year intervals studied here. Moreover, it is possible that reducing the rate of recurrence may carry risks for subsystem supporters of a program portfolio. Representatives from districts in which program benefits have been recurrent are typically among the strongest supporters of a policy subsystem (cf. Hamman, 1993:561–5). Reducing the rate at which benefits are recurrent in the same districts may risk alienating these core subsystem supporters. Such a loss in support might not be offset by the political support obtained from expanded district coverage or legislators who anticipate new awards in their districts.

Table 4.3. *Regression estimates for the average change in diversity of program recipients: 98th-101st Congress*

Variable	Coefficient	Standard error	T-value
Constant	-0.212	0.155	-1.36
Change in			
Number of programs in portfolio	-0.135	0.005	-2.37**
District coverage	0.027	0.0009	2.87**
N	72		
R square	0.123		

*$p < 0.05$ **$p < 0.01$

As expected, the findings in Table 4.3 show that the change in the diversity of program recipients is significantly related to change in district coverage and the number of programs in a subsystem portfolio. The addition of new programs to a subsystem portfolio decreases the mean program recipient diversity score. The average number of program recipient categories drops by 0.1 per program with the addition of one new program. The negative affect that new programs have on program diversity suggests that the programmatic expansion of a policy subsystem is targeted, in part, at minimizing the collective action costs of subsystem interest groups. Expanding district coverage increases the diversity of program recipients. The average number of program recipient categories increases 0.3 per program with the addition of ten new districts.

The findings in Table 4.3 provide an additional explanation for why universalization of benefits is absent in the findings of Chapter 3. Significant expansion of district coverage comes at the expense of satisfying core subsystem supporters. Although small increases in district coverage entail only minor expansion of program recipient diversity, significant expansion – beyond half the legislature – would risk significant collective action problems for core subsystem supporters.

Table 4.4 reports the regression estimates for the average change in program portfolio appropriations. If money matters in the design and operation of policy subsystem portfolios, we should observe changes in appropriations to covary with changes in district coverage, program diversity, and the number of programs in a subsystem's portfolio. This is not the case. None of the coefficients in Table 4.4 are statistically significant, nor does the model account for any significant portion of the varia-

67

Table 4.4. *Regression estimates for the average change in program portfolio appropriations: 98th-101st Congress*

Variable	Coefficient	Standard error	T-value
Constant	316	365	0.864
Change in			
Number of programs in portfolio	-2.48	2.79	-0.888
District coverage	-84.6	137	-0.614
Program recipient diversity	4.67	23.2	0.201
N	72		
R square	0.013		

Note: Appropriations in millions of constant 1982 dollars.
$^*p < 0.05$ $^{**}p < 0.01$

tion in the average change in program portfolio appropriations. What this indicates is that program appropriations are not systematically related to the design of policy subsystem portfolios.

CONCLUSION

In this chapter we have developed the logic underlying our policy subsystem model. Our findings confirm the existence of policy subsystems that operate to promote the collective and individual interests of subsystem actors. District coverage of program portfolios increases with the addition of new programs and the diversity of program recipients. Program diversity decreases with new programs and increases with district coverage. Interestingly, however, there is no evidence that appropriations positively impact district coverage or the reduction of collective action costs for program beneficiaries. Program portfolio appropriations have a negligible effect on promoting subsystem strategies. Our findings suggest a number of questions about the operation of policy subsystems, particularly the trade-off between different subsystem goals and the importance of money in the operation of policy subsystems.

Strategies designed to achieve greater district coverage were found to be unproductive and in one instance counterproductive to another subsystem goal. District coverage increases slowly with the addition of new programs and is unresponsive to increases in program portfolio appropriations. Attempting to increase district coverage through the acquisition of new programs is not likely to achieve substantial success. Furthermore, the cost of increasing district coverage through the acquisition of new programs comes at the cost of an increase in recipient diversity. As we discovered in Chapter 3, the absence of universalized program portfolios suggests that subsystem actors may prefer not to increase district coverage, since this comes at the expense of disadvantaging their core supporters. This conclusion is corroborated by the fact that changes in new program acquisitions diminish the diversity of recipients. It would appear, therefore, that policy subsystems place a greater premium on controlling the collective action costs of their interest group beneficiaries than on expanding district coverage.

It is noteworthy that the average size of program appropriations is not related to the pursuit of subsystem goals of district coverage, recipient homogeneity and recurrence. Although policy analysts are often preoccupied with the fiscal size of domestic assistance programs, this attention may not be the central focus of all subsystem actors. In Chapter 7 we examine the possibility that political benefits that accrue to legislators from the distribution of program benefits are tied to the number of awards distributed to recipients in their district rather than the monetary size of these awards.

How then do policy subsystems expand their base of support? The answer to this question may be related to the behavior of interest groups. In Chapter 6 we examine the possibility that PAC contributions from interest groups can be substituted for district level benefits as an incentive for legislators to support subsystem portfolios.

5

Policy subsystem adaptability and resilience in the Reagan period

In this chapter we turn our attention to the durability of policy sub-systems. Specifically, we examine how subsystem actors respond to bud-getary assaults on their program portfolios. In Chapter 4 we outlined the logic underlying our policy subsystem model. We found that policy sub-systems operated in a predictable fashion, seeking a balance between maximum district coverage and minimum diversity of program recipients. Generally, however, we found that policy subsystems place a greater em-phasis on minimizing the collective action problems of their interest group stakeholders than expanding district coverage, or program appropria-tions. We found that program appropriations were unrelated to either district coverage or recipient homogeneity. Our examination of subsystem strategies in Chapter 4 did not, however, differentiate between policy subsystems that were well supported and those under challenge. We might reasonably expect that the pursuit of subsystem strategies is made mea-surably easier when the fiscal and/or political climate is supportive rather than hostile.

The 1980s were a difficult decade for many policy subsystems at the federal level. During much of the decade, "politics as usual" was sus-pended, in part, as a consequence of the Reagan administration's active efforts to curtail spending in many areas of domestic policy. In part, it was a consequence of the fiscal constraint imposed by mounting budgetary deficits, a constraint expressed vividly in the Gramm–Rudman deficit reduction agreement. Taken together, these forces reached deep into the day-to-day functioning of many domestic policy subsystems. As a number of scholars have shown, a host of domestic programs and entire agencies were made vulnerable to cutbacks, and some to outright termination (e.g., Ellwood, 1982; Palmer and Sawhill, 1984; Chubb and Peterson, 1985; Rubin, 1985; Nathan and Doolittle, 1987; Conlan, 1988; Bickers, 1991).

This chapter focuses on the budgetary climate during the Reagan period and its impact on the programmatic activities of federal agencies in four cabinet level departments. The chapter is different from most analyses of the Reagan era in several respects. First, the chapter does not focus solely on policy activities that fell out of favor with the election of Ronald Reagan. Instead the chapter compares the fate of agencies targeted for cuts with those that the administration proposed to receive budgetary increases. We track how the program portfolios of the forty-six agencies included in the study changed over the decade of the 1980s in order to see how policy subsystems fared, not just in the short-term, but over the long-term as well. We are thus able to point to specific differences in how agencies and their backers, both those favored and those opposed by the administration, responded to the changes in their political environments. Second, the chapter treats the issue of how agencies are affected by changes in their political environments as a question of program portfolio maintenance and adaptation. Specifically, it asks how subsystem actors, responding to changes in the political environment, adapt their program portfolios to reduce the risk of a catastrophic loss and to ensure growth.

We should note, however, that the data presented here hint at, but cannot fully reveal, the groping, experimentation, and excitement of the groups of people that were faced with the sudden loss of funding for programs of concern to them as they were forced to respond to the new climate with new strategies and newfound resolve. This type of contextual detail can only be found in well-written case studies of the period (e.g., Rubin, 1985). The metaphor of a portfolio of programs, however, directs attention to two aspects of these responses that might otherwise be overlooked.

In the first place, the portfolio idea suggests that the focus should not be on one program only, but on the way the full set of program activities that are of concern to groups of actors is managed and invested in, to minimize the probability of incurring catastrophic losses and to produce positive returns over an extended period of time. The question is, How is the group of programs that an agency administers utilized, not simply to achieve prestated policy objectives, but also to create and maintain necessary levels of political support for the continuation and expansion of the activities of subsystem actors? Second, the portfolio idea suggests that the relevant unit of analysis should be broadly construed to encompass the full range of claimants on a group of programs. The agency is not the sole entity with a concern for a group of programs. So are the other actors in a policy subsystem. Each of these actors is forced by a crisis, such as that posed during the Reagan period, to reassess how much of their resources (time, political capital, money, etc.) they want to have invested in a group of programs. The answer will depend both on the amount of risk that they are willing to tolerate and on the alternatives to which those resources might be put.

71

These portfolios exist in a political environment, and thus the viability of the overall portfolio is determined by how much of their political currency the various actors in a policy subsystem are willing to invest, given the political environment at the time. The political environment created by the Reagan administration's budget proposals is thus a unique opportunity to examine policy subsystems at work. Each policy subsystem has different groups of actors that have to make their own calculations as to how much to invest in a portfolio of programs. Each policy subsystem also is affected, to a greater or lesser extent, by the increased risk of loss.

POLICY SUBSYSTEM STRATEGIES

Several behavioral responses by policy subsystems might be expected when an agency's funding is threatened by budgetary cutbacks. First, we might expect the various participants in a threatened policy subsystem to mobilize aggressively to secure additional programs to shore up the existing portfolio. Small or large, new programs allow a policy subsystem to use its portfolio to reach out directly to constituent groups that might otherwise not have a strong stake in the agency's fate. This strategy, though likely to be central in the development of a stronger, more defensible portfolio, may be difficult to accomplish in the short run, since there are usually substantial barriers to the creation of new programs. Also, this strategy, one might assume, would pose more of a problem for small agencies and those with few programs, as an additional program would represent a much larger relative jump in such portfolios than in one already possessing a number of programs. Consequently, it will be important to control for initial size of program portfolios, both in terms of numbers of programs and in funding levels.

Second, we might expect that policy subsystems, when threatened by cuts, would seek to reallocate available budgetary authority to provide benefits to as many congressional districts as possible. This response, however, may be muted by functional specificity of the agency's existing programs, by the scarceness of the agency's available pool of funds, and by the need to keep existing recipients working within the policy subsystem, which mitigates against drastically lowering benefit levels to existing recipients. In recognition of these factors, controls are included for the agency's initial funding level and for the number of congressional districts receiving assistance at the outset of the period.

Third, we might expect that in an embattled policy subsystem efforts would be made by the agency and other subsystem actors to help its interest groups to overcome their collective action problems so that they might be as effective as possible in defending the subsystem's interests in the legislative process. If our earlier discussion is on track, then making the groups of recipients for each program more homogenous should reduce the collective action problems of the groups attempting to organize on behalf of the agency's programs. The extent to which the recipients of programs can be made more homogeneous will be a function both of the average level of recipient diversity within programs, as well as the overall diversity of recipients across the full set of programs within the portfolio. Also likely to be a constraint on the reduction of the average recipient diversity of programs is the amount of funding available to spend on the portfolio of programs. Controls for these constraining variables are thus included in the models presented here.

To fend off proposed budget cuts, policy subsystems may adopt another set of strategies, which we are unable to examine in detail. This category is composed of "guerilla warfare" tactics. These, by their vary nature, are difficult to measure or test directly, and thus are not examined in the empirical portion of this chapter. Nevertheless, the use of these tactics is common enough to warrant mention. One such tactic is to inhibit efforts to cut a policy subsystem's programs by holding up, through creative use of legislative procedures, any nominee that the administration proposes to become the head of the agency. This helps forestall cuts by preventing the administration from being able to place its people directly in the agency, where they might be able to dismantle it from the inside. Another strategy is to offer up a "sacrificial lamb," that is, to suggest, under protest, that the administration cut a particular program but save the rest of the programs in the portfolio. This strategy can be particularly advantageous since it allows the subsystem to choose for elimination a program that might be inconsequential to the key players in the policy subsystem, but which satisfies the demands of the administration for cuts. It also allows the policy subsystem to claim, with apparent plausibility, that it has borne its "fair share" of cuts if or when it is targeted for cutbacks in a future budget cycle.

It is also possible that some subsystems might recast their policy goals in light of the administration's agenda. This can be done by deemphasizing some programs and their goals, while emphasizing, and perhaps redefining, other programs and their goals. Such changes may be mostly rhetorical, little more than a disguise, but may nonetheless be effective, because they may suggest that the policy subsystem's programs should be treated as part of the president's mandate, rather than as part of the policy legacy that he wants to eliminate. This latter strategy may not always be a viable option, since its success will depend on how closely the administration actually looks at the policy subsystem's portfolio of programs, as well as how easily a portfolio of programs can be justified on new policy grounds without upsetting and alienating existing supporters.

To the extent that policy subsystems are able to pursue these strategies, we would expect that they should be able to fend off the administration's proposed cutbacks. Specifically, the expectation is that significant differences should exist in the use and effectiveness of these strategies between agencies threatened by cutbacks and those not threatened. Threatened agencies, one assumes, would make special efforts to ensure that every response haś as much payoff as possible. The measure of "payoff" (i.e., adjustment success) used here is the increase or decrease in the amount of money that a threatened agency is able to spend as a result of its use of the strategies just described. The focus here is not on absolute increases or decreases in agency outlays. Instead, the focus is on relative differences in the amount of increase or decrease between agencies that were threatened with cutbacks and those that were not. This focus on relative differences allows an analysis of the efficacy of the adjustment strategies that threatened versus nonthreatened policy subsystems employ.

RESEARCH DESIGN

This chapter examines the responses of policy subsystems to the budgetary climate during the Reagan period by examining the programmatic adjustments of agencies in four cabinet-level departments: Agriculture, Education, Health and Human Services, and Commerce. The four departments included here were selected because they contain a wide variety of agencies, involved not just in the provision of redistributive social services but other types of domestic assistance as well, including distributive programs. Also these departments contain agencies that the administration proposed for cuts as well as agencies favored for budgetary increases. A few offices and agencies are excluded from each department, either because the office or agency provides administrative or other services to the department itself (e.g., Office of the Secretary, Office of the Legal Counsel), or because no information was available relating to the response of the agency to the proposed changes in appropriations. A full list of agencies included in the study, along with a description of the coding rules that were employed, is found in Appendix 5.

The support or opposition of the administration to an agency's portfolio of programs is measured in two ways. The simplest, and crudest, measure is simply the direction of change from the actual appropriation level for an agency's program activities in fiscal year (FY) 1981, the last budget wholly prepared in the Carter administration, to the proposed appropriation level for an agency's activities in FY1983, the first budget prepared entirely by the Reagan administration. This was the budget that the administration submitted to Congress in January 1982 (see Stockman, 1986). A more sensitive measure of the administration's support or opposition to the agency was also constructed using the percentage increase or decrease from the actual appropriation level in FY1981 to the proposed level in FY1983 for each agency's program activities. In four cases where agencies did not exist in 1981 (and thus had appropriations of zero), the percentage increase or decrease utilizes FY1982 as the baseline year. Data for these measures are drawn from the FY1983 *Appendix to the Budget of the United States Government,* which is prepared by the Office of Management and Budget in the Executive Office of the President. All of the figures used here represent the sum of the actual (FY1981) or proposed (FY1983) obligations (costs) of all program activities listed in each agency. For purposes of this analysis, these figures, as well as all other financial information, have been deflated to constant 1982 dollars, using the implicit price deflator for government purchases of goods and services. Obligation levels for FY1981 and FY1983 are reported in Appendix 5 for each of the agencies.

What these data show is that the Reagan administration favored real reductions in most of the program portfolios included in this study. Of the 46 agencies included here, the administration proposed cuts in 31. As part of its overall plans to eliminate the Department of Education, all six Education agencies were to be abolished entirely, with their programs to be terminated or transferred to other agencies, some of which did not then exist, but were to be newly created. Of the remaining 25 agencies with proposed cuts, 12 were in Agriculture (out of 17 USDA agencies with domestic assistance programs), 4 were in Commerce (out of 6 agencies with domestic assistance programs), and 9 were in Health and Human Services (out of 17 with domestic assistance programs). Among the 25 agencies in these three departments, none was to be abolished. Compared with obligation levels in FY1981, the average cutback was to be 25.9 percent in constant dollars by FY1983. Of the 15 agencies that the administration proposed for real increases, 4 did not exist in 1981; the 11 remaining agencies were to receive an average increase from FY1981 to FY1983 of 26.3 percent, with a maximum proposed increase of 176 percent.

How and when subsystems respond to threatened budgetary cutbacks may be affected by the nature of agency personnel. Lynn (1984) reports that administrative appointees in the first Reagan administration were initially eager to implement President Reagan's efforts to curtail government spending. With time, however, they were frustrated by entrenched agency personnel who resisted efforts to cut program budgets. "Although some kind of externally provoked change was the rule rather than the exception in these agencies, their experiences also demonstrate convincingly that change is a slow, costly process attended by controversy and exceedingly demanding of executive effort" (Lynn, 1984:361).

One issue on which we have chosen to remain agnostic is the question of how long is the period of adjustment required for a policy subsystem to respond to threatened cutbacks. Part of the difficulty in making adjustments is that the window to secure statutory amendments is a function of when a program is scheduled to come up for reauthorization. But part of the difficulty is that mobilizing disparate groups of actors takes time and may involve significant hurdles. Indeed the threat represented by the administration's proposal to cut an agency's budget may throw all of the actors in the policy subsystem into disarray. The level of consensus about what directions to pursue may not be high. Some of the actors may prefer to jump ship, rather than mobilize resources to defend the policy subsystem and its portfolio of programs. Thus it may take a period from a few months to several years for policy subsystem actors to mobilize sufficient resources and gain enough support from actors in the larger political environment to obtain additional programs, gain the administrative discretion or changes in statutory formulas to expand the geographic distribution of program assistance, or alter the agency's decision rules to channel recipients of programs into more homogeneous recipient populations. It is also important to note that some policy subsystems may prove too inept or too weak to make such adjustments. Collapse should never be ruled out.

The analysis here models the adjustment process over three different lengths of time. For each regression, the beginning period for the adjustment process is taken to be the 98th Congress (1983–4), which, given the lead time needed to move ideas from the proposal stage through the legislative process to administrative action, is the first Congress in which the Reagan administration could be expected to have had a relatively free hand. Agency decisions during the 97th Congress, while doubtless influenced heavily by the Reagan administration, would have been determined in large measure by legislation passed during the Carter period. Each adjustment process is modeled over three progressively longer time periods: first, the period from the 98th through the 99th Congress; second, the period from the 98th through the 100th Congress; and third, the period from the 98th Congress through the 101st Congress. In some cases, the adjustment process may work relatively quickly; in others, the process may take more time. In every case, however, policy subsystems operating under the threat of greater cutbacks are expected to respond more dramatically than subsystems operating under a lesser threat or with the support of the administration.

Data on the responses of the policy subsystems are drawn from *Federal Assistance Awards Data System* (see Appendix 2). Information on the agency with responsibility for each program was identified from the *Catalog of Federal Domestic Assistance* (see Appendix 1). The rule was to code the most discrete organizational unit listed (i.e., lowest on the government manual organizational chart) in the catalog with responsibility for a program as the administrative agency.[1]

To examine the degree to which program portfolios are altered in response to the threat of budgetary cutbacks, these data were organized as follows. First, the data were aggregated by pairs of years, 1983–4, 1985–6, 1987–8, and 1989–90, which correspond to the 98th, 99th, 100th, and 101st Congresses, respectively. Second, five variables were computed to describe the program portfolios of the agencies in each Congress: the number of domestic assistance programs administered by each agency; the number of congressional districts that contain recipients of at least one of the agency's programs; the average annual appropriations for the agency's programs (deflated to constant 1982 dollars); a portfolio diversity index that is simply the number of different recipient categories receiving at least some (one dollar or more) assistance from the program; and an average program diversity index that is the average of the diversity index calculated for each program administered by the agency. The latter two measures have a potential range of 1 to 12, with a score of 1 indicating that all of the assistance went to just one type of recipient, and a score of 12 indicating that at least some assistance went to all 12 types of recipients that are recorded in the Bickers and Stein data base.[2] The portfolio diversity index reflects the number of different categories of recipients receiving assistance from any one (or more) of the agency's programs. The average program diversity index is measured by calculating a recipient diversity index for each program, and then averaging the index across the number of programs administered by the agency. Finally, the third step in organizing the data was to compute change measures for each of these five variables. Change measures were calculated for each of the three adjustment periods described here: the 98th through the 99th, the 98th through the 100th, and the 98th through the 101st Congress.

A set of regression models is specified with a dummy variable to indicate whether an agency was threatened by the Reagan administration with cutbacks (the excluded category is nonthreatened agencies). To test each of the expected strategies, each model includes this "threat" dummy variable, which is interacted with our measures of the extent to which each of the three strategies is used. In each model, the interaction term reflects the amount of change in the dependent variable for threatened agencies. By setting up a regression model in this form, the slope coefficients for each of the interaction terms estimate the difference in efficacy of a strategy for a threatened agency compared with a nonthreatened one; the *t*-ratios indicate the statistical significance of the strategy's efficacy for threatened agencies compared with nonthreatened agencies. Such a model should permit us to view clearly how successful threatened agencies are

77

when using these strategies compared with similarly situated non-threatened agencies.

Table 5.1 reports means for the five variables, broken down into agencies that the Reagan administration proposed for budget decreases and budget increases. In brief, what these data indicate is that agencies that the administration proposed to cut, on most dimensions, had larger and more varied program portfolios than agencies that had been slated for increases. In numbers of programs, numbers of congressional districts receiving assistance from the agencies, average recipient diversity, and overall portfolio diversity, agencies that were threatened with cutbacks were generally larger. Only in dollar size do the threatened agencies appear smaller than the nonthreatened agencies. This is somewhat misleading, however, because two of the nonthreatened agencies (the Social Security Administration and Health Care Financing Administration) have among the most expensive programs in the federal budget. When outlays for these two agencies are excluded, the average outlays of nonthreatened agencies are only one-fifth those of threatened agencies. It is also apparent from these data that the nonthreatened agencies were, on most dimensions, not as aggressive as threatened ones in responding to the fiscal environment of the Reagan period. Threatened agencies were more successful in obtaining additional programs and distributing assistance to additional congressional districts. Neither group of agencies was terribly successful in reducing the diversity of recipients, with some movement toward greater homogeneity and some toward greater heterogeneity. The one dimension on which nonthreatened agencies appear clearly to have done better was in expansion of outlays. Once again, however, these numbers are upwardly biased by the inclusion of Social Security and Health Care Financing. When these two agencies are removed from the calculation, it becomes apparent that outlays by threatened agencies expanded at a substantially greater pace (on the order of 66 to 1) than did the outlays of nonthreatened agencies.

The first set of regressions focuses on changes in the number of programs in agency portfolios as a function of the size of the Reagan administration's proposed budgetary increase or decrease (from FY1981 to FY1983), the agency's FY1981 obligations, and the number of assistance programs that the agency possessed in the 98th Congress. The results of these regressions are reported in Table 5.2. The results indicate a couple of patterns. First, the administration's proposed changes do not have an immediate impact on changes in the number of programs in the agency portfolios. But as the adjustment period extends outward in time, there is

Table 5.1. Threatened and nonthreatened agencies during the early Reagan administration: Effect on number of programs, district coverage, recipient diversity, and budget outlays

	Average number of programs		Average number of districts		Average program diversity		Average overall agency diversity		Average total program outlays	
	Threatened	Not threatened	Threatened	Not threatened	Threatened	Not threatened	Threatened	Not threatened	Threatened	Not threatened
Congress										
98th	8.40	2.90	198.30	135.50	4.3	4.2	7.5	5.8	1,282,443,274	17,541,540,302
99th	9.20	3.20	207.90	174.70	4.2	4.2	7.1	6.0	1,599,589,225	20,264,067,817
100th	9.90	3.30	207.30	138.50	3.6	4.0	6.6	6.1	1,849,582,745	21,985,031,761
101st	11.20	3.30	215.30	161.80	4.0	4.4	7.3	6.5	2,005,185,534	25,812,716,043
98th–99th	0.70	0.13	12.17	1.53	0.07	−0.31	0.00	−0.15	277,885,070	2,722,527,515
98th–100th	1.48	0.20	9.06	−6.40	−0.55	−0.46	−0.55	−0.08	567,139,470	4,443,491,459
98th–101st	2.74	0.20	17.00	13.80	−0.21	−0.33	0.14	0.25	722,742,260	8,271,175,741
Number of observations										
98th	31	15	31	15	29	14	29	14	31	15
99th	30	15	30	15	30	13	30	13	30	15
100th	31	15	31	15	31	13	31	13	31	15
101st	31	15	31	15	31	13	31	13	31	15
98th–99th	30	15	30	15	28	13	28	13	31	15
98th–100th	31	15	31	15	29	13	29	13	31	15
98th–101st	31	15	31	15	29	12	29	12	31	15

Table 5.2. Regression estimates for change in the number of programs in portfolio

Model	Adjustment period	Independent variables	Estimated coefficient	T-value
2.1	93th - 99th	Constant	0.605	2.183*
		Proposed change in agency budget (%)	0.0017	0.349
		FY81 agency obligations (millions of constant dollars)	-0.00002	-2.722**
		Number of programs in 98th Congress	0.0132	0.544
		Mean of dependent variable	0.511	
		Number of observations	45	
		R square	0.154	
2.2	93th - 100th	Constant	0.394	1.072
		Proposed change in agency budget (%)	-0.0076	-1.197
		FY81 agency obligations (millions of constant dollars)	-0.00003	-2.809**
		Number of programs in 98th Congress	0.1073	3.319**
		Mean of dependent variable	1.065	
		Number of observations	46	
		R square	0.355	
2.3	93th - 101st	Constant	0.797	1.203
		Proposed change in agency budget (%)	-0.029	-2.508*
		FY81 agency obligations (millions of constant dollars)	-0.00003	-1.533
		Number of programs in 98th Congress	0.1015	1.744
		Mean of dependent variable	1.913	
		Number of observations	46	
		R square	0.271	

*$p < 0.05$ **$p < 0.01$

clear movement toward additional programs among agencies that were the most threatened. Compare, for example, the results of model 2.1 with model 2.3. When examining changes in the number of programs from the 98th to the 101st Congress, the regression coefficient indicates that among agencies that had 100 percent cuts proposed, the average increase in the number of programs, all other things being equal, is almost three programs. What this means is that threats to cut an agency's budget have what might be viewed as a perverse, if predictable, result. Threats provoke policy subsystem responses that, at least over an adjustment period of three or four Congresses, culminates in significant additions to program portfolios.

The second pattern in these regression results is that the larger an agency's outlays in 1981, the fewer additional programs it tends to obtain. Over each of the adjustment periods, the relationship between net program increase and obligation size is negative. Said differently, what these data indicate is that agencies with smaller budgets are more active in seeking and obtaining additional programs. At the same time, however, agencies with a large number of programs appear to be able to add additional programs more easily than agencies with few programs. The estimates in models 2.2 and 2.3 indicate that, on average, one program is added over a period of three to four Congresses for every ten programs in an agency's portfolio at the outset of the period. These findings are consistent with our portfolio thesis. Moreover, much of the dynamic of adding programs to agency portfolios appears to operate independently of the threat of budget cuts.

The second set of regressions deal with changes in the geographic coverage as a function of the Reagan budgetary proposals and the other factors we have discussed. These regressions are reported in Table 5.3. For each adjustment period, the sign of the regression coefficient on the proposed budget change is negative, indicating that efforts to expand assistance to additional congressional districts may covary with the size of the cutbacks that are proposed for an agency, but this effect is not statistically significant. Consequently, the regression results should be interpreted to indicate that there is no measurable or detectable difference between threatened and nonthreatened agencies in the extent to which they expand assistance payments to additional congressional districts. The regression estimates do show, however, that expansion of an agency's geographic coverage is a relatively generalized phenomenon. Over the three adjustment periods tested here, the average change across all agencies in the number of districts receiving benefits, all other things equal, ranged from increases of nine additional districts to increases of thirty-six additional districts.

When we turn to the analysis of efforts to reduce the diversity of the

Table 5.3. *Regression estimates for change in district coverage*

Model	Adjustment period	Independent variables	Estimated coefficient	T-value
3.1	98th - 99th	Constant	18.25	2.154*
		Proposed change in agency budget (%)	-0.0704	-0.572
		FY81 agency obligations (millions of constant dollars)	0.000088	0.391
		Districts benefited in 98th Congress	-0.0684	-1.598
		Mean of dependent variable	8.622	
		Number of observations	45	
		R square	0.061	
3.2	98th - 100th	Constant	9.03	0.975
		Proposed change in agency budget (%)	-0.1476	-1.097
		FY81 agency obligations (millions of constant dollars)	0.000148	0.602
		Districts benefited in 98th Congress	-0.0537	-1.152
		Mean of dependent variable	4.022	
		Number of observations	46	
		R square	0.042	
3.3	98th - 101st	Constant	36.04	2.894**
		Proposed change in agency budget (%)	-0.125	-0.693
		FY81 agency obligations (millions of constant dollars)	0.000238	0.719
		Districts benefited in 98th Congress	-0.1404	-2.241*
		Mean of dependent variable	15.96	
		Number of observations	46	
		R square	0.109	

*$p < 0.05$ **$p < 0.01$

types of recipients receiving assistance from each of the programs in an agency's portfolio, evidence for the hypotheses we have discussed is less persuasive. As Table 5.4 shows, the sign on the coefficients for the effect of the proposed budget changes on changes in average program recipient diversity is in the expected direction, but the estimates are statistically insignificant. Moreover, the magnitudes of the coefficients are small. These regression estimates suggest, however, that there are two partially countervailing processes that may be at work. In the first place, most agencies appear to experience net increases over time in the average diversity of the recipient groups that benefit from each of their programs. At the same time, there is a negative relationship between the diversity of program recipients at the beginning of the adjustment period and the change in the average diversity of program recipients over time (controlling for, among other things, the overall recipient diversity across all programs within the agency at the outset of the period). This latter dynamic indicates that there may be a regression toward the mean effect that pushes agencies with low recipient diversity upward in diversity and pulls agencies with high levels of recipient diversity downward.

The final set of regressions shifts the question away from the factors that explain the use of the strategies available to policy subsystems and focuses, instead, on the relative efficacy of the strategies for threatened versus nonthreatened agency portfolios. The results of these regressions are reported in Table 5.5. The estimates indicate that, all other things being equal, nonthreatened agencies tended to experience much larger growth in real outlays than the threatened agencies. Nonthreatened agencies, on average, saw real outlay increases of $1.8 billion over the period of the 98th to 99th Congress, $2.3 billion from the 98th to the 100th Congress, and $8.1 billion from the 98th to the 101st Congress. By contrast, threatened agencies, on average, saw real increases of about $200 million from the 98th to the 99th Congress, $400 million from the 98th to the 100th Congress, and $200 million from the 98th to the 101st Congress. But not everything was equal. The strategies employed by threatened agencies had a much different "bang for the buck" than the same actions when taken by nonthreatened agencies.

DISCUSSION

The regressions in this chapter show that program portfolios are managed by subsystem actors in a decidedly different manner in cases where agency budgets are targeted for cutbacks than in cases where agency budgets are to receive increases. The policy subsystems surrounding threatened agencies utilized the addition of new programs more effectively than did nonthreatened agencies to expand their assistance outlays. This boost to

83

Table 5.4. *Regression estimates for change in recipient diversity of programs in portfolio*

Model	Adjustment period	Independent variables	Estimated coefficient	T-value
4.1	98th – 99th	Constant	1.583	3.169**
		Proposed change in agency budget (%)	0.00053	0.123
		FY81 agency obligations (millions of constant dollars)	-0.000007	-0.937
		Overall recipient diversity of portfolio in 98th Congress	0.0172	0.209
		Average recipient diversity of programs in 98th Congress	-0.385	-3.122**
		Mean of dependent variable	-0.0488	
		Number of observations	41	
		R square	0.306	
4.2	98th – 100th	Constant	1.21	1.863
		Proposed change in agency budget (%)	0.0034	0.599
		FY81 agency obligations (millions of constant dollars)	-0.000004	-0.385
		Overall recipient diversity of portfolio in 98th Congress	-0.013	-0.122
		Average recipient diversity of programs in 98th Congress	-0.353	-2.213*
		Mean of dependent variable	-0.524	
		Number of observations	42	
		R square	0.219	
4.3	98th – 101st	Constant	1.898	3.007**
		Proposed change in agency budget (%)	0.0029	0.533
		FY81 agency obligations (millions of constant dollars)	-0.000001	-0.135
		Overall recipient diversity of portfolio in 98th Congress	0.038	0.371
		Average recipient diversity of programs in 98th Congress	-0.534	-3.466**
		Mean of dependent variable	-0.244	
		Number of observations	41	
		R square	0.354	

* $p < 0.05$ ** $p < 0.01$

threatened agencies from additional programs persists regardless of the length of the adjustment period examined, but its magnitude tends to attenuate as the adjustment period lengthens. Over the period from the 98th to the 99th Congress, the addition of one program, all other things being equal, produced average increases in the outlays of threatened agencies of $2.3 billion more than the increases in outlays of nonthreatened agencies. Over the period from the 98th to the 100th Congress, the boost for threatened agencies over nonthreatened agencies from the addition of one program was approximately $1 billion. Over the period from the 98th to the 101st Congress, the size of the boost was about $900 million, but was no longer statistically significant.

The story to be told about increasing a portfolio's congressional district coverage may be suggestive of the long-term adjustment strategies in which policy subsystems engage. Over the relatively short adjustment period from the 98th to the 99th Congress, nonthreatened agencies, all other things equal, were able to spend $97 million in outlays for each additional congressional district, whereas the threatened agencies obtained no additional outlays for each additional congressional district. At one level, this suggests that threatened agencies treaded water. It also means, however, that threatened agencies were utilizing their existing resources to provide benefits to additional districts. Over the adjustment period extending through the 100th Congress, the same basic pattern held, except that the additional outlays per each additional congressional district was only $25 million for nonthreatened agencies and the difference was not statistically different from zero. The effect on outlays per district for threatened agencies continued to be $0, which like the effect for their nonthreatened counterparts was not statistically significant.

Over the adjustment period extending through the 101st Congress, a pattern favoring threatened agencies had begun strongly to emerge. Among formerly threatened agencies, the payoff for each additional congressional district assisted was $133 million in added outlays; but among nonthreatened agencies, gains from spreading assistance to additional districts had disappeared and were essentially zero. While threatened agencies could only tread water in the short run, they were able to translate increased geographic breadth into large budgetary bonuses over the long haul. Although the length of the adjustment period necessary was unpredicted, this result is quite compatible with the argument that expansions in geographic coverage builds political support for the policy subsystem over time.

The findings with regard to decreasing program recipient diversity provide only weak support for this part of the argument developed earlier. The estimates for the diversity regressors are statistically insignificant,

Table 5.5. Regression estimates for change in annual portfolio obligations (millions of constant 1982 dollars)

Model	Adjustment period	Independent variables	Estimated coefficient	T-value
5.1	98th - 99th	Constant	1,820	3.651**
		Targeted agency (1 = targeted for real cuts, 0 = else)	-1,628	-2.639*
		Change in		
		Congressional district coverage by portfolio	97	3.437**
		Number of programs in portfolio	-2,296	-5.618**
		Average program recipient diversity	-353	-1.294
		Interaction of targeted agency and change in		
		Congressional district	-97	-3.311**
		Number of programs	2,287	4.874**
		Average program recipient diversity	287	0.699
		Mean of dependent variable	622.6	
		Number of observations	41	
		R square	0.512	
5.2	98th - 100th	Constant	2,307	2.405*
		Targeted agency (1 = targeted for real cuts, 0 = else)	-1,912	-1.578
		Change in		
		Congressional district coverage by portfolio	25	1.156
		Number of programs in portfolio	-1,037	-2.222*
		Average program recipient diversity	-275	-0.662
		Interaction of targeted agency and change in		
		Congressional district	-26	-0.924
		Number of programs	1,024	1.888
		Average program recipient diversity	313	0.481

Mean of dependent variable		836.34	
Number of observations		42	
R square		0.177	
5.3 **98th - 101st**			
Constant		8,069	3.792**
Targeted agency (1 = targeted for real cuts, 0 = else)		-7,849	-3.192**
Change in			
Congressional district coverage by portfolio		-134	-2.365*
Number of programs in portfolio		-898	-1.212
Average program recipient diversity		2,584	2.299*
Interaction of targeted agency and change in			
Congressional district		133	2.152*
Number of programs		953	1.221
Average program recipient diversity		-2,632	-1.946
Mean of dependent variable		1,447.2	
Number of observations		41	
R square		0.290	

*$p < 0.05$ **$p < 0.01$

except for the longest adjustment period examined. In the one case where the estimates are statistically significant, the coefficients point in the expected direction and the magnitudes of the effects are nontrivial. Specifically, over the adjustment period that extends through the 101st Congress, a threatened agency that was able to decrease by one recipient category the diversity of all the programs in its portfolio was able to gain an average increase of $2.6 billion, all other things being equal. A non-threatened agency doing the same thing, on average, would gain only $50 million in outlays. At least in this one model, the implication is that threatened agencies are able, through the reduction of recipient diversity, to garner far more support for additional outlays than are nonthreatened agencies. How much weight to give this particular finding is an open question, given the overall weakness of the diversity findings. In general, however, it is appropriate to conclude that cumulatively the strategies employed by threatened policy subsystems are efficacious in producing budgetary gains.

CONCLUSION

What are we to make of these findings? One conclusion that is both simplistic and wrong is that the Reagan administration's proposals to cut the budgets of domestic assistance agencies had no effect. Indeed they did. The effects of the administration's proposals began to be seen almost immediately and grew stronger with time, but the effects were not the ones desired by the administration: the agencies that were to be eliminated survived, and grew; the agencies that were to have their budgets pared back, in many cases suffered short-run cuts but, in most cases, managed to overcome the cuts with time. The irony, which from the point of view of the administration must have seemed perverse, is that the agencies that had been targeted for cuts did better over the long haul than did the agencies whose budgets the administration had proposed to increase.

These findings suggest a different conclusion. They suggest that the unintended consequence of the administration's early budgetary proposals was to energize policy subsystems throughout the executive branch. The regression results reported here provide strong evidence of this response. Over the course of the next several years, agencies that had been threatened with cutbacks by the Reagan administration moved to obtain new programs at rates far in excess of nonthreatened agencies, and these new programs were constructed in ways that, on average, paid far larger benefits than the new programs obtained by nonthreatened agencies. Threatened and nonthreatened agencies alike managed to distribute their assistance payments to more congressional districts. But, with time, it was clear that threatened agencies were using this expanding coverage to obtain outlay increases that more than offset earlier outlays given to non-threatened agencies.

Finally, the evidence that agencies altered the recipient composition of programs to reduce collective action problems faced by interest groups proved relatively weak and inconsistent. The one strong finding was that, over a relatively long adjustment period, when average recipient diversity was decreased, the effect on the ability of the agencies to obtain outlay increases was dramatic and strong. What we see during the Reagan period is that policy subsystems most threatened by budgetary cutbacks tended to respond strategically by altering their portfolios of programs in ways that, over the long haul, not only protected the portfolios but led, in many cases, to the growth of the portfolios. These policy subsystems proved remarkably resilient.

6

PAC contributions and the distribution of domestic assistance programs

In this chapter we examine the relationship between interest groups and legislators. Our focus is how this relationship promotes support for programs by legislators. A reason that legislators may support programs is that they may benefit from the activities of interest groups that have a stake in those programs, whether or not program benefits go to their districts. Interest group contributions may serve as the functional equivalent of programmatic benefits in enhancing the electoral fortunes of legislators. We precede first with a discussion of our own explanation for the interest group–legislator finance relationship and then proceed to a review of the literature on interest groups and their influence on policy decisions. This explanation should be viewed in terms of the larger set of relationships among actors within policy subsystems. As argued earlier, agencies and legislative committees play important roles in helping interest groups overcome their collective action problems. Data collected on interest group activity with respect to nine public laws passed during the 99th and 100th Congresses are used to examine these dynamics.

THE LEGISLATOR–INTEREST GROUP FINANCE RELATIONSHIP

To understand how interest groups might operate to supplement programmatic benefits to a district, we need to consider the set of relationships among actors in the policy subsystem. Our principal thesis is that policy subsystems and their main product, program portfolios, affect the goals and objectives of each actor in the subsystem. Legislators seek reelection through the electoral support of constituents. Interest groups facilitate this goal by informing their members about programmatic benefits, as well as by providing financial and nonfinancial resources to legislative campaigns. Interest groups thereby seek to increase the probability that legislators will reciprocate with their energies and their votes on

90

issues that concern their membership (cf. Hall and Wayman, 1990). Specifically, interest groups use the allocation of campaign contributions and other forms of electoral resources in order to obtain benefits to their members in the form of legislation that makes desired alterations in existing programs, creates new programs, provides more generous appropriations, liberalizes mandates, and so on. Note that the benefits sought by interest groups tend to be conferred on them indirectly, inasmuch as the legislation directly affects the agency in a policy subsystem, which in turn is responsible for passing on the largess of the legislature to those constituencies that the interest groups represent.

As will be explained, campaign contributions by an interest group's PAC may, for certain purposes, operate in lieu of programmatic benefits to a district. Indeed, campaign contributions may be more effective than an agency's allocation of program benefits to a district in giving legislators an incentive to support programs. Unlike programmatic benefits to the district, campaign contributions are fungible and bankable, since they can be used in ways and at times that the legislator deems likely to have the greatest positive impact on his or her reelection bid. In addition to campaign contributions by an interest group's PAC, interest groups can employ a variety of strategies to influence legislative support for programs. We will highlight some of the key findings of the literature on interest groups and identify some of the strategies that interest groups and PACs adopt in trying to build support for the programs in which they have a stake.

PREVIOUS RESEARCH

The 1974 amendments to the Federal Election Campaign Act (FECA) established the modern era of federal campaign financing. After the major changes in the law brought about by the *Buckley* v. *Valeo,* 424 U.S. 1 (1976) decision, the basic structure governing congressional and presidential elections has remained relatively intact. In spite of this stability in the laws governing campaign finance, Sorauf (1992) observes significant changes in the level of campaign contributions and the distribution of these moneys by type of candidate. The enormous rise in PAC contributions observed in the 1970s reached a plateau in the 1980s and has remained relatively stable over the last decade. More important for our research is the change in the distribution of PAC contributions by type of candidate. Contributions to incumbents grew during the 1980s, while contributions to challengers dropped markedly.[1] Sorauf interprets these changes in PAC activity as evidence of "an impressive amount of political learning and adaptation." PACs confronted "the realities of incumbent advantages and challenger futility" (1992:19). Like Sorauf, we view these trends as suggestive of the strategies that interest groups pursue to influence legislative policy decisions.

An important strategic consideration for any interest group is to whom it should direct campaign resources. The findings in the literature suggest that interest groups have a preference for supporting incumbents sympathetic to their issue positions. J. Wright (1989) argues that interest groups choose between a maintenance strategy, in which resources are allocated to legislators in districts where the interest group has an organizational presence, and an expansionary strategy, in which resources are allocated to districts where the interest group does not have a presence. The maintenance strategy is essentially defensive, whereas an expansionary strategy seeks to broaden the support base by inducing the assistance of legislators who might otherwise be indifferent to the interest group's concerns. The literature is indeterminate as to the frequency that these strategies are pursued. J. Wright (1985) found that PACs prefer to give money to districts where they have strong local activists in order to reward local fundraising activities. Likewise Sabato (1985) and Sorauf (1985) also find that the wishes of local interest group organizers often guide the allocational strategy of the national PAC. By contrast, Grenzke's (1988) finding that substantial PAC money flows from sources outside a legislator's district suggests that interest groups often adopt expansionary strategies. She argues that because legislators receive large out-of-district and out-of-state contributions, the U.S. political system is no longer realistically described "using a narrow, district-based conceptualization of representation" (1988:95).

The evolution in PAC strategies has produced a curious mixture of expected and unexpected results. As expected, PAC contributions are found to be electorally advantageous. As a general rule, PAC contributions go disproportionately to incumbents, victors, and people in positions of legislative influence (i.e., senior members, committee chairs). In particular, PAC contributions appear to help ensure that incumbents are unopposed. This generalization, however, varies over time and by type of PAC. Sorauf (1992:16) found that PAC contributions to incumbents increased significantly between 1978 and 1990. Schlozman and Tierney (1986:235–6) found that corporate PACs prefer the incumbency strategy more than ideological PACs. This difference may reflect the distribution of different policy concerns, an issue we address in the next section.

The most unexpected and nonintuitive finding about PAC contributions concerns the impact on legislative voting behavior. Contrary to widespread public and journalistic perception, the evidence is ambiguous that financial contributions of organized interests are systematically related to the voting decisions of legislators, either in committee or on the floor. Grenzke (1989a), J. Wright (1985), Wayman (1985), and Welch

(1982) find no correlation between contributions and votes of legislators. Others, such as Chappell (1982), Kau and Rubin (1982), Silberman and Durden (1976), and Frendreis and Waterman (1985) have found a statistically significant, but substantively weak, relationship between the two. A problem with most of these studies is the inability to show that legislators would have voted differently in the absence of the campaign contributions.

Evans (1986) is one of very few to find a strong relationship between contributions and votes, but does so only when she focuses on consensual issues. Evans demonstrates PAC contributions and interest group lobbying have significantly different effects on distributive policies, which she defines as consensual, than on regulatory and redistributive policies, which she defines as conflictual. The latter tend not to be significantly responsive to PAC contributions. She argues that the reason for this condition is that:

One group tries to get something at the other's expense and both have the resources for a fight. In such cases, many representatives will have to oppose a supporter no matter what they do, and, by and large, contributions by PACs on one side may be matched by PACs on the other side. Hence, the contributions may effectively cancel each other out. (Evans, 1986:117)

By contrast, potential opponents of distributive bills are thought to be unable to generate sufficient collective action to influence legislators' votes on these policy issues.

Thus, in spite of the wide dispersion of people affected by the legislation in many or all congressional districts, the fact that they typically are not organized makes it difficult for them to counteract the power of campaign contributions. (Evans, 1986:117)

Salisbury et al. (1987) and Schlozman and Tierney (1986:278) report very similar results and note that interest groups tend to form coalitions around distributive public policy issues. Writing about "specialized producers, with relatively narrow policy agendas," Salisbury et al. report that interest groups

tend to avoid becoming embroiled in adversarial encounters. As becomes the protagonists in a system of distributive policies, they try instead to confine their efforts to building whatever support they can for their primary policy goals. These live-and-let-live efforts are complicated in some domains by the presence of peak associations, organizations that seek to transcend the limited membership potential of specialized groups. (1987:1229)

These findings raise a predicament. In conflictual situations, it may be rational to invest resources, even if the expected outcome is merely a draw, since the alternative is a high probability of defeat. But the finding that PACs are more effective on consensual issues is nonobvious. Why should interest groups invest their resources on issues where they are likely to prevail without making an investment? In consensual situations, where significant opposition is absent, it appears irrational to expend scarce resources. The implicit presumption, here, is that the purpose of PAC contributions is to influence legislative votes. Yet this may not be the primary objective in every case. Other aspects of the legislative process may be as important to interest groups when considering consensual issues. J. Wright's (1990) study of lobbying activities and PAC contributions provides supporting evidence for such an alternative perspective. Wright finds that PAC contributions do not directly affect legislators' committee votes. PAC contributions, however, have an indirect effect on representatives' policy decisions through the lobbying efforts of interest groups. PACs contribute to vulnerable and sympathetic congressional candidates. In turn, previous contributions mark legislators for interest group lobbying activity.

Hall and Wayman (1990) offer a refinement on this perspective, which shifts the focus from votes to other activities of legislators. They argue that "the object of rational PAC allocation is not simply the direction of legislators' preferences but the vigor with which those preferences are promoted in the decision making process" (1990:802). They maintain that interest group resources are intended to "mobilize legislative support and demobilize opposition, particularly at the most important points in the legislative process. . . . the goal is not simply to purchase support but to provide incentives for supporters to act as agents at the extreme, to serve as coalition leaders on the principal's behalf" (1990:800). Rather than examining one single stage in the process – for example, committee or floor votes – they find that PAC moneys flow disproportionately to those legislators active in the shaping and positioning of legislation sympathetic to a PAC's interests throughout the legislative process. Their empirical investigations confirm that PAC contributions flow disproportionately to those members of House committees most actively involved in legislative committee work. Committee members have a significant influence on the content and funding of domestic assistance programs. Committee members also have significant indirect influence over the agencies responsible for administering and implementing domestic assistance programs. This perspective underscores the general thesis that a significant amount of policy making takes place among subsystem actors before and after committee and floor votes have taken place.

SUBSYSTEM MODEL OF INTEREST GROUP INFLUENCE

A number of generalizations about the influence of PAC contributions on legislative policy outputs can be integrated with our own policy subsystem thesis. Our argument is that the strategies of interest groups in building legislative support for programs are likely to be influenced by two factors: the breadth with which distributive benefits are allocated and the degree of controversy associated with the policy arena.

The first factor is the extent to which the portfolio allocates distributive benefits to a majority or minority of legislative districts. Recall that the underlying premise of the universalism literature is that distributive benefits have a special attraction to politicians because this type of benefit allows credit taking. Narrowly distributed benefits do not offer these electoral advantages to a majority of the legislature. Absent broadly allocated distributive benefits, interest groups must provide another incentive for members to support their programs. For example, legislators from New York had little direct incentive to support a Super Collider Project in Texas once the location of the project was announced and contracts and subcontracts were negotiated. Though ultimately unsuccessful, interest groups and others who supported this narrowly distributed project found it necessary to provide other material incentives to legislators outside of Texas to support the project. Some of this took the form of PAC contributions. The logic of universalism suggests that, for program portfolios with narrowly allotted distributive program benefits, PACs must compensate for the shortfall in benefits with broadly distributed campaign contributions.

The second factor has to do with the degree of controversy associated with programs in a policy subsystem. Although agencies and interest groups may design program portfolios to minimize conflict, it is not possible to anticipate all controversies that may arise. Controversy is dangerous for a policy subsystem. The venue for controversy may involve an expansion in the scope of conflict beyond the normal boundaries of the subsystem (Schattschneider, 1960). Amendments unfriendly to the committee's recommendations may be offered from the floor. Disputes on the floor may displace policy consensus. Interest group competition may produce a frenzy of legislative maneuvers and contentious floor votes. Conflict causes legislators to reexamine their standing position in support of the policy subsystem. Program supporters may be thrown on the defensive when fissures of controversy arise where consensus previously prevailed. Interest groups must seek at least a simple majority of legislators to be on their side, and probably prefer oversized majorities to ensure success. As one side in a policy controversy mobilizes, so too must the opposing side. The result is a contagion of escalating mobilization. The net result may appear to be near universalization of PAC contributions to members of the legislature, but without achieving unanimity of opinion or legislative behavior.

Consensus is not a static condition. It may have to be painstakingly nurtured in the interstices of the policy subsystem. Indeed, the actors in a subsystem are ill advised to take the appearance of consensus as a cue for

Table 6.1. *Expected strategies of PAC coalitions*

Distribution of benefits	Subsystem environment	
	Consensual	Conflictual
Narrow	Contributions to at least a majority of legislators	Contributions to at least a majority of legislators by each contending coalition of PACs
Broad	Minimal PAC activity	Contributions to at least a majority of legislators by each contending coalition of PACs

inaction. The job of interest groups is to engage in a maintenance effort to signal their supporters in the legislature about the issues that are salient to the subsystem. Where there is consensus, interest groups are more likely to focus their activities on agency decision making and working with members of committees and their staffs. In other words, interest groups adopt maintenance strategies to rally the erstwhile faithful to shepherd programs through the legislative process. The high cost of maintaining a well-funded PAC is an imprudent use of interest group resources except where distributive program benefits are narrowly allocated. Absent controversy we expect that committee recommendations should go unchallenged in the full legislature, and votes should approach unanimity, with a minimum of partisanship and legislative maneuvering.

We thus expect the choice of interest group strategy to be a function of the interaction of the degree of conflict or consensus in the subsystem and the extent to which a portfolio of programs has broad versus narrow district coverage. Although the two dimensions, in reality, are continuous, we have treated them as dichotomous categories for ease of presentation. We examine here one important facet of interest group activities – the pattern of PAC contributions.

Table 6.1 summarizes our expectations about the behavior of subsystem actors as a function of the geographic coverage of their portfolio and the degree of consensus or conflict that exists in the subsystem's political environment. The upper left-hand section of Table 6.1 is defined by the combination of narrow district coverage and consensual subsystem environment. Because of the consensual environment, we expect that legislators receiving PAC contributions will be those with a preexisting interest in the subsystem's portfolio. By this we mean that PAC contributions should flow to members whose districts are receiving benefits from one or more programs in the subsystem portfolio or to members who sit on one of the committees with jurisdiction over the portfolio. Due to the narrowness of coverage by these programs, we may observe that PAC moneys will be distributed to a sufficient number of legislators to ensure that more than 50 percent of the legislature receives distributive benefits or PAC contributions. This assumes that PAC contributions are the functional equivalent to distributive benefits in giving legislators an incentive to support a portfolio.

The lower left-hand section is defined by broad coverage of distributive benefits and a consensual environment. These conditions define the traditional notion of universalized benefits. Legislative support for these programs is thought to be provided by the extension of distributive program benefits to a majority of the legislature. The need for active PACs is diminished and indeed may be nonexistent, except insofar as PAC contributions are used to signal members about the salience of issues. To the extent that PACs are active in support of these programs, their contributions should flow to legislators who are members of the committees with jurisdiction over the programs.

The upper right-hand section of Table 6.1 is defined by narrow district coverage and a conflictual policy environment. These portfolios provide program benefits to few districts. This denies most legislators the opportunity for credit taking. As with the consensual situation, PAC contributions might compensate for the narrowness of district coverage, but conflict introduces the dimension of inter-PAC competition. Each competing set of PACs will have an incentive to contribute to majorities of the legislature. In this situation, the problem for PACs is ensuring that their contributions successfully induce legislators to support their issue positions. Lobbying in such cases is likely to be aggressive. Interest groups on the different sides of the conflict are likely to focus their activities on legislators without a clear stake in the policy subsystem. Such legislators would include those whose districts do not receive distributive benefits from the portfolio of programs and legislators that do not serve on the committees with jurisdiction over the portfolio.

The lower right-hand section defines a portfolio with broad coverage and a conflictual environment. Broad district coverage suggests that most legislators have an incentive to support these programs. When conflict emerges within the subsystem, we expect aggressive activity by the contending sets of interest groups. Because the number of legislators with a stake in the subsystem is high, PAC contributions are likely to be broadly distributed. Likewise, lobbying activities will focus on those legislators with a stake in the subsystem, as well as all other legislators.

Underlying the lobbying efforts of interest groups and their PACs is the expectation that their actions will positively influence the vote choices of legislators. As the literature review has suggested, this is an open question. Only those studies that have focused on votes that deal with concentrated costs or benefits have found significant relationships between PAC contributions and the vote choices of legislators. We think that the failure to observe consistent results stems from the lack of nuance in this literature. Not all votes and policy choices are alike. It is important to differentiate among the types of votes legislators cast in order to capture the underlying variables that influence those votes.

In this chapter we differentiate between votes cast on issues concerning the distribution of costs and/or benefits to narrow segments of society and votes that deal mainly with other issues. Arnold (1990:13ff.) makes a similar differentiation, arguing that the potential policy preferences of voters relates to two attributes of policies. The first is the incidence of costs and benefits, which may fall on the public generally, specific geographic locations, or particular groups. The second is the complexity of "the causal chain that links a policy instrument with policy effects" (p. 13). On complex issues – where the linkage between a policy and its potential effects involve a multistage and uncertain process – voters are unlikely to hold legislators responsible for their policy actions. Consequently legislators are likely to be most responsive to narrow interest groups on issues when neither concentrated costs nor concentrated benefits fall on the general public and when the issues involve complex causal linkages between the policy changes and their effects. Votes on complicated policy questions involving costs and/or benefits for narrow segments of society may be significantly influenced by interest group activity, given the disinterest of the general public and the high stakes to interest groups. On these votes, legislators may rely on interest groups both for information and guidance on how to vote. The important point is that even where interest groups are active on issues, we expect their influence to be felt only on certain types of votes, specifically those that involve the allocation of concentrated costs and benefits.

The typology of portfolios presented in Table 6.1 suggests that, under certain conditions, PACs activity may be either minimal or quite aggressive and competitive. It is therefore necessary to consider how PAC activity varies by type of portfolio in examining the relationship between campaign contributions and legislative votes. PACs need not be aggressive nor are they expected to be especially influential on consensual policies with broad district coverage. Party, incumbent vulnerability, and membership on committees with jurisdiction over the bill are expected to have a greater influence on vote choices for these policies. Given the nonconflictual nature of consensual and narrow policy portfolios we do not expect to observe competition among opposing PACs. Rather, PAC influence should be limited to a single PAC cluster attempting to expand its base of narrow program beneficiaries by spreading its contributions to at least a majority of the legislature. Conflictual and narrow policies are expected to generate significant PAC activity. Here we expect to observe multiple PAC clusters making contributions to different majorities of House members. Their influence should be visible mainly on votes involving the allocation of specific benefits or costs for particular types of groups.

DATA BASE

The propositions presented in the preceding section are examined with a sample of nine portfolios. To select these portfolios, we first identified all public laws passed during the 99th (1985–6) or 100th (1987–8) Congress that authorized, reauthorized, or amended domestic assistance programs. This information was coded from the 1990 *Catalog of Federal Domestic Assistance*. A total of forty-nine public laws were identified. These laws were rank ordered on the basis of the total district coverage provided by the bundle of programs authorized by the public laws. After a random start, every fourth law was selected, netting thirteen public laws with total district coverage (i.e., from distributive as well as redistributive programs) ranging from a low of 44 congressional districts up to 435 districts. Of the thirteen public laws, two were appropriation bills, which provided moneys to programs and agencies in many different policy subsystems. These two laws were dropped from the sample. A third public law was dropped from the sample because the legislation listed in the catalog as having provided authority for the programs was incorrectly identified.[2] A final public law was dropped after determining that it was not a law but merely a House report. This produced a sample of nine public laws with a total of eighty-two domestic assistance programs for the following analysis. The list of these programs and the public laws that provided or altered their authority is contained in Appendix 6. This appendix also indicates whether the programs provided distributive benefits during the Congress in which the public law was passed.

For each public law, we first determined whether the program benefits were distributive or not. To be defined as distributive, at least half of the program's transactions had to be in the form of either project grants or cooperative agreements and the program was not explicitly designed to allocate benefits on the basis of income or unemployment status. This method is identical to that employed in Table 2.1 where distributive programs were identified as those in which an agency is given discretion for awarding benefits and there is no requirement that moneys be targeted to the poor or unemployed. We then calculated the number of congressional districts that received benefits from distributive programs authorized by

Table 6.2. *Public law categorization*

Distribution of benefits	Subsystem environment	
	Consensual	Conflictual
Narrow	PL99-319. Legal advocacy and Protective Services for the Mentally Ill Act (0)	PL99-499. Superfund Reauthorization Act (44)
	PL100-241. Alaska Native Claims Settlement Act (0)	PL99-603. Immigration and Nationality Extension and Reauthorization Act (0)
	PL100-485. Family Welfare Reform Act (0)	PL100-242. Housing and Community Development Reauthorization Act (0)
Broad	PL99-443. Small Business Innovation and Research Act (348)	PL100-4. Clean Water Reauthorization Act (379)
	PL99-457. Vocational Rehabilitation of the Handicapped Act (383)	

Note: Numbers in parentheses indicate number of congressional districts receiving PAC particularized benefits from programs reauthorized by the public law during the congress that the law was enacted. See Appendix 6 for a list of programs (re)authorized by each public law.

each public law. Portfolios that bestowed distributive benefits to 218 or more districts were classified as broad. Those providing benefits to fewer than 218 districts were classified as narrow. Each public law portfolio can be located in one of the four sections of Table 6.2, based on the breadth of district coverage and the degree of conflict.

Using the *Congressional Information Service Index* (CIS index), we identified the committees that held hearings on each public law. Based on these hearings, we determined the extent to which the persons providing testimony appeared to be in conflict with one another. This characterization is admittedly subjective, since it involves an attempt to interpret the tenor of the debate. Our coding, however, correlated closely with other indicators of conflict, including the number of different interest groups involved in the hearings and the number and divisiveness of votes taken on each issue.

The members of these committees were identified from *Congressional Quarterly*. This information is used below to determine if committee members are disproportionately advantaged by grant allocations and/or PAC contributions. The CIS index was also used to identify the organizational affiliation of each person who testified at any congressional hearing on the public law. We then matched the interest groups that participated in the hearings with groups listed in the Federal Election Commission (FEC) *Committee Master File* to identify those groups that had a political action committee. PAC contributions to incumbent House members in the 99th Congress were compiled for PACs whose parent interest groups were involved in these hearings. The same was done for PACs associated with interest groups involved in public laws passed during the 100th Congress. This information was used to code whether legislators received contributions during the Congress from any PAC whose parent interest group played a role in the hearings on the public law.

As discussed earlier, interest groups tend to form coalitions, particularly around contentious policy issues (Salisbury et al., 1987; Schlozman and Tierney, 1986:27). We have used factor analyses of PAC contributions to identify the clusters of interest group coalitions that form around each of our nine public laws. For each public law, a separate factor analysis was conducted on PACs whose parent interest groups testified on the public law. If a PAC provided a contribution to a member of Congress, that member was coded 1 for that PAC and 0 if no campaign contribution was received by the member from the PAC. The factor analysis examines the interrelations between PACs to identify similar patterns in the distribution of campaign funds to House members. In other words, the factor analysis identifies correlations in the contribution patterns across a set of PACs.[3] As expected, the factor analysis reveals different numbers and types of PAC clusters for each of the public laws. Listed in Table 6.3 are the extracted factors for each public law and a description of these factors, based on those PACs with high loadings on each factor. Note that for the public laws that were characterized as consensual, no factors could be extracted. In fact, in two cases there were no PACs present at all. In the other two consensual cases, there were only one and three PACs, respectively, that made contributions to House members.

To test whether PAC contributions affect legislators' vote choice, we utilized probit analysis to regress the roll call votes cast by House members on the following variables: the member's party affiliation, membership on a committee that held hearings on the public law, the legislator's electoral margin in the last election, whether the member's district received a distributive program benefit from the public law, and the support each member received from the different PAC clusters. This last variable comprises a set of dummy variables, equal to the number of PAC clusters identified in our factor analysis. To determine which legislators, if any, are favored by a coalition of interest groups, we have constructed a measure

Table 6.3. *PAC coalitions and contributions to House members, by subsystem environment and breadth of particularized benefit distribution*

Public law	PAC coalition 1	PAC coalition 2	PAC coalition 3
Consensual			
Narrow			
PL99-319. Legal Advocacy and Protective Services for the Mentally Ill Act	No PACs		
PL100-241. Alaska Native Claims Settlement Act	3 PACs, No common factors (227)		
PL100-485. Family Welfare Reform Act	Labor (328)		
Broad			
PL99-443. Small Business Innovation and Research Act	1 PAC (20)		
PL99-457. Vocational Rehabilitation of the Handicapped Act	No PACs		
Conflictual			
Narrow			
PL99-499. Superfund Reauthorization Act	Liberal-labor-environmental (249)	Insurance-real estate-steel (310)	Petrochemicals-cleanup contractors (358)
PL99-603. Immigration and Nationality Extension and Reauthorization Act	Labor (219)	Hotels-ranchers-hospitals (357)	Travel industry-agriculture-transportation (37)
PL100-242. Housing and Community Development Reauthorization Act	Homebuilders-banking-realtors (385)	Labor (223)	Savings & loans-mortgagers-independent banking (292)
Broad			
PL100-4. Clean Water Reauthorization Act	Hotels-ranchers-utilities (375)	Liberal-labor-environmental (215)	

Notes: Numbers in parentheses indicate number of House members receiving PAC contributions. See Appendix 7 for a list of PACs in each PAC coalition.

from our factor analysis that indicates whether a legislator received a campaign contribution from any of the PACs in the PAC clusterings that are reported in Table 6.4.[4] The PAC variables were coded 1 if the legislator received contributions from any PAC in a coalition of interest groups, and 0 if not. Our portfolio explanation suggests that members with a stake in the program (i.e., those receiving benefits) are likely to have a close relationship with interest groups that lobby on behalf of the program.

As might be expected, legislative proposals where there was conflict generated a much larger number of roll call votes than did the proposals where there was consensus. In all, fifty-two roll call votes were recorded on these nine public laws. Appendix 8 provides a description of these roll call votes. The number of votes varies, from only one roll call on each of the two public laws that were characterized as being consensual and providing broadly distributed particularized benefits, to an average of twelve votes on the three public laws that were characterized as being conflictual and narrowly distributed.

Appendix 9 reports the full probit results on the roll call votes. The probit regressions include from zero to three PAC variables, depending on the number of PAC coalitions active in the process leading up to the passage of the public law. For two public laws (PL99-319, PL99-457), there was no PAC activity. For the roll calls on these public laws, the PAC variables were excluded from the regressions. For two other public laws (PL100-241, PL99-443), so few PACs were active that the factor analysis did not indicate that a PAC cluster existed. The probit analyses of roll calls for these two public laws include dummy variables for the contributions of the individual PACs rather than a PAC cluster. Each probit regression also included dummy variables for party, membership on a committee that held hearings on the public law, and the receipt of distributive benefits from programs reauthorized by the public law, as well as a continuous variable measuring the legislator's margin of victory over his or her major party opponent in the last election. If no programs providing distributive benefits were involved in the public law, the dummy variable measuring the receipt of such benefits was excluded from the probit regression.

To get a picture of the substantive impact of PAC contributions on the vote choices of legislators, we computed the difference in the probability that a legislator would vote affirmatively or negatively on the roll call, based on whether or not the legislator received contributions from a PAC. The difference in the vote probability due to the receipt of PAC moneys was estimated for a "typical" House member – that is, a Democrat, not sitting on a committee that held hearings on the public law, receiving no distributive benefit from any programs that were reauthorized by the public law, and winning by the average margin in his or her last election. Using the estimates produced by the probit regressions, we calculated the

Table 6.4. *Summary of probit results for impact of PAC contributions on voting behavior of House members*

	Consensual		Conflictual		Total
	Narrow	Broad	Narrow	Broad	
All roll call votes					
Number of votes	12	2	35	3	52
Average number of votes per public law	4	1	11.67	3	5.78
Proportion of PAC variables significant	0.60	n.a.	0.44	0.33	0.45
Average absolute change in vote probability	0.125	n.a.	0.105	0.019	0.103
Roll calls directly involving concentrated costs or benefits					
Number of votes	3	0	17	0	20
Proportion of PAC variables significant	1.00	n.a.	0.53	n.a.	0.55
Average absolute change in vote probability	0.289	n.a.	0.118	n.a.	0.125
Other roll calls					
Number of votes	9	2	18	3	32
Proportion of PAC variables significant	0.50	n.a.	0.35	0.33	0.37
Average absolute change in vote probability	0.084	n.a.	0.093	0.019	0.086

Notes: The probit regressions include from 0 to 3 PAC variables, depending on the number of PAC coalitions active in the process leading up to the passage of the public law. The PAC variables were coded 1 if the legislator received contributions from any PAC in a coalitions of PACs, and 0 if not. If no PACs were active, the PAC variables were excluded from the regression. Significance of variables was established at the two-tailed 0.10 alpha level.

Each probit regression also included dummy variables for party membership on a committee that held hearings on the public law, and the receipt of particularized benefits from programs reauthorized by the public law, as well as a continuous variable measuring the legislator's margin of victory over his or her major party opponent in the last election. If no programs providing particularized benefits were involved in the public law, the dummy variable measuring the receipt of such benefits was excluded from the probit regression.

The difference in the vote probability due to the receipt of PAC moneys was calculated for a "typical" House member, i.e., a Democrat, not sitting on a committee that held hearings on the public law, receiving no particularized benefit from any programs that were reauthorized by the public law, and winning by the average margin in his or her last election. The probability of voting affirmatively was calculated for the "typical" member, first assuming the receipt of no PAC moneys and then assuming that PAC moneys were received. The absolute change in the vote probability was then calculated for each roll call vote.

See Appendix 8 for a description of the House roll call votes. See Appendix 9 for full probit results on all House roll call votes.

probability of voting affirmatively for the "typical" member, first assuming the receipt of no PAC moneys and then assuming that PAC moneys were received. The absolute change in the vote probability was then calculated for each roll call vote.

As discussed in a previous section, our expectation is that roll calls involving concentrated costs or concentrated benefits are likely to be more susceptible to successful PAC influence. To test this proposition, we subjectively categorized the substantive content of each roll call vote (see Appendix 8). We grouped roll calls on the basis of whether they appeared to involve concentrated costs or benefits. To be sure, some votes may be "disguised" (e.g., procedural votes). The allocation of concentrated costs or benefits may be hidden to avoid attention being drawn publicly to the consequences of the vote.

DISTRIBUTION OF PAC CONTRIBUTIONS

Our discussion of the findings proceeds in two parts. First we describe the subsystems located in each section of Table 6.2. This discussion focuses on the distribution of campaign contributions and how this relates to the distribution of distributive benefits and the scope of conflict over the legislation. Second, we examine the impact of PAC contributions and the receipt of distributive benefits on the voting behavior of legislators.

Consensual-narrow

Three public laws were identified as consensual and providing distributive benefits to fewer than half of the House. It was hypothesized that for portfolios characterized by consensus and providing distributive benefits to a small number of legislative districts, interest groups would compensate for the lack of broad district coverage by spreading campaign contributions to at least a majority of the legislature. We expected that the distribution of PAC contributions would disproportionately favor members whose districts received distributive benefits, and members who sat on committees that held hearings on the public law.

The first law, the Legal Advocacy and Protective Services for the Mentally Ill Act (PL99-319), provided no distributive benefits to House districts during 1985–6. It did, however, reauthorize one formula program, which provides benefits to the mental health departments in all fifty states. Testimony in the committee hearings primarily focused on the need for greater Justice Department enforcement of the civil rights of institutionalized persons. With the exception of a few witnesses from state mental health facilities, most witnesses voiced support for greater federal intervention on behalf of the institutionalized. None of the persons who testified represented interest groups with an associated PAC. This public law does not provide evidence for the hypothesis that interest groups compensate for narrow benefit coverage by providing broadly distributed campaign contributions.

The second public law, the Alaska Native Claims Settlement Act (PL100-241), also provided no distributive program benefits to House districts during 1987–8. The public law terminated restrictions on the sale of shares in native Alaskan corporations to nonnative Alaskans. The debate over this proposed legislation entailed a painstaking effort to construct a compromise over which there could be consensus. Initial positions of native Alaskan organizations, environmentalists, and sportsmen organizations were significantly divergent. The debate turned on the issue of who would exercise sovereignty over Alaskan corporations if shares were sold to nonnatives. As hearings progressed and the proposed legislation was amended, the positions of the various interest groups appeared to converge toward a compromise. The three interest groups with PACs illustrate this point. The Bristol Bay Native Corporation strongly favored the proposed bill throughout the hearings. The Sierra Club and the National Rifle Association (NRA) initially opposed the draft legislation, though for different reasons. By the end of the hearings, however, their objections were largely alleviated because the proposed legislation was amended to permit native Alaskans the option of continued control over these corporations even if shares were sold to nonnatives.

The hypotheses advanced here suggest that, given narrowness of distributive benefits, interest groups are likely to concentrate their PAC contributions on key legislators, including members of committees with jurisdiction over the legislation. As expected, the PACs in this case provided contributions disproportionately to members of the committee that held hearings on the bill. Eighty-two percent of the members of the House Committee on Interior and Insular Affairs received campaign funds from one or more of the PACs, whereas only 50 percent of the remaining House membership received campaign funds from these PACs. Moreover, the expectation that under conditions of narrow district coverage PACs must provide campaign contributions to at least a simple majority of the House members is borne out. Though certainly odd bedfellows, the PACs of the Sierra Club, NRA, and Bristol Bay Native Corporation made overlapping contributions to 227 districts.

The third and last public law that falls into the consensual-narrow cell is the Family Welfare Reform Act (PL100-485). This portfolio included eight programs, none of which provided distributive benefits. All of the programs involved redistributive benefits, including Aid to Families with Dependent Children (AFDC), Medicaid, Supplemental Social Security Insurance, and other redistributive entitlement programs. During the 100th

Congress, benefits from nondistributive programs were allocated to recipients in all 435 House districts. Contrary to what one might believe, the debate over the welfare reform proposal was not highly contentious. The nonconflictual nature of the debate may owe, in part, to the efforts of Senator Moynihan, chief sponsor of the bill in the Senate. Senator Moynihan's original proposal did not set out new spending proposals. To the contrary, the proposed legislation sought to reduce welfare costs by instituting new efforts to recover child support payments from delinquent parents of welfare dependent children. Other parts of the proposed legislation included job training and educational programs for welfare recipients with provisions to continue assistance while the recipient participated in the educational program.

Campaign contributions from ten PACs were made to 328 House members. The nonconflictual nature of the debate on welfare reform is corroborated by the factor analysis. Only one PAC cluster, comprised of six PACs, was extracted from the contribution pattern of the ten PACs whose parent interest groups were involved in this debate. This PAC cluster is composed of labor unions, professional social workers, nurses, and public employees. Contributions from the PAC cluster went to 231 House members. Contrary to our expectation, PACs did not significantly favor committee members over noncommittee members in making campaign contributions. The primary expectation, however, is fulfilled: contributions from PACs flowed to well over a simple majority of House members.

Consensual-broad

Consensual portfolios with broad distribution of particularistic program benefits have little need for PAC contributions. Two public laws fall into this cell and appear to confirm the hypothesis. The first, the Small Business Innovation and Research Act (PL99-443) involved thirty-seven programs, all of which provided distributive benefits. Together these programs provided benefits to 383 districts during the period 1985-6. The programs that this legislation affected were those in agencies that fund substantial civilian research and innovation activities. The proposed legislation required that up to 10 percent of the appropriated funds for each of these programs be allocated for small business innovation projects. With the exception of some academic researchers who expressed concerns with possible diversion of moneys from their research agenda, a significant portion of those testifying supported the proposed legislation. Quite a number of those testifying before House committees spoke about the economic benefits that spread to the community as a result of stimulating small business development. There was only one interest group testifying that possessed a PAC, the KMS Fusion Inc. Political Action Fund. This

PAC provided campaign contributions to twenty house members. There was no clear pattern to the distribution of these campaign moneys by committee membership or receipt of program benefits. These findings are consistent with the hypothesis that PAC activity will be minimal for portfolios falling into this cell.

The second portfolio that appears in this cell, the Vocational Rehabilitation of the Handicapped Act (PL99-457) epitomizes consensus. During the hearings on this proposed legislation the main concern raised by witnesses was not over the basic merits of the legislation, but the need for more funding and the desire of some to transform the programs into a permanent entitlement. All but one of the portfolio's eleven programs provided distributive benefits. Together these programs provided benefits to a total of 348 districts during 1985–6. There were no campaign contributions made to any House member by PACs whose parent interest group testified on this legislation. This is consistent with the hypothesis that PACs should play a minimal role on this type of nonconflictual legislation.

Conflictual-narrow

Among portfolios with conflictual environments and narrowly allocated distributive benefits, we expect to observe competitive PAC activity, where each set of PACs is attempting to build its own legislative majority. The first public law in this cell is the Superfund Reauthorization Act (PL99-499). In 1985–6 Superfund included one program that provided distributive benefits to forty-four districts, all with Superfund cleanup sites. During the reauthorization hearings, there were two primary threads of debate. The first, and less contentious, was the need for greater safety training for firefighters and workers involved in the handling and disposal of toxic substances. The second, and far more contentious, issue concerned the assignment of liability for toxic waste and its removal. Petrochemical and other industrial interests sought partial indemnification for toxic wastes at their current or former facilities. Those responsible for cleanups were concerned that in the future standards might become more rigorous or testing procedures more precise and they would be held liable for past cleanups that failed to meet future standards. Environmentalists were adamant that cleanups be undertaken with the most rigorous standards, regardless of the specific allocation of liability to companies, past and present, that may have contributed to the problem.

The factor analysis of PAC contributions indicated that there were at least three distinct clusterings of PACs involved in the Superfund debate. These included a liberal-labor-environmental PAC cluster, an insurance-real estate–steel industry PAC cluster, and a petrochemical-cleanup contractor PAC cluster. Collectively, all PACs involved in this legislative conflict provided campaign contributions to 384 members. Individually the three clusters of PACs provided campaign contributions to well over a simple majority of legislators. The liberal-labor-environmental PAC cluster funded the campaigns of 249 House members. The insurance–real estate–steel industry PAC cluster contributed to the campaigns of 310 House members and the petrochemical-cleanup contractors gave to 358 House members. These findings unambiguously support our hypothesis.

The second public law located in the conflictual-narrow cell is the Immigration and Nationality Extension and Reauthorization Act (PL99-603). As of 1985–6 when this legislation was under consideration, there was only one existing domestic assistance program affected by this proposed legislation – food stamps – that provided nondistributive benefits to all fifty states. This legislation was fraught with controversy. Commercial interests, including the National Association of Manufacturers, agricultural growers, hotels, restaurants, building contractors, and hospitals, focused on enforcement of the proposed legislation. Their concern was with the added cost of doing business that would be imposed by new compliance requirements. State and local officials were worried about the increased local cost of illegal immigration that the bill would produce. State officials opposed the proposal to use welfare applications as a means of monitoring the residency status of applicants. Minority groups, especially Hispanic organizations, feared that the law would produce discrimination against legal aliens and Hispanic citizens. Labor organizations believed that provisions of the proposed legislation lacked adequate protection for American workers. Surrounding all these commercial concerns were the ideological agendas of groups advocating English as the official language as well as anticommunist groups worried over the possibility of an influx of refugees from leftist governments.

The factor analysis of PAC activity on this legislative proposal identifies three PAC clusters. The first is the easily recognized labor PAC cluster. Unlike the PAC cluster identified in the Superfund debate, this group of PACs is composed exclusively of labor unions. The second PAC cluster includes hotels, restaurants, ranching interests, and hospitals – all employers of low-wage workers. The third cluster is composed of interests from the travel, transportation, and tourist industries. Together all PACs contributed to the reelection campaigns of 387 House members. The labor PAC cluster contributed to 219 members, the second PAC cluster contributed to 375, and the third PAC cluster gave contributions to 37 members. Most of the members who received campaign contributions from this third PAC cluster were located in California, as were most of the PACs that composed this cluster. Given the breadth of campaign contributions from the first and second PAC clusters, it is not surprising that these contributions are distributed to similar proportions of committee members and noncommittee members alike.

The third public law with narrow district coverage and a conflictual policy debate is the Housing and Community Development Reauthorization Act (PL100-242). During the 1987–8 period, three programs were included in this portfolio, all providing nondistributive benefits. Two of these programs were income tested to provide housing subsidies for low-income families. These benefits, though nondistributive, were provided to all 435 districts through a block and formula mechanism. Distributive benefits, for which members of Congress might take credit, are absent from the programs in this portfolio. Debate on this legislation was heated, no doubt in part because it followed on the disclosure of official corruption charges against Samuel Pierce, the former secretary of Housing and Urban Development (HUD) under President Reagan. HUD Secretary Jack Kemp was aggressively attempting to sell off the federal government's stock of public housing to residents and other private interests. Debate focused on a variety of issues related to Kemp's privatization goals, ranging from restrictions on the use of public housing properties after federally subsidized mortgages were paid off, to restrictions on prepayment of federally subsidized mortgages, the fear that restrictions against racial discrimination would be unenforceable if housing projects were privatized, restrictions on builders of public housing to abide by collective bargaining agreements, and the use of federal mortgage subsidies to shore up the savings and loan industry.

As the nature of these conflicts suggests, there was a wide range of different types of interest groups involved in the debate over the Housing and Community Development Reauthorization Act. The factor analysis revealed three clusterings of political action committees. Cluster one is made up of home builders, large banking institutions (e.g., American Banking Association), mortgage bankers, and realtors. The second PAC cluster comprises the AFL-CIO, United Auto Workers, and one senior citizens' PAC. The third PAC cluster includes the thrift industry, savings and loans, independent bankers, and the mortgage insurance industry. Collectively, all PACs operating in this legislative arena provided contributions to 390 members of Congress. Those in the first PAC cluster gave to 385 House members; contributions from the second cluster went to 223 members; and contributions from the third cluster were provided to 292 House members. Contributions from the second and third PAC clusters favored committee members. The labor PAC cluster contributed to the campaigns of 55 percent of committee members, compared with campaign contributions to 49 percent of the remaining House members. The thrift PAC cluster contributed to the campaigns of 72 percent of committee members, compared with contributions to 64 percent of the remaining members in the House. Contributions from the first PAC cluster, representing the banking and realty industry, showed no obvious favoritism for committee members.

Conflictual-broad

Only one public law is identified in the fourth section of Table 6.2, described by a broad distribution of particularized benefits and conflictual policy environment. This public law is the Clean Water Reauthorization Act (PL100-4). Five programs are in this portfolio, three provided non-distributive benefits and two provided distributive benefits. Distributive benefits from the Construction Grants for Wastewater Treatment Works program and Construction Management Assistance program were distributed to 379 districts. A significant controversy over environmental regulations dominated the testimony given at congressional hearings on the proposed legislation. The regulatory issue concerned allowable levels of toxicity and the timetable for discontinuing the dumping of sewage in the oceans and the Great Lakes. The principals in this policy debate were commercial interests (e.g., Chemical Manufacturers Association) who lobbied against the acceleration of the deadline for discontinuing ocean dumping, and environmental groups and public employee and trade unions (e.g., Sierra Club and American Federation of Government Employees) who had promulgated recommendations for discontinuing ocean dumping. PAC contributions were forthcoming from both sides of this policy debate as each interest group sought to influence the regulatory, rather than distributive, component of this public law.

Twenty-two PACs whose parent interest groups testified made campaign contributions to a total of 390 House members. Two distinct PAC clusters emerged from our factor analysis. The first PAC cluster is composed of heavy industries (e.g., General Motors, Monsanto), public utilities (e.g., Edison Electric), the construction industry, and the mining and natural resource industry (e.g., COALPAC and Forest Industry PAC). This first PAC cluster contributed to the campaigns of 375 House members. The second PAC cluster is dominated by labor unions and environmental organizations. Together these PACs gave to 215 House members. There is no evidence that either PAC cluster contributed disproportionately to committee members or members whose districts received distributive program benefits under this public law. The main conclusion, however, is that both sides in this policy debate attempted to make contributions to at least a majority of House members, although it should be noted that the labor and environmental groups fell short of a simple majority by three votes.

IMPACT OF PAC CONTRIBUTIONS

The logical question is, What impact do these PAC contributions have on the policy decisions of House members? To assess the influence of PAC contributions on the voting behavior of legislators, we employ probit regressions on the roll call votes taken on each of the nine public laws. Table 6.4 reports a summary of the impact of PAC contributions on the voting behavior of House members. This table is based on the probit results that are reported in Appendix 9. Across all of the roll calls, nearly half (45 percent) of the PAC variables were significantly related to the votes cast by House members. The substantive effect of PAC contributions is hardly trivial. On average, PAC contributions changed the probability of a legislator's roll call vote by 10 percent. However, the strongest predictor of roll call voting is party. In 82 percent of the roll calls studied, the party affiliation of the legislator was statistically significant in predicting his or her vote choice. On average, party accounts for a 39 percentage point difference in the probability that a legislator will vote yes or no on the roll call. The big surprise is how seldom the receipt of distributive program benefits is significantly related to legislators' voting behavior. In only 27 percent of the roll calls on public law where there were preexisting distributive benefits did the receipt of such benefits in a district significantly affect the voting choices of the incumbents from those districts. On average, the receipt of distributive program benefits accounts for only a 5 percentage point difference in the probability that a legislator will vote yes or no on the roll call.

Where distributive benefits are broadly distributed, the legislators demonstrate much different behavior than when benefits are narrowly distributed. In each of the two public laws involving broadly distributed program benefits in a consensual policy area – the Small Business Innovation and Research Act and the Vocational Rehabilitation of the Handicapped Act – there was only one roll call vote taken. In each, the vote was unanimous. Neither vote raised the question of how concentrated costs or benefits should be allocated. Instead they were procedural motions to suspend the rules and adopt the bills on final passage. In the presence of widespread consensus and broadly distributed program benefits, legislators do not require additional cues or incentives from PACs in deciding how to vote. It should be noted that program portfolios in this cell represent the classic universalism story. Oversized voting coalitions form to adopt a bundle of projects providing distributive benefits to virtually all members of the legislature.

In the one instance of a public law providing broadly distributed particularized benefits where there was conflict – the Clean Water Reauthorization Act – there were two PAC coalitions present. Interestingly, across all

112

three votes that were taken, only two of the PAC variables were significant. In no case did the PACs lead legislators to vote in opposite directions. In fact, two of the three votes were nearly unanimous, with 98 and 94 percent of the House members voting affirmatively. On the other vote, the probability a legislator would support the measure increased 4 percentage points if the member received a contribution from the coalition of PACs representing builders, ranchers, and utilities and 8 percentage points if the member received a contribution from the cluster of liberal, labor, and environmental PACs. Again, when there is breadth to the number of legislative districts receiving distributive benefits, PACs appear to have little influence on voting behavior, even if the issue involves some controversy.

The influence of PACs is most clearly visible in consensual subsystems where the specific issues at stake involve the allocation of concentrated costs or benefits. Where consensual issues do not directly involve the allocation of concentrated costs or benefits, 50 percent of the PAC variables are significantly related to legislative vote choices. For votes on consensual issues involving the allocation of concentrated costs or benefits, all PAC variables were significant. It should be noted, however, that relatively few questions involving concentrated costs or benefits are brought to the floor of the House if the subsystem environment is basically consensual. Only three of the twelve votes on consensual public laws involved concentrated costs or benefits. As noted before, consensual issues produce relatively few roll call votes. They also produce little competitive PAC activity. This means that there are fewer votes and PAC clusters available for analysis. This should not be construed, however, to mean that interest groups have little impact on votes over consensual issues. When consensus prevails, difficult issues are typically resolved internally within the subsystem, where interest groups are likely to be especially active and influential.

In consensual policy environments, the average influence of PAC contributions is an 8 percentage point difference in a legislator's vote choice when balloting on questions that do not directly affect costs or benefits. PAC contributions change the probability of a legislator's vote 29 percentage points, on average, when the issue consists of the allocation of concentrated costs or benefits. One way to interpret this difference in the effect of PAC contributions on legislative voting is to view the 8 percentage point figure as a kind of baseline and the 21 point jump to 29 percent as an estimate of the true influence of PAC contributions. On issues for which there are no concentrated costs or benefits, the correlation between the receipt of a PAC contribution and voting in a particular way may simply reflect the nonrandom manner with which PACs choose legislators to finance. In other words, the magnitude of this correlation may represent not the influence of PACs on voting decisions, but the predisposition of the legislators, independent of any special lobbying effort by the PAC.

An example may help illustrate the point. Consider PL100-485, the Family Welfare Reform Act. The PAC coalition identified in the factor analysis is comprised of five PACs: the AFL-CIO's Committee on Political Education Political Contributions Committee, the American Federation of State, County, and Municipal Employees, the American Nurses Association PAC, the National Association of Social Workers PAC, and the Service Employees International Union Committee on Political Education PAC. As might be expected, these PACs disproportionately favor liberal Democrats. The voting pattern on the motion to pass the Family Welfare Reform Act, and thereby change the AFDC program into a Family Support Program (Vote 475), suggests that liberal Democrats composed the faction most likely to vote in favor of the bill. Democrats were 63 percentage points more likely to vote affirmatively on the bill than were Republicans. Recipients of PAC contributions from these labor groups were 24 percentage points more likely to vote affirmatively than nonrecipients. But given the enthusiasm among liberals for the proposed policy change, it is unlikely that the PAC contributions "caused" legislators to vote differently. Instead liberal Democrats were likely to favor the bill and they were also the types of incumbents that the labor groups would choose to support. On issues of such general concern, the causal variable is the predisposition of the legislator, which probably is responsible for both the PAC contribution and the vote choice. On issues that deal with concentrated costs or benefits, PACs have an incentive to call upon the legislators that received PAC contributions to solicit their votes. The ability of PACs to broaden a vote coalition beyond that of the legislators that are predisposed to support the PACs' positions can be estimated by netting the change in probability on votes that do not involve concentrated costs or benefits from the change in probability on votes that do. On consensual issues, this estimate of the true impact of PAC contributions on legislative voting behavior is 21 percentage points.

Not surprisingly, conflictual policy debates generate a large number of roll calls, often centering on narrow controversies embedded in the proposed legislation. In these policy debates, PACs play an important role. As expected, the proportion of PAC variables that are statistically significant is higher when the substantive content of a vote turns on a question of how costs or benefits should be allocated than when the vote turns on other questions. On votes concerning concentrated costs or benefits, 53 percent of the PAC variables were found to be significant in influencing legislative vote choices. On other votes, the proportion of PAC variables that were significant fell to only 35 percent. In this type of charged political environment, the overall magnitude of PAC influence is attenuated because the PAC coalitions tend to offset each other. Consequently the net influence of the PACs is not much greater on votes involving concentrated costs or benefits than in the baseline set of votes where costs or benefits are not explicitly at stake. On average, the absolute change in the vote probability due to the receipt of PAC moneys is 12 percentage points on roll calls where the questions directly involved concentrated costs or benefits. Where the questions did not expressly involve these issues, the receipt of PAC moneys is associated with a 9 percentage point change in the probability that a legislator would vote in a particular way.

The offsetting influence of PACs as a result of PAC competition is visible in the following example. Consider the following vote that was taken on the legislation authorizing the set of Superfund programs. Vote 417 expressly involved the allocation of concentrated costs and benefits. It was an amendment that allowed persons harmed by the release of toxic substances to bring lawsuits against the responsible parties in the federal court system. The PAC coalitions were involved in a bidding process, that approached a standoff. On vote 417, contributions from all three PAC clusters that participated in this policy debate were found to be significant. The liberal-labor-environmental PAC coalition made contributions to 249 House members, which, on average, increased the probability that a legislator receiving a contribution would vote in favor of the amendment by 31 percentage points. The second PAC coalition, comprising insurance, real estate, and steel interests, distributed contributions to 310 House members. These contributions reduced the probability that a member would favor the amendment by 25 percentage points, on average. The third coalition, made up of petrochemical and cleanup contractors, was the most aggressive in making contributions, providing campaign assistance to 358 House members. These contributions were associated with an average reduction of 43 percentage points in the probability that a legislator would support the amendment. The net result is that the probability of a legislator receiving contributions from all three coalitions supporting the amendment is 12 points lower than a similar legislator who received no contributions. This cross-pressuring of legislators is common on conflictual issues when the allocation of concentrated costs or benefits is at stake. In almost two-thirds of the votes taken on narrowly distributed, conflictual public laws, where the question explicitly involved costs or benefits, at least two of the PAC variables were significant and in opposite directions.

CONCLUSION

In Chapter 3, we confronted a research quandary. Although there was strong theoretical reason to expect universalism of benefits, we found scant empirical evidence to support this condition. Very few individual programs provided benefits to more than a majority of districts. When we shifted to portfolios of programs, we again found that substantially fewer than half the portfolios distributed benefits to majorities of districts. If the basic premise of the universalism thesis is that legislators support programs because benefits to a district increase the probability that the legislator will be reelected, then why should majorities of legislators cast their votes to support programs that do not benefit their districts? What is the incentive of legislators to support narrowly distributed programs? In Chapter 4 we argued that a legislator may support programs because he or she benefits from the activities of interest groups that have a stake in those programs, whether or not program benefits go to the legislator's district. The argument was that interest group resources may serve as the functional equivalent of programmatic benefits in enhancing the electoral fortunes of incumbents.

Table 6.3 supports this supposition. In five of the six program portfolios where distributive benefits are narrowly distributed, PACs provided contributions to more than a simple majority of legislators. In the three instances where the policy environment was characterized by conflict, each of the PAC coalitions, with only one exception, individually provided contributions to at least 218 House members. Four of the nine PAC coalitions operating in these three policy debates provided contributions to more than 300 members. We find a much different pattern when distributive benefits are broadly distributed and the policy environment is consensual. Here there is minimal PAC involvement. If the policy environment is conflictual, we find substantial numbers of legislators receiving PAC contributions, but do not find that these contributions make much difference in the voting behavior of the members.

The findings summarized in Table 6.4 support our hypotheses about the conditions under which PAC contributions influence legislative voting behavior and show that PAC contributions do influence legislators' voting behavior. Because other researchers have failed to confirm a significant relationship between PAC contributions and legislative voting behavior, our finding is itself noteworthy and in need of further emphasis. The legislative proposals studied here were selected as a probability sample from the universe of public laws adopted in the 99th and 100th Congresses. This has not been the practice in the literature. Researchers have often chosen conflictual policy issues with which to study the influence of PAC contributions on legislative voting behavior, reasoning that PAC influence is best observed where there is competition for the attention of legislators. This sampling strategy may have biased previous research findings. Our own findings, however, show that the influence of PAC contributions varies with the nature of the policy issue and the scope of the costs or benefits associated with each roll call. Although the level of PAC activity in conflictual policy arenas is considerable, the magnitude of its influence is modest when compared with PAC influence on consensual roll calls. An important conclusion to be drawn from these findings is that PAC activity does not ensure a concomitant level of PAC influence. It is among consensual roll call votes where distributive benefits have narrow district coverage that PAC contributions exhibit their greatest influence. In the arena of conflictual policies, contending PAC contributions are often offsetting, reducing the influence any one PAC coalition has on the vote choices of legislators.

7

Congressional elections and the pork barrel

It is an enduring belief in American politics that legislators who "bring home the bacon" are rewarded for their efforts at the ballot box. This is reflected in the attention of the political science profession, which has invested heavily in explaining and testing for a relationship between the particularized benefits legislators secure for their districts and the electoral margins with which incumbents are reelected. Mayhew (1974), who first elaborated on the logic underlying the electoral connection with distributive policy benefits, observed that "how much particularized benefits count for at the polls is extraordinarily difficult to say, but it would be hard to find a Congressman who thinks he can afford to wait around until precise information is available. The lore is that they count" (p. 57).

We argue that the lore about the relationship between benefits and electoral support contains an important element of truth, which previous research may have failed to detect due to misconceptualization or misspecified empirical tests, or both. Following Fiorina (1981a:546–51, 556), we treat the relationship between distributive benefits and electoral support as dynamic over time and conditioned by institutional, partisan, and electoral differences among individual legislators. We argue, however, that a properly conceptualized view of the electoral connection must integrate both a macroview of the behavior of legislators and a microview of the responses of voters. In this chapter we develop an argument in which not all legislators have the same incentives to utilize their positions within policy subsystems to enhance their electoral margins. We also argue that the extent to which voters are influenced by the provision of distributive benefits is likely to vary greatly and depend on how politically attentive each voter is and the voter's sources of political information and interest group affiliations. In short, both the predisposition to engage in pork-barrel strategies and their effects are likely to be conditional.

This chapter examines this relationship both at the macrolevel, in which the focus is the connection between electoral margins and the al-

118

location of domestic assistance awards, and at the microlevel, in which the focus is the awareness by various groups of constituents of the extent to which federally financed projects have benefited their congressional district. We find that a "pork-barrel" connection between distributive benefits and electoral support exists, but only in a mediated and conditional way. Although legislators are able to obtain electoral benefits from policy subsystems, the conditions that determine when legislators seek such benefits do not apply to all legislators, at least not all the time.

PREVIOUS RESEARCH

Few studies have detected even a modest relationship between electoral measures of congressional support and the distribution of particularized benefits to congressional districts (see, however, Fiorina, 1981a). Anagnoson (1982) found that the timing of award announcements, but not the awards themselves, were driven by electoral factors. Related research has shown that a member's tenure, committee assignments, and leadership positions in the House of Representatives are often unrelated to his or her district's receipt of distributive policy benefits (Rundquist and Griffith, 1976; Ray, 1980). In a nuanced explanation, Arnold (1979) has shown that members on certain committees and coalition leaders in the legislature are sometimes rewarded with agency awards, which are not available to other members until after a program is well established. These findings stand in sharp contrast to the conventional wisdom, which presumes that there is an unambiguous connection between particularized benefits and electoral support. In part, the lack of clear findings can be attributed to the way in which researchers have conceptualized the electoral connection. We argue that the previous research on this issue has suffered from one or more defects. We discuss four problems in the previous research.

Causal direction

The first problem in the literature is the assumption that the causal direction in the electoral connection moves from the legislator's efforts to extract distributive benefits for his or her constituents to enhanced electoral margins. The assumption apparently is that district-level benefits increase the incumbent's visibility and electoral support from informed and/or benefited constituents. An alternative specification is suggested by Jacobson's (1978) finding that campaign spending among incumbents is inversely related to reelection margins. Jacobson explains this finding in terms of vulnerable incumbents responding to their predicament with increased campaign spending. Spending is a response to electoral weakness. Following this logic, it may be that legislators who are vulnerable to electoral defeat seek to acquire new grant awards for their district as a way of demonstrating their efficacy and value to district voters. Absent an electoral threat, members may not have a strong political incentive to expend their time and political capital to extract new grant awards for their district. On this view, the causal order is asymmetric. Legislators that are likely to face an uphill reelection battle may attempt to bring more awards into the district, which in turn should increase the probability that voters will support them in the voting booth. Secure legislators, by contrast, may be unwilling to expend time and energy in an effort to increase the number of projects benefiting the district, given the high probability that voters will support them regardless of any short-run changes in the flow of projects to the district.

Variability of electoral connection

Second, most of the research has assumed that the electoral connection is either invariant for all legislators, or varies only with the member's capacity to extract benefits from the federal largess (e.g., seniority, committee position, leadership posts).[1] For example, Owens and Wade (1984) found a strong relationship between congressional influence and district benefits, albeit for a nontraditional measure of congressional influence and one that was policy specific. Feldman and Jondrow (1984) introduced controls for tenure and party, but did not investigate their interaction with federal spending and electoral margins. Although these studies raise the possibility that not all legislators have an equal capacity to influence the flow of awards to their districts, they ignore the possibility that legislators may not have equal need to use the grant system to improve their electoral fortunes. Vulnerable incumbents – that is, those most in danger of failing to be reelected – should have a greater incentive than their more secure peers to extract district-level benefits as a means of enhancing their electoral fortunes. The fact that most research has not shown a strong and independent relationship between incumbent electoral margins and district-level benefits may be due to the small number of vulnerable incumbents (cf. Ferejohn, 1977; Erikson, 1976; Fiorina, 1977). Moreover, this observation may help explain why previous research (Rundquist and Griffith, 1976; Ray, 1980) has not found a significant relationship between district outlays and a member's influence in the legislature.

Vulnerable members are not likely to occupy positions of significant influence, but instead are most likely to have little seniority, to be members of the minority party, and to sit on the least influential committees (Fenno, 1973). This condition raises a conundrum. Those members with the greatest electoral need for district-level benefits may be least able to obtain these resources.

Voter attentiveness

A third problem is that not all voters are equally attentive to or affected by the flow of new grant awards to their district. Voter awareness of new grant awards to the district should vary with voters' general attentiveness to politics and the substantive nature of the grant award. Teachers might be expected to be more aware of new grant awards for education, whereas environmentalists should be attuned to the flow of moneys to the district for environmental protection. Interest group affiliation and interest in politics may be significant intervening variables between the probability a voter will support an incumbent and the distribution of benefits to the district. The specification of these possible linkages is discussed later in the chapter.

Dollars versus awards

The fourth problem in the literature is the tendency to focus on dollars as a measure of the grant-seeking efficacy of legislators. Most previous studies have operationalized district-level benefits in terms of dollars received, hypothesizing that electoral margins increase monotonically with federal spending in the district (an exception is Anagnoson, 1982). A dollar measure of district-level benefits assumes that all federal moneys are equally beneficial to a member's reelection. It is difficult to imagine that an increase in unemployment benefits or food stamp outlays is positively related to an incumbent's electoral margins since increases in outlays for these programs tend to be triggered by conditions that signal an economic downturn in an area, a situation that tends to be negatively related to support for incumbents (Fiorina, 1978; Kinder and Kiewiet, 1979).[2] By focusing on discretionary programs, as we do in this chapter, we are not examining programs that are automatically triggered by downturns in economic conditions. For discretionary programs, what drives awards to a district is demand for federal assistance (cf. Stein, 1981; Rich, 1989).

As Owens and Wade (1984) found, changes in outlays appear to be related to electoral margins only in policy areas where project awards bring new, highly visible benefits to the district, for example, in the public works sector. The example of public works suggests that a member might prefer to maximize the number of grants and projects awarded to his or her district rather than the amount of money allocated. A single award for $10 million may be less advantageous than ten $100,000 awards. Each award provides an opportunity for a legislator to demonstrate his or her efficacy. Whereas an extremely large project may produce extensive positive externalities in the district, a variety of fiscally modest grant awards provides many different constituencies the opportunity to identify a project that is closely tied to their interests. The potential electoral advantage of program awards over dollar outlays may help overcome a significant disadvantage vulnerable incumbents confront when seeking reelection. These officeholders are often least able to secure significant dollar outlays to their districts since they are less likely to possess significant influence in the legislature. However, the procurement of program awards of lesser financial magnitude may be well within their legislative reach and still provide significant electoral benefits.

THE FEDERAL AID SYSTEM

Congressional influence over the distribution of awards originates with the program's enabling legislation, appropriations of funds to agencies, and subsequent congressional oversight activities. For entitlement programs, which comprise a small number of programs but the lion's share of domestic spending, Congress is directly responsible for specifying the formula by which funds are to be allocated. For these programs, agencies have no discretion in determining eligibility standards and award levels. Recall from Chapter 2 that most programs are discretionary, distributive grants. In these programs authority to select aid recipients, as well as to determine eligibility standards and award levels, is delegated to federal agencies. Typically, such agencies provide awards to a significant majority of applicants for discretionary program assistance, which is made possible by the relatively small amounts of money allocated in most program awards (Stein, 1979, 1981; Rich, 1989).

To have an electoral impact, the timing of these awards is critical. For grant awards to affect electoral margins, the time between the submission of a grant application and the announcement of an award must fall within the two-year cycle of congressional elections. Anagnoson (1982:554–5) reports that for the agencies he studied, the processing time was around twenty months. He notes that this was longer than the average processing time for most other federal agencies.

It is rarely necessary for a member of Congress to create a new program in order to provide his or her constituents program benefits. In fact, few new programs are created during most two-year election cycles (Bickers, 1991). In seeking awards for their districts, members of Congress typically turn to existing programs. It is important to distinguish between the award that is made to a recipient and the dollar amount of that award. Funding for a project may extend over several years, with different amounts allocated to the recipient at different points in time, depending on the current costs of the project. Each of these payments is treated by the federal government as an award transaction. A new transaction represents the initial payment that inaugurates a project. Subsequent payments are recorded by federal agencies as continuing transactions. During a given year, a district receives new and continuing award transactions. We will distinguish between the first award transaction for a project and the total number of transactions required to fulfill project obligations. The total flow of grant moneys to a district represents the sum of ongoing projects that may have commenced in previous years, as well as any spending on new projects begun during a given year.

Vulnerable incumbents are more likely to receive grant awards simply because they are more likely to promote aggressively grant applications from their districts. Republican incumbents are as likely to be successful in this as Democrats, in large part because agencies take special pains to avoid appearing partisan in their review and award activities (Anagnoson, 1982; Rich, 1989; Hird, 1990). The key is how hard a legislator works in identifying and assisting potential grant applicants in his or her district. As a consequence, feeding at the public pork barrel can be, and is, a bipartisan affair.

ELECTORAL CONNECTIONS

Three assumptions are central to the thesis that link electoral margins to the distribution of benefits to a member's district. The first assumption is that legislators can influence the distribution of program benefits to their district. The second assumption is that constituents in the district are aware of the benefits flowing to their district. Finally, it is assumed that constitutents reward a legislator for securing program benefits by voting for the legislator's reelection.

As noted already, the first assumption has met with mixed empirical results. Although some researchers have identified a relationship between a member's committee assignments and the distribution of moneys to his or her district (Plott, 1968; Goss, 1972; Ferejohn, 1974; Ritt, 1976; Arnold, 1979), others have found these relationships to be spurious and often a function of district need (Rundquist and Griffith, 1976; Ray, 1980). Rich (1989) and others (Anagnoson, 1982; Arnold, 1979) have found district needs are often better predictors of the distribution of district-level benefits than measures of legislative influence (e.g., seniority, committee, and leadership positions).

The second assumption, that constituents in the district are aware of the benefits, is also unrealistic, at least for many constituents. It has been common wisdom in political science for a generation that many voters know very little, and care less, about their legislative representatives. Many voters are disinterested about their legislator's role in securing projects for the district.[3] To be sure, legislators are not shy about broadcasting their districts' good fortunes, regardless of their role in securing the largess. Legislators attempt to use television, radio, and newspapers as media to communicate their accomplishments. The evening news broadcast and daily headlines are opportunities for candidates to be noticed by their constituents, however brief and superficial. Repeated news coverage should enhance both voter recognition and evaluation of the incumbent.

A difficulty with this is that the legislator is competing for the attention of voters. The media may not share with the legislator the judgment about the newsworthiness of a project. Even if the project announcement is covered, the broadcast space allotted may be short. Moreover, not all constituents have the same incentive to bear the cost of monitoring information about the flow of moneys into the district. Most programs do not provide benefits directly to individual voters, but rather distribute benefits to universities, hospitals, nonprofit organizations, government agencies, or school districts. Many of the awards that flow to individuals stem from entitlement programs, such as Medicare, Social Security, and other pension programs, rather than from distributive programs. Also many awards are not the subject of daily newspaper accounts or featured prominently on the evening television news, making it difficult for even the most informed voters to know what types of benefits flow to their district.

Yet some constituents are motivated consumers of political information. Members of organized interest groups and other political activists are likely to be better informed than the general public about the activities of their representative. This population of politically aware constituents is likely to supply most of an incumbent's active political support and opposition, including campaign contributors and volunteers, as well as potential challengers. Reaching this group of constituents may be a sufficient reason for a legislator to engage in grant-seeking activity. They may be the target audience.

Third, the assumption that voters reward their representatives on election day for securing district benefits is not as obvious as it might seem. The electoral impact of helping to direct benefits to the district is likely to be muted to the extent that voters are unaware of the benefits and to the extent that voters do not credit their member with securing them. The theoretical problem is how to account for the relationship between a representative's efforts to secure particularistic benefits and changes in the likelihood that voters will support the incumbent. Our hypothesis is that the impact of grant awards on electoral support for incumbents is a product of a cumulative evaluation among members of the politically attentive subpopulations within a district, rather than a simple Pavlovian response to a particular award.

The explanation of the electoral connection between district-specific benefits and reelection margins that we construct and test in this chapter is composed of four parts. Vulnerable incumbents, those with narrower electoral margins, are expected to shepherd more new grant awards into their district than nonvulnerable incumbents. In part two, the expectation is that new awards have a cognitive impact on constituents, but not on all constituents. Rather, politically aware and active constituents should be most cognizant of new awards to the district. In part three, constituent awareness of new grant awards should positively affect evaluations of incumbents. Finally, in part four, a positive evaluation of the incumbent should produce a higher probability that constituents will vote for the incumbent. Our explanation suggests that it would be a mistake to expect an unmediated or direct relationship between increases in the flow of new grant awards and increases in electoral margins. Instead, the relationship between new awards and electoral support is expected to be mediated by an alteration in how select subpopulations of constituents evaluate the incumbent.

RESEARCH DESIGN

Before we undertake empirical tests of our explanation of the electoral connection, we test the hypothesis that changes in the number of new awards to a district directly affect an incumbent's electoral margins. The key independent variable in this analysis is measured as the change in the proportion of new discretionary awards to the total number of discretionary awards from one Congress to the next. The rationale for this measure of particularized benefits is discussed in the next section. Included in this regression analysis are also controls for the incumbent's electoral margin in the 1986 general election, and the number of terms the incumbent has served in Congress. Conventional thinking would suggest a positive relationship between new awards and electoral margins. Our expectation, however, is that such a relationship will not be found.

Following this analysis, we turn to our alternative explanation of the electoral connection. In analyzing the first part of our argument, we regress change in the proportion of new to total discretionary awards from the 1985–6 period to the 1987–8 period on four variables, of which three are designed to tap the relative vulnerability of incumbent members of the House of Representatives. The first variable relating to vulnerability is the incumbent's electoral margin in 1986; the second is the incumbent's share of total campaign spending in the 1986 electoral cycle; and the third is the number of congressional terms the member has been in office. Our assumption is that vulnerability decreases with number of terms for two reasons. First, the member gains greater name recognition from successive reelections. Second, over time the member is able to move into increasingly important positions on committees, which permits the member more effectively to help program applicants obtain awards. We have also included a dummy variable measuring the legislator's party in order to control for the extent to which Democratic and Republican members of Congress differ in their ability to manipulate the grant system for electoral purposes.

The second part of our argument addresses the extent to which voters are aware of the flow of new grants into the district. The question is whether all constituents, or a subset comprised of politically attentive constituents, know about the activities of the incumbent in securing new awards for the district. Two subpopulations are identified in the analysis: members of organized interest groups and respondents who claim to have a high level of interest and information about government and politics. The model also includes control variables for the incumbent's share of total campaign spending, incumbent tenure, and the party of the incumbent.

The third part of our argument examines constituent evaluations of incumbents. Specifically we are interested in the impact of awareness of new awards on evaluations. Our expectation is that awareness of increases in the proportion of new awards is the key factor in raising constituent evaluations. Constituent awareness of new awards is expected to be the mediating variable that determines whether the efforts of a legislator to bring awards into the district will produce positive evaluations. Control variables in this analysis include the respondent's party affiliation, specific likes or dislikes about the incumbent, attentiveness to government, and interest group membership, as well as the incumbent's share of campaign spending and the incumbent's tenure.

The fourth part of our argument relates to the impact of constituent evaluations of the incumbent on the constituent's vote choice. As in the explanation of constituent evaluation of incumbents, we do not expect a strong relationship between change in the number of new awards and vote choice. Instead, we think the impact of new awards on vote choice operates through cognitive influences. The two cognitive variables through which this effect should operate are expected to be constituent awareness of new awards and voter evaluation of the incumbent. Control variables in this model include the respondent's party affiliation, whether the respondent has specific likes or dislikes about the incumbent, incumbent share of campaign spending, and the incumbent's tenure.

DATA AND OPERATIONAL MEASURES

Data for this chapter come from a number of different sources. Information on the distribution of federal program outlays is drawn from the *Federal Assistance Awards Data System* (FAADS), which we have discussed previously (see Appendix 2). We identify the total number of discretionary program awards to each district in a specific year. As in Chapter 3, what we focus on is the number of award transactions, not the number of dollars awarded. Programs included in this chapter are those where there is some degree of discretion in the making of awards. This excludes programs that are generally considered entitlements, such as Social Security, Medicare, Medicaid, Food Stamps, and AFDC, as well as Railroad Retirement and other pension programs. Table 7.1 contains a brief depiction of the volume and dollar sizes of discretionary assistance awards during the 99th and 100th Congresses.

Because we are interested in the flow of new awards, grant awards have been divided into those which have been made as part of an ongoing project and those which are the first award in the project. The measure employed below is based on the ratio of new awards to the total number of both new and ongoing awards received in a district. We measure the change in this ratio from the 99th Congress to the 100th Congress using the formula of $NW_{100}/AD_{100} - NW_{99}/AD_{99}$, where NW = the number of new grant awards to a congressional district during the 99th (100th) Congress, and AD = The total number of grant awards to a congressional district during the 99th (100th) Congress. We recognize that our measure of the change in the flow of awards to districts is somewhat more cumbersome to interpret than a level of awards measure, but it is preferable on theoretical grounds. First, congressional districts vary enormously in the number of awards that they typically receive, with urban districts and some agricultural districts receiving far more awards than suburban districts. By employing a proportional measure, differences in the "normal" volume of grants is eliminated, allowing the changes in the number of grants to show up as relative changes in the "normal" flow of awards. Second, the difference in the proportion of new grant awards to total awards between one Congress and the next measures within-district change. We are measuring the change in this proportion between the 99th Congress and the 100th Congress within districts. This measure assumes that voters make retrospective comparisons about the state of affairs in their district. An alternative measure would focus on the level of awards across districts. Such a measure, however, would assume that voters are capable of comparing their district to all other districts. We think such between-district comparisons place unrealistic and heroic expectations on voters.

Table 7.1. *Distributive grant awards by congressional district, 99th and 100th Congresses*

	Number of new awards by congressional district		Total number of awards by congressional district		Proportion of new to total awards		Average size of award (nominal dollars)	
	99th Cong.	100th Cong.	99th Cong.	100th Cong.	99th Cong.	100th Cong.	99th Cong.	100th Cong.
Minimum	26	23	390	146	4.00%	10.75%	$7,254	$10,629
Quartile 1	281	192	1,090	863	21.17%	21.92%	$45,741	$68,453
Median	488	359	1,752	1,326	34.11%	25.96%	$79,723	$96,283
Quartile 3	1,143	769	2,937	2,523	46.76%	31.31%	$140,196	$139,861
Maximum	6,172	3,824	18,144	19,125	75.06%	63.81%	$1,470,900	$2,289,806

Note: All figures calculated by authors. Assistance program awards exclude entitlements.

Data on campaign spending, party affiliation, electoral margins, and tenure come from Makinson's (1992) reference volume on the sources of campaign finance dollars for House and Senate elections. This volume contains detailed data on PAC contributions to incumbents in the 1988 election, including the types of PACs, the committee memberships of each incumbent, the proportion of campaign expenditures supplied by PACs, the vote percentages received by each incumbent and his or her major party opponent, and a variety of other data. Tenure is measured as the number of terms served in the House. There were 396 incumbents who were elected in 1986, served in the 100th Congress, and ran for reelection in 1988. It was necessary to exclude members who did not run for election in both 1986 and 1988 in order to have measures of their electoral margins at the beginning and the end of the 100th Congress.

Individual level data come from the 1988 *National Election Study* (Center for Political Studies, 1988). Respondents were queried about, among other topics, their vote choice for Congress, evaluations of their congressional representative, their party and interest group affiliations, their knowledge of politics, and awareness of projects in the district for which the House member is responsible.[4] Evaluations of the two major party candidates are measured with a feeling thermometer question of the two major party candidates. The thermometer score for the candidate who was the incumbent is used in this analysis. We have also included as control variables dichotomous measures of whether a constituent expressed a like or dislike for the candidate who was the incumbent. Additionally, we have identified whether a person is of the same party as the incumbent. This is a trichotomous measure, where 1 indicates same party identification, 0 indicates a constituent who identifies himself or herself as an independent, and −1 indicates that the respondent was of the opposite party of the incumbent.

Appendix 10 reports the individual questions and other items used in our analysis. There were 1,775 respondents interviewed in the *National Election Study* who resided in congressional districts where incumbents stood for reelection. Among these voters, 987 reported voting for a congressional candidate in the 1988 election. The sample of respondents covers 125 congressional districts.

FINDINGS

Table 7.2 focuses on the macrolevel effect of changes in the proportion of new to total discretionary awards on the incumbent's overall electoral margin in 1988. Consistent with our expectation, but contrary to the conventional wisdom, change in the proportion of new to total grant

Table 7.2. *OLS regression estimates for electoral margins of House incumbents in 1988*

Variable	Coefficient	Standard error	T-value
Constant	-49.58	6.14	-8.08***
Electoral margin for			
House incumbent, 1986	0.291	0.038	7.62***
Change in the proportion			
of new to total awards	-1.99	7.22	-0.28
Party affiliation of			
House member	-1.25	2.10	-0.59
Incumbent's share of total			
campaign spending, 1987-8	95.81	7.07	13.56***
Incumbent tenure	0.221	0.274	0.81
Mean of dependent variable	48.0		
Number of observations	396		
R square	0.496		

*$p < 0.1$, one-tailed   **$p < 0.05$, one-tailed   ***$p < 0.01$, one-tailed

awards is not related to electoral margins.[5] This suggests that the impact of particularized benefits on electoral support is not direct, at least not at this aggregate level. The OLS regression estimates indicate that only prior electoral margins and incumbent share of spending are significantly related to 1988 electoral margins. Neither tenure nor party was significantly related to 1988 incumbent electoral margins.

Table 7.3 reports the ordinary least squares regression estimates for our first step of the electoral connection model. It focuses on the effect of electoral vulnerability on the change in the proportion of new awards to total awards from the 99th to the 100th Congress. Where others have failed to detect a strong relationship between margins and domestic spending, we find that when grants are measured, not by dollars, but by change in the proportion of new to total awards, there is a significant, negative relationship.[6] When grant awards are measured in terms of the percentage change in dollars, we fail to obtain a single significant coefficient for any of the independent regressors reported in Table 7.3. These findings were replicated with the dependent variable as the absolute change in nominal dollars to a district and also with the dependent variable as the absolute change in real dollars to a district. In every case the dollar measure was unrelated to the independent variables, including the degree of vulnerability in the previous election.

Table 7.3. *OLS regression estimates for change in the percentage of new to total grant awards from the 99th to the 100th Congress*

Variable	Coefficient	Standard error	T-value
Constant	-0.128	0.034	-3.69***
Electoral margin for House incumbent, 1986	-0.00072	0.00034	-2.11**
Party affiliation of House member	0.0554	0.0145	3.82***
Incumbent's share of total campaign spending, 1985-6	0.0636	0.0515	1.24
Incumbent tenure	.00154	0.00193	0.796
Mean of dependent variable	-0.077		
Number of observations	396		
R square	0.057		

$*p < 0.1$, one-tailed $**p < 0.05$, one-tailed $***p < 0.01$, one-tailed

As hypothesized, Table 7.3 shows that the electoral margin in 1986 is significantly related in the negative direction to new grant awards. In districts where incumbents suffered from close margins in 1986, there is a statistically significant, albeit modest, increase in the proportion of new awards to total awards flowing to the district. The share of campaign spending by incumbents in the 1986 election was not significantly related to changes in the proportion of new to total awards from the 1985–6 period to the 1987–8 period. Interestingly, Republican legislators had significantly larger increases in the proportion of new to total awards between the two periods than did Democratic legislators. Upon further analysis of this differential, we found that Republicans in general have a lower total number of grants flowing to their district; consequently their efforts to increase the number of new awards in the 1987–8 period translated into a generally higher proportion of new to total awards than most Democratic members were able to achieve. Tenure in the House is not significantly related to the change in the proportion of new to total awards.

Voter awareness of new awards is a dichotomous measure and thus our analysis involves a probit regression. Table 7.4 reports the estimates and probabilities for voter awareness of new awards.[7] Increases in the proportion of new awards to the district raises awareness among constituents that their incumbent has brought new projects into the district. This rela-

131

Table 7.4. *Probit estimates for voter awareness of new projects in the district*

Variable	Coefficient	Standard error	T-value	Change in probability
Constant	-.808	.266	-3.04***	
Party affiliation of House member	-.262	.089	-2.95***	-.058
Incumbent's share of total campaign spending, 1988	-.534	.293	-1.82**	-.034
Interest group affiliation	.480	.079	6.12**	.122
Information about politics and government	.535	.079	6.76***	.138
Incumbent tenure	.016	.011	1.37*	.025
Change in the proportion of new to total awards	.474	.259	1.83**	.034
Mean of dependent variable	0.16			
Number of observations	1,704			
Pseudo R square	0.059			

Note: For the two continuous independent variables (i.e., incumbent share of campaign spending and the change in the proportion of new to total grant awards), we have calculated the change in the probabilities when each independent variable is set to one standard deviation above and below the mean values for these measures. For each of the dichotomous independent variables, the effect of each variable is evaluated at the o and 1 values. Pseudo R square is calculated by taking the square of the Pearson product moment between the observed dependent variable and the predicted probabilities for the dependent variable as estimated by the probit regression.

$*p < 0.1$, one-tailed $**p < 0.05$, one-tailed $***p < 0.01$, one-tailed

tionship, however, is relatively modest. Though statistically significant, there is only a 3.4 percent change in the probability that a constituent will be aware of new projects when the proportion of new awards moves from one standard deviation below to one standard deviation above the mean. As expected voters who are either members of interest groups or who are well informed politically are significantly more likely to be aware of new projects in their district. These effects are the strongest observed in the model. Group membership increases the probability that a respondent will be aware of new projects by 12 percent, holding all other variables at their mean values. Knowledge of government and politics increases awareness of new projects by 14 percent. These variables indicate that members of these two politically attentive subpopulations are far more

Table 7.5. *OLS estimates for incumbent thermometer rating*

Variable	Coefficient	Standard error	T-value
Constant	49.02	3.19	15.36***
Party affiliation of House member	4.05	0.620	6.57***
Incumbent tenure	.315	.143	2.19***
Incumbent share of total campaign spending, 1988	5.71	3.64	1.57*
Interest group affiliation	0.066	1.04	0.063
Information about politics and government	0.037	1.06	0.034
Incumbent likes	19.99	1.03	19.42***
Incumbent dislikes	-13.43	1.47	-9.12***
Awareness of new projects in the district	4.54	1.31	3.47***
Change in proportion of new to total awards (99th-100th)	4.01	3.02	1.33*
Mean of dependent variable	64.1		
Number of observations	1,429		
R square	0.338		

*$p < 0.1$, one-tailed **$p < 0.05$, one-tailed ***$p < 0.01$, one-tailed

sensitive to alterations in the flow of new awards to the district than are other members of the public.

One curious and unexpected finding in this analysis is that respondents in districts represented by Republicans are significantly less likely to recall new awards. The probability that voters will be aware of new projects in their district is nearly 5.8 percent lower in districts represented by Republicans. The fact that constituents in districts represented by Republicans are less likely to be aware of new awards may reflect the preference of conservative voters for less government spending. Republican incumbents may be reluctant to broadcast the flow of new awards into the district to their Republican constituents in the face of latter's strong preference for reduced government spending. Republican incumbents therefore may be more selective than their Democratic counterparts in claiming credit for new grant awards. Perhaps Republican House members limit their broadcasting of new awards to project beneficiaries.

Table 7.5 reports the regression estimates for constituent evaluation of the incumbent. As expected, constituent evaluations of the incumbent are not related to change in the proportion of new awards. Instead, evalua-

Table 7.6. *Probit estimates of individual votes for incumbent congressional candidates*

Variable	Coefficient	Standard error	T-value	Change in probability
Constant	-2.11	0.369	-5.71***	
Party congruence	0.508	0.067	7.61***	0.266
Incumbent tenure	0.063	0.018	3.57***	0.107
Incumbent share of total campaign spending, 1988	1.57	0.383	4.11***	0.103
Incumbent likes	0.309	0.123	2.50***	0.073
Incumbent dislikes	-0.832	0.140	-5.94***	-0.249
Incumbent thermometer	0.018	0.003	5.80***	0.181
Voter awareness of new projects in district	0.472	0.160	2.96***	0.097
Change in proportion of new to total awards (99th-100th)	0.513	0.314	1.63*	0.040
Mean of dependent variable	77.2			
Number of observations	987			
Pseudo R square	0.310			

Note: For the two continuous independent variables (i.e., incumbent share of campaign spending and the change in the proportion of new to total grant awards), we have calculated the change in the probabilities when each independent variable is set to one standard deviation above and below the mean values for these measures. For each of the dichotomous independent variables, the effect of each variable is evaluated at the 0 and 1 values. Pseudo R square is calculated by taking the square of the Pearson product moment between the observed dependent variable and the predicted probabilities for the dependent variable as estimated by the probit regression.

$*p < 0.1$, one-tailed $**p < 0.05$, one-tailed $***p < 0.01$, one-tailed

tions of the incumbent are related to a cognitive variable – that is, constituent awareness of new awards. A constituent who believes that the incumbent is responsible for new projects in the district rewards the incumbent with an increased thermometer rating of 4.5 degrees. It is interesting to note that evaluations of incumbents by members of interest groups and people who are watchers of government and politics do not vary from the population in general. The evaluations of these politically attentive subpopulations are mediated instead by the increased likelihood that they are aware of new projects, as shown in Table 7.4. Other variables included as controls in the model have predicted affects on the thermometer ratings. People in the same party as the incumbent, people that had specific likes about the incumbent, and longer tenured incumbents scored higher on the thermometer ratings. People from the opposite party and those with specific dislikes evaluated the incumbent more poorly.

The final regression asks whether the effect of particularized benefits on electoral support for incumbents is direct or mediated by cognitive and evaluative factors. Table 7.6 reports probit estimates and probabilities of electoral support for incumbent House candidates in 1988. As hypothesized, voting for incumbents is positively related to cognitive information about new projects in the voter's district. Voter awareness of new projects in their district increases the probability of voting for the incumbent House member by 9.7 percent, when all other variables are held to their mean values. Voter evaluations of the incumbent are also significantly related to the probability of voting for the incumbent. The probability of voting for the incumbent increases 18.1 percent when evaluations of the incumbent increase from one standard deviation below to one standard deviation above the mean.

Most important, change in the proportion of new awards to the district is not significantly related to a constituent's vote choice. Instead, the effect of changes in the flow of new awards is mediated by both cognitive information about new projects and the impact that new awards have on how constituents evaluate incumbents. The estimates for the control variables are consistent with previous expectations. The likelihood of voting for the incumbent is also affected by whether the voter is in the same or a different party than the incumbent, whether a voter has specific likes or dislikes about the incumbent, the number of terms that the incumbent has served, and the incumbent's share of total campaign expenditures.

CONCLUSION

Previous research has led to the appearance of a disjuncture between the folklore and scholarly wisdom about the relationship between particularized benefits to congressional districts and electoral support for incumbents. We are skeptical about the scholarly wisdom. First, we are skeptical about the appropriateness of a dollar measure of particularized benefits. It is the occurrence of an award, not its dollar size, that is usually salient to constituents. An awards measure that involves within-district comparisons rather than between-district comparisons is conceptually more appropriate in identifying how new awards capture the attention and electoral support of constituents. Second, we are skeptical about treating all incumbents alike. Not all incumbents have the same incentive to seek an increased flow of particularized benefits to their districts. Those who are electorally vulnerable are most likely to seek an increase in projects to their district. Electorally vulnerable incumbents seek new particularized benefits in order to shore up sagging electoral margins by winning the attention and support of their constituents. Third, we are skeptical about treating all constituents as equally attentive to the grant-seeking activities of incumbents. Politically attentive constituents – for example, members of interest groups and those that are high consumers of information about government and politics – are more aware of increases in new awards. Fourth, it is this awareness of new grants that is likely to have an impact on a constituent's vote choice, primarily due to the impact of awareness of new grants on how the constituent more generally evaluates the incumbent. In sum, this model holds that the electoral payoff from an increase in the flow of new projects is mediated by both constituent awareness of new projects and constituent evaluations of incumbents.

The findings reported in Tables 7.2 through 7.6 support our alternative model. What is important to notice about these results is that they require a more nuanced interpretation of the electoral connection and its consequences for governance. The electoral connection is not about all incumbents, nor is it about all constituents. To the contrary, we find that only some incumbents, namely those who are most vulnerable, are likely to seek increases in new awards. Certain constituents, those who are politically attentive and members of interest groups, are most likely to be aware of new awards to the district and to more favorably evaluate to alterations in the flow of new awards. New grant awards help with very specific constituencies in the district, such as members of influential interest groups and key political figures in the district. The support of these individuals may produce tangible, but indirect, electoral benefits. These individuals provide campaign contributions and campaign volunteers, and may be influential in the decision of challengers to enter the fray.

The normative preoccupation with the electoral connection has, in part, focused on the inefficiency and profligacy that it fosters. What we find, however, is that the electoral connection, while real, is not universal. This does not mean that inefficiency and profligacy do not exist. It does suggest that a critique of the politics of the pork barrel needs to address several questions. Are the projects that benefit districts with vulnerable members different, not simply in number, but also in size and type, than those that benefit other districts? Are awards to districts with vulnerable incumbents targeted to constituencies chosen not on the basis of conventional measures of need, but rather on their voting strength or the electoral resources they can provide? Would increasing the vulnerability of some members, for example, by the adoption of term limitations and campaign reform legislation increase, rather than decrease, the number of new grant awards? If so, the adoption of these reforms might have the unintended consequence of increasing the inefficiency and profligacy in the system. We turn to these questions in the concluding chapter.

136

PART IV

8

Policy subsystems in practice and democratic theory

Americans have a love–hate relationship with their government. They tell pollsters that they disapprove strongly of Congress as a whole, but vote to reelect their own members of Congress. They decry the role of special interests in influencing congressional decision making, but oppose public funding of federal campaigns. They believe that much of what the government does is unnecessary and wasteful, but demand that programs benefiting themselves be protected. The policy subsystems that we analyze in this book contribute to this ambivalence about our political system. They are viewed as insulated from popular control, self-serving, and a major contributor to the country's runaway deficits. At the same time, they are given responsibility for designing and implementing policies in response to public problems.

MYTHS ABOUT FEDERAL ASSISTANCE PROGRAMS

Given this ambivalence, it is important to separate the real problems from the mythology associated with policy subsystems. Perhaps the biggest myth is the contention that policy subsystems in general are a major contributor to the federal deficit. The fact is that a very small number of domestic programs account for virtually all of the growth in domestic spending. Figure 8.1 shows that three programs – Social Security, Medicare, and Medicaid – are responsible for the vast majority of the growth in domestic spending during the 1980s.[1] These three programs account for 85 percent of all growth in spending for domestic financial assistance programs from 1983 through 1990. The average annual rate of change, in real per capita dollars, for these three programs was 3.5 percent. For all other financial assistance programs, the average annual rate of change was only 1.3 percent. This in spite of the fact, discussed in Chapter 2, that the number of discretionary (nonentitlement) programs providing direct forms of financial assistance grew in number by 42 percent, from 435

139

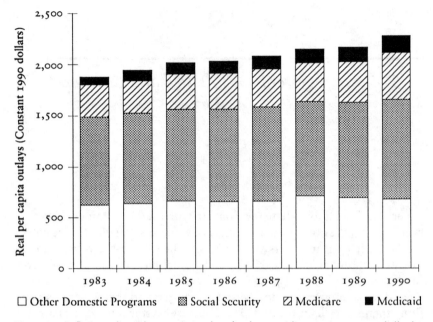

Figure 8.1. Inflation-adjusted per capita outlays for three entitlement programs and all other domestic financial assistance programs, 1983–90.

programs to 620 programs, during the eight-year period from 1983 through 1990. If the three big entitlement programs had grown by the same rate over this eight-year period as all other direct assistance programs, the deficit in 1990 would have been 54.6 billion dollars smaller than it was. It is important not to generalize from the experience of the policy subsystems that contain these large entitlement programs to that of all other policy subsystems. There are scores of subsystems throughout the federal bureaucracy. While these subsystems have been active in a variety of ways during the 1980s, very few experienced the kind of expenditure growth that characterized these redistributive entitlements.

A second myth is that once created domestic assistance programs grow inexorably and never die. For the twenty-year period between 1971 and 1990 there were an average of fifty-seven programs created and thirty-six programs terminated each year (Bickers, 1991). This means that for every eleven programs created, seven other programs were terminated. The size of terminated programs was not trivial. During this twenty-year period, the average size of a terminated program was only slightly smaller than that of newly created programs. For this twenty-year period, the average annual rate of growth in spending for continuing assistance programs was 2.5 percent (in constant dollars), which was considerably less than the rate of inflation during this period. There is little truth to the contention that programs never die and grow without limit. Although such growth may be visible in a handful of programs, most programs begin in obscurity and never reach far beyond their starting point.

A third myth concerns the geographic scope of domestic assistance programs. In most programs, eligibility is limited to a small number of recipients. Our own portfolio theory provides a rationale for why subsystem actors would want to limit the scope of eligibility within programs. The reason is that subsystem actors have an incentive to help interest groups overcome their collective action problems so that they might better organize on behalf of the programs. One consequence of this is that the geographic scope of many federal programs tends to be narrow. Recipients tend not to exist in every congressional district. By crafting programs in this way, the effect is to limit the number of congressional districts in which there will be eligible recipients. An overwhelming majority of federal assistance programs are distributed to a relatively small number of congressional districts. Chapter 3 shows that three-quarters of all federal assistance programs distribute benefits to recipients in fewer than 150 congressional districts. Most program portfolios are more broadly distributed, but still go to fewer than half of the congressional districts. Viewed as a whole, the majority of policy subsystems dispense benefits from a pork barrel that is surprisingly limited in its geographic reach.

A fourth myth concerns the relationship between the flow of assistance moneys to congressional districts and the margin with which incumbents are reelected. It is generally thought that those legislators who "bring home the bacon" are rewarded for their efforts with reelection by large margins. Because all members are assumed to seek reelection, all members are thought to have a incentive to maximize the amount of distributive benefits they obtain for their districts. We find in Chapter 7, however, that the amount of money is not relevant. The reelection margins of legislators are unrelated to the amount of federal assistance moneys that pass to a member's district. What does matter is the number of new projects, and only for those members who are electorally vulnerable. Vulnerable members seek new grant awards as a means of gaining positive recognition from their constituents, penultimate to receiving their votes. Although domestic programs are being utilized to help legislators get reelected, the budgetary cost of this activity, it turns out, is electorally irrelevant.

NORMATIVE CONCERNS

If the budgetary impact of policy subsystems has been exaggerated, other aspects of their impact on American politics are nonetheless troubling. What troubles us is how their operation impinges on basic democratic

principles in American politics. Three issues seem to be most problematic:
(1) the accountability of policy subsystems; (2) the congruence of voter
preferences with subsystem outputs; and (3) the subsystem's impact on the
election of representatives.

Accountability

To the extent that subsystems are successful at managing their program
portfolios, there is an accountability problem. The hallmark of successful
policy subsystems is that the actors internal to the subsystem are able to
mutually assist each other in gaining the resources to pursue their individual interests. Interest groups and members of congressional committees
are active partners in helping agencies win program authorizations that
are used to benefit interest groups and the reelection efforts of legislators.
What this means, as we saw in Chapter 5, is that presidential efforts to
control agencies may be successfully challenged by policy subsystems.
Normatively, one can legitimately ask if policy subsystems should be subject to presidential oversight or should be permitted wide latitude in their
areas of expertise. A constitutional argument can be made that the president should be responsible for the activities of the executive branch, including the agencies that participate in policy subsystems.

The problem, of course, is that presidents have never exercised exclusive control over executive branch agencies. In practice, control over
executive branch agencies throughout American history has been subject
to continual pulling and hauling between Congress and the president.
Congress, too, has traditionally asserted its constitutional responsibility in
making policy and overseeing its implementation (Dodd and Shott, 1979;
Cronin, 1975; Skowronek, 1982). A second problem with presidential
control of agencies is rooted in the limited resources and expertise of
presidents and their advisors. No matter how much effort they might
invest in policy questions, presidents are unable to become expert in all
policy arenas. Moreover, they are unlikely to be able to view policy questions from the diverse perspectives of the many groups that may be affected by a policy proposal. Charles Lindblom explains this limitation on
the capacities of centralized policy analysis: "No person, committee, or
research team, even with all the resources of modern electronic computa-
tion, can complete the analysis of a complex problem. Too many interact-
ing values are at stake, too many possible alternatives, too many consequences to be traced through an uncertain future" (Lindblom, 1979:518).
According to Lindblom, centralized control over the policy-making process is not only infeasible but dangerous. What Lindblom terms the intelli-
gence of democracy is the mutual adjustments that "will achieve a coordination superior to an attempt at central coordination, which is often so

complex as to lie beyond any coordinator's competence" (Lindblom, 1979:523).

Congruence of preferences and policies

Shepsle and Weingast (1981) argue that universalism will produce a supply of particularized program benefits in excess of the true level of demand for government expenditures. They argue that the reason for this condition is that legislators seeking reelection from single-member legislative districts prefer to bring particularized benefits to their districts because the taxes raised from across the country are spent primarily in the legislator's district to produce benefits. Legislators have little incentive to hold down the costs of the program, because the district pays a small proportion of the total cost but receives the entire benefit. We find that Shepsle and Weingast's empirical expectation about the existence of universalism is not confirmed. However, the normative problem about the lack of congruence between the public's preferences and the supply of particularized benefits may, in fact, be even worse than predicted by Shepsle and Weingast.

Under conditions of universalism every district receives at least some benefit, albeit of different levels. We find in Chapter 6 that legislators will support programs for which their district receives no particularized benefits when interest groups mobilize campaign contributions to persuade them. In the districts that do not receive program benefits, constituents bear a full share of the tax cost of the program. The role of an interest group in promoting its policy agenda may be at odds with the preferences of constituents who will be forced to bear the tax costs of the benefits received by interest group members. Even in those districts that receive particularized benefits, the presence of the benefits may have more to do with the preferences of an interest group that lobbied on behalf of the programs than with preferences of voters in the districts. Legislators may vote for programs that none of their constituents want. By providing legislators an alternative motivation for supporting programs, interest groups distort the relationship between legislators and their constituents.

Incumbency advantage

The third problem is that policy subsystems constrain the choices of voters in selecting their representatives. Subsystems provide a steady flow of electoral resources to legislators. These resources take two primary forms: particularized benefits from an agency to the district and campaign contributions from interest groups to incumbents. Together these resources enhance reelection of incumbents; moreover, these subsystems are self-correcting. When legislators are vulnerable, subsystems enable legislators to extract additional resources with which to remedy their electoral vulnerability. Most members of Congress rarely appear to be vulnerable, in part due to the successful operation of the subsystems in which they are participants. This is doubly advantageous to incumbents, since participation in the subsystem provides them with resources to avoid the rise of strong challengers, and offers a vehicle for mounting effective campaigns on those rare occasions when strong challengers do arise. In short, policy subsystems make democracy safe for incumbents.

REFORM PROPOSALS

In this final section of the book we ask how different proposals for reforming American politics might fare in light of our own empirical findings. The reforms include: a balanced budget amendment to the U.S. Constitution; a line-item veto for the president; term limitations for members of the U.S. Congress; campaign finance reform; and reforms of the congressional committee system.

Balanced budget amendment

One mechanism proposed for reducing the size of the federal government's deficit is a constitutional amendment requiring balanced budgets. Although various proposals for a balanced budget amendment have been advanced,[2] common to all these proposals is the imposition of a budget constraint on policy makers. Upon first consideration, we might speculate that a balanced budget requirement would lead to the elimination of many discretionary spending programs. This speculation is probably false. If our own subsystem story is correct, the imposition of a balanced budget requirement might not severely affect discretionary spending programs. Recall that our findings in Chapter 5 demonstrated that most of the agencies targeted by the Reagan administration for severe budget cuts were not only able to resist these assaults on their budgets, but in fact were able to increase the number of programs in their agency portfolios.

An attack on policy subsystems sets in motion an adaptive response. By threatening agency budgets, subsystem actors are given strong incentives to overcome their collective action problems in order to countermobilize. Day-to-day conflicts between interest groups and agencies are suppressed in order to fend off the threat to the subsystem as a whole. Insofar as programs are in jeopardy, recipients of the program benefits will need and want aggressive interest group representation to preserve the programs. Consequently, the value of interest groups to their membership increases. This insecurity-induced mobilization means that interest groups will be

144

able to open the sluice gates of their PACs to support legislators who are sympathetic to the plight of the programs that the groups support.

What is likely to transpire is that the howls of protest from the chorus of policy subsystems will prevent drastic budgetary cuts from being levied on discretionary programs. Although much rhetoric will be expended about cutting unnecessary government spending, Congress ultimately will be forced to look elsewhere to find politically palatable sources of funds to balance the budget. Moreover, viewed in the aggregate, discretionary programs represent such a small portion of federal outlays that cuts in these programs would not make a serious dent in the deficit. In the end, most policy subsystems that surround discretionary programs will survive more or less intact.

In practice, Congress and the president will have to look elsewhere for funds to balance the budget. One option is to attack entitlement programs. Many, if not most, entitlements are likely to prove as untouchable as most discretionary policy subsystems – for the same reasons. Proposals to cut entitlements will provoke the type of adaptive response that is characteristic of subsystems with distributive programs. This is particularly true of entitlements serving politically engaged constituencies, for example, the elderly. The heavy midterm losses of Republican House members in 1982 were blamed by many pundits on the Reagan administration's threat to cut Social Security benefits. Groups representing entitlement beneficiaries are typically able to mobilize quickly and effectively to protect their benefits against external threats. The exceptions to this are entitlements that benefit constituencies that are politically inefficacious. Housing assistance, Medicaid, food stamps, Aid to Families with Dependent Children – programs that provide assistance to the poor are easier targets because the beneficiaries of these programs are difficult to organize for political action and have few resources that can be mobilized to protect their interests in the political arena.

A second option for budget balancers is to look for cuts in defense spending. Given the size of defense appropriations in the past decade, it is small wonder that this portion of the budget is an attractive place for spending cuts. The problem, however, is that increasingly cuts in defense spending have become politically indistinguishable from cuts in domestic spending. Base closings, force reductions, and weapons system cancellations directly reduce federal outlays that provide jobs, maintain property values, and undergird local economies. As the politics of military retrenchment intensifies and becomes more transparently an extension of domestic politics, it is likely that the same type of subsystem response to threats will prevail. Groups representing affected publics will mobilize to preserve their benefits. Members of Congress that represent these impacted groups and regions will fight to keep defense spending at current levels.

And the Pentagon will take an active role in orchestrating the defense of military spending in local communities.

A third option is to raise new taxes. This choice has little to do with policy subsystems and much to do with public opinion and electoral politics. The rhetoric that prevents the use of tax hikes to balance the budget calls for spending cuts to occur first. Yet, spending cuts always come at the expense of identifiable publics, who are quick to mobilize against assaults on the programs that provide benefits to themselves. If the country awaits spending cuts before taxes are increased, it will be a long time before the promised land of balanced budgets is seen.

A fourth option is for the government to engage in cost shifting, by placing requirements on individuals and private firms to assume responsibility for goods and services previously financed by the federal government. Unfunded federal mandates are a well-worn practice between the federal government and state and local governments, where the federal government imposes performance requirements on subnational units of government. The cost of these requirements is borne by the state and local government, not the federal government. This same type of cost shifting may be increasingly imposed on private citizens and businesses.[3] The original Clinton health care proposal required most private businesses to provide health insurance to their employees. The original counterproposal by moderate Republicans required that, not businesses, but private citizens buy health coverage for themselves. What is significant about both these proposals is that a major new social initiative is to be paid not out of federal tax revenues, but by shifting the costs to either the private sector or families. This cost shifting through unfunded mandates is a form of silent taxation.

Line-item veto

As a deficit reduction tool, the line-item veto might give the president a useful new tool. It would allow the president to excise surgically wasteful government spending. To be effective in reducing the deficit, however, the line-item veto would have to be used to cut moneys out of policy areas that involve major spending programs. We have shown that distributive programs, while large in number, do not represent a very significant portion of the total budget. While the president could use the line-item veto to ax distributive programs that serve constituencies that are in opposition to his agenda, such cuts would net little in the way of budgetary savings. To use the line-item veto for meaningful deficit reduction, the president would have to go where the money is, which would require an attack on entitlements. From a president's point of view, this might not seem such an appealing prospect. Entitlements, almost by definition, have large

146

constituencies – some of which vote in large numbers. A president clearly could be held accountable were he or she to single-handedly cut entitlements. This is particularly true for the largest entitlements, which disproportionately benefit the elderly. As a deficit reducer, the line-item veto may be more symbolic than substantive.

The line-item veto has also been proposed as a solution to the problem of accountability (U.S. GAO, 1992; Watson, 1993). The argument is that it would give a president substantially more power over subsystems. There may be some truth to this argument. The president becomes a player at the table along with the actors that are tied to the subsystem. It would allow the president to speak on behalf of the public as a whole in trying to reign in errant agencies and their subsystem supporters. More mundanely, it would mean that subsystem supporters would have to "pre-clear" their proposals with the White House to ensure that a new program, a change in a program's structure, or funding for an existing program would not be vetoed. This means that subsystem actors will have to make rational expectations forecast about what is likely to be acceptable to the president. Positively, this might lead to self-imposed constraints on what subsystem actors deem to be acceptable proposals. Negatively, the problem is that presidents are poorly equipped to make micromanagement decisions about the minutiae of most programs. The line-item veto is no magic wand. It does not bestow on a president the ability to know all the pertinent information or to empathize with the diverse perspectives of those with a stake in a portfolio of programs. It would, however, make subsystems more accountable to the president.

Term limits

The proposal to limit the number of terms members of Congress can serve has been forwarded as a means of increasing accountability of legislators to their constituents. This proposal is a favorite among Republicans and conservatives (Will, 1992). It is important to consider the impact of term limits on policy subsystems. Underlying the belief that term limits will increase accountability is the presumption that incumbents are electorally advantaged by their incumbency, which in turn isolates them from preferences of their constituents. Perversely, term limits may have the opposite effect on accountability.

The immediate effect of term limits is to create a larger class of electorally vulnerable legislators. The increased turnover, mandated by such a proposal, means that there would be a large number of relatively new legislators who are inexperienced at holding their seats and less known by their constituents. As our findings in Chapter 7 demonstrate, vulnerability has significant consequences for utilization of program portfolios. Vulnerable incumbents feel compelled to build up a base of support in the district. To do this they seek opportunities to claim credit for federal spending in the district. Resort to the pork barrel increases the likelihood that there will be greater demand for spending on the type of projects that offer opportunities for credit taking but may not address basic needs in the district.

Vulnerable members are also likely to be more aggressive in extracting campaign funds from interest groups that have a stake in policy sub-systems. In his analysis of spending in House election campaigns, Jacobson (1980) shows that it is the most vulnerable incumbents who spent the most money. If more members are vulnerable due to term limits, more members will have to look for funds to finance their reelection bids. This places a premium on interest groups and the funds that their political action committees have to offer. The needs and demands of interest groups may become more prominent in the decision making of legislators. Increased vulnerability is, therefore, likely to make legislators more dependent on PACs and thus more accountable to the interest groups that have campaign funds to offer than to the voters in their own districts. We suspect that this is not the intention of the advocates of term limits.

Campaign finance reform

Critics of Congress have argued for a host of campaign finance reforms. With these reform proposals, the devil is in the detail. Several questions must be asked about the fine print buried at the bottom of these proposals. How much does the reform reduce overall spending levels? Does the proposal restrict the types and sources of campaign funds that will be available? Are PAC contributions eliminated entirely or simply relabeled as something else? Some of these proposals are more ambitious than others in reforming the existing method of campaign finance. Some are no more than incumbent protection plans. To bring about meaningful reforms of the existing system of funding campaigns, a campaign finance plan would have to reduce the influence of PAC dollars in congressional elections. A simple limit on PACs would not be meaningful if there were a loophole, for example, that permitted coordination of gifts from individual contributors by the interest group.

The presumption underlying campaign finance reform proposals is that interest groups have obtained a competitive advantage over voters in vying for the attention of legislators. The argument is that by reducing the role of special interests in elections, incumbents will be more accountable to the needs and interests of the voters in their districts. As with the proposal to impose term limits, campaign finance reform might make congressional races more genuinely competitive. This is likely to produce, however, the same response already discussed – as races become more competitive, and vulnerability increases, incumbents may resort increasingly to the pork barrel to help them win elections.

What is distinctive about campaign finance reform is that it increases vulnerability, while removing campaign funds that PACs have to offer. This introduces a new dynamic. Currently, members can utilize policy subsystems to enhance their reelection bids in two different ways. One, they can obtain distributive benefits for their districts. Two, they can exchange support of programs for PAC contributions from the interest groups that have a stake in a set of federal programs. The latter does not require that the legislator's district receive program benefits. As Chapter 6 shows, this exchange relationship is an important mechanism for creating support coalitions for narrowly distributed program portfolios. With campaign finance reform, however, a legislator will not have an incentive to support policy subsystems unless the legislator's district receives direct benefits from the portfolio of programs. These benefits must be of sufficient number and stature to enhance a legislator's reelection prospects. This implies that each subsystem will have to be aggressive in putting program benefits in the districts of a majority of the legislature – something that relatively few subsystems currently do. Most program portfolios distribute their benefits to a minority of congressional districts. Subsystems will be forced to garner legislative support for their program portfolios by giving each legislator benefits. Subsystem actors will be unable to rely on a combination of program benefits to recipients in the districts of a minority of legislators and PAC contributions to a majority of legislators. Ironically, in the absence of other reforms that curtail the actions of subsystems, campaign finance reform may lead to the type of universalizing behavior that produces inefficient and profligate federal spending.

Institutional reforms

In *Renewing Congress* (Mann and Ornstein, 1992), the American Enterprise Institute and the Brookings Institution offer a number of reforms that are designed to enhance the efficiency and effectiveness of Congress. The major focus of these reforms is to improve the quality of deliberation in both houses of Congress. Toward that end, the recommendation is to reduce the size of committees, limit the maximum number of committee assignments for full committees and subcommittees, phase out select committees, introduce committee assignment rotation through the adoption of leaves of absence and term assignments, and reduce the use of proxy voting for absent members by committee chairs. The 104th Congress, led by the Republicans, has adopted some of the reforms, including a slight reduction in the number of standing committees and the prohibition on proxy voting. The Republicans, however, failed to adopt the more far-reaching of these proposals.

These proposals would alter the legislative venue in which subsystems operate. By decreasing the number of standing committees and increasing their functional policy scope, multiple subsystems would be thrown together in the new committees. Instead of dealing with members of a subcommittee who were attentive to the concerns of the subsystem, under the proposed reforms subsystem actors would be forced to make their case to a broader and perhaps less sympathetic set of legislators. To the extent that the reforms have their intended effect and legislators spend more time deliberating in committee, scrutiny of subsystem proposals would increase. Some subsystems, currently characterized by consensus, might be challenged by committee members new to the policy subsystem. The result might be increased conflict. This might not be unhealthy. Such a change would introduce new ideas and force subsystem supporters to justify their claims on the public purse. Subsystems now characterized by conflict would probably continue to exhibit conflict under the proposed reforms. The reforms would expand the scope of conflict by shifting debate out of relatively small subcommittees into the larger and more heterogeneous environment of newly formed committees or subcommittees. Because the newly constituted committees might be more representative of the entire House, the decisions of the committees would be likely to be accepted by the full House (Krehbiel, 1991). Arguments that otherwise would have spilled onto the floor of the House, consuming time and energies of the entire institution, might in some cases be resolvable in the new committees. Obviously in many cases, conflicts that existed previously would continue to exist despite the reforms. Nevertheless, improving the quality of deliberation and opening subsystems to a wider array of viewpoints is likely to enhance accountability of subsystems to elected representatives and help ensure that decisions from within the subsystem are more representative of broader publics. Unlike most of the other reforms that we have considered, internal reform of the committee structure in Congress offers what we think is a promising avenue to address the troubling aspects of subsystems.

CONCLUSION

In the course of writing this book we have been impressed by the durability and persistence of policy subsystems. Moreover, we have discovered that much of the conventional wisdom about subsystems is exaggerated, and in some instances wrong. Subsystems and their program portfolios play a crucial role in undergirding and structuring the ability of diverse interests in society to overcome their collective action problems, the strategies of organized groups, the behaviors of officials within agencies, and the opportunities and resources of legislators in seeking reelection. One conclusion we draw is that policy subsystems are so intrinsic to the way American democracy operates that it is foolish to argue that they can be legislated out of existence.

What makes the study of policy subsystems important is they highlight tensions in the practice of American democracy. Reforms of subsystem activities must recognize this tension. Subsystems exist within the context of democratic institutions and practices in America. At the same time, subsystems require constant vigilance to assure that basic democratic values are preserved and cultivated.

Descriptive data base of domestic assistance programs

The underlying source for the data base on U.S. domestic assistance programs that we have constructed is the *Catalog of Federal Domestic Assistance* (CFDA). In this appendix we discuss the data file that contains descriptive information on programs for each year from 1971 through 1990.

The data file derived from the CFDA contains no geographic detail nor is it a record of the specific awards made by federal agencies. Instead it describes the types of recipients that are eligible for assistance, the form of the assistance provided, the amount of money that the agency is authorized to spend on assistance awards, policy areas served by the program, and information about the history of the program.

The catalog was first published in 1965 by the Office of Economic Opportunity. From the outset, its purpose was to serve potential applicants and recipients of federal programs as a guide in applying for federal assistance. In its early years, the catalog underwent considerable evolution in coverage, content, and programmatic detail, making year-to-year comparisons across programs virtually impossible. By 1971, the catalog was being published by the Bureau of the Budget and had matured into essentially the form that it continues to take today (in the early 1980s it was shifted to the General Services Administration). Several points should be noted about the catalog and, by extension, the data file that is based on it.

First, the operational definition of a domestic assistance program used in the catalog provides a reasonable approximation to the formal definition of a program offered in Chapter 1. In the catalog, a program is an activity or function of an agency that provides assistance or benefits to a category of recipients to accomplish a specific purpose. Other government sources employing different definitional schemes were considered but rejected for this study. One alternative was budget accounts data, which have the merit of being cast at the level that Congress appropriates moneys. Budget accounts, however, are subject to frequent revision and reorganization and do not employ standardized program definitions. A second alternative was the Social Security Administration classification of social welfare expenditures, which has the merit of existing over a relatively long period of time. Unfortunately, this classification scheme has not been published at a detailed programmatic level since 1966 nor have its program categories been updated since 1966 to reflect growth in the range of social welfare activities of the federal government. In comparison to these other sources, the catalog provides a relatively standardized operational definition of programs, while adapting to programmatic changes in the domestic activities of the U.S. government. It also tends to produce the most discrete definition of programs because of its rule that agency activities that provide assistance to distinct beneficiary groups should be categorized as separate programs (see also Browning, 1986:55–9).

The second point to note is that, although the catalog encompasses the lion's share of domestic activities of the federal government, it is not fully comprehensive. Some types of government programs are systematically excluded from this data source. Among these are nondomestic programs, including foreign aid, defense procurement contracts, and other defense activities. Also excluded are federal procurement contracts for items that the government itself consumes, such as office buildings and equipment, and government debt retirement. Two categories of domestic programs are excluded from the catalog but probably should not be. One involves programs that are designed to address one-time-only problems of named persons or entities (e.g., the New York City, Chrysler, and Lockheed bailouts). The rationale for excluding this category of programs appears to be that they are not available to the public at large since they are equivalent, in a sense, to activities mandated by private bills. The second category of excluded domestic programs are those that are administered by quasi-governmental bodies. These include activities of such agencies as the Resolution Trust Corporation, the Post Office, and the Smithsonian Institution, among others. To be sure, the line between quasi-governmental and nongovernmental can be so fuzzy that excluding programs administered by these agencies might be justified as a reasonable and straightforward coding rule. Nonetheless, such a rule eliminates an unknown number of activities that probably should be counted as federal programs.

Third, caution should be exercised when interpreting expenditure data for direct loans, guaranteed loans, and insurance programs. Two kinds of figures can be reported for these programs: one represents the total value of assets that are underwritten by the government; the second represents only those payments that the government makes to cover losses. These programs, collectively known as contingent liability programs, involve payouts only when a covered loss has been incurred. Only a small portion of the assets experience the sort of contingency that requires the government to pay its potential liability. The government financed bail-out of the savings and loan industry, for example, represents such a contingency. Ordinarily, most of these potential liabilities never require government payments. Unfortunately, the government is not consistent in which of these two numbers are reported. We have made an effort in coding these contingent liability programs to report the amounts that Congress appropriates to cover payments, not the total value of assets that are underwritten. The amount Congress appropriates is far less than the full amount of contingent liabilities, since only a small proportion of the risk to the government typically eventuates in payments.

Finally, one other point should be mentioned with respect to this data source. The catalog is subject to both underreporting and overreporting of programs. These problems stem from a variety of factors, including inadequate record keeping by agencies, the political incentives of agencies to misstate the number of programs actually being implemented, confusion over the definitions and coding rules used in the catalog, and so on. The overall bias that these problems introduce into estimates of the size of the government is difficult to assess since the downward bias produced by underreporting may be offset by the upward bias produced by overreporting. We should note, however, that at least some programs that had existed prior to the publication of the catalog were not included in the catalog until the early 1970s, suggesting that the overall bias in the early years of the catalog is probably to understate the scope of the government's domestic activities.

The data file that is based on catalog information comprises more than 21,000 program observations from 1971 through 1990. The average number of programs in each year was 1,048. For each observation, several pieces of information were coded: its identification number, its structural type (e.g., formula, project, insurance), the range of eligible applicants (e.g., states, local, and municipal governments, institutions of higher education, individuals), criteria used in selecting recipients (e.g., racial criteria, income/unemployment, geographic location), the policy area(s) served by the program (e.g., agriculture, education, environmental quality, health, housing, income security), the presence of matching requirements, the previous fiscal year authorization level, and the current fiscal year authorization level. Using the cross-walk table that is included in the basic catalog each year and the historical profile of programs that has been included in the catalog in recent years, an effort was made to trace programs through number reassignments and agency transfers. With this information, an identification number was assigned to each program in order to track it throughout its history from its creation (or 1971) through its termination (or 1990). This tracking identification number was used as

155

the basis for extensive cleaning of the data, as well as the coding of several additional variables.

The coding of information from the catalogs for the 1971–90 period variables was completed in two waves of coding. Most of the variables in the data file are drawn from the individual program records. This information was coded in the first wave. A couple dozen additional variables were later added in a second wave of coding, which drew information from indexes and appendixes that are included in the annual catalogs. The first wave of the coding enterprise was staffed by eight student coders, plus one person preparing electronic coding forms, one person acquiring microfiched or paper copies of all catalogs ever published, and a graduate student supervisor. As part of this coding process, a machine-generated test of all data entries was undertaken to detect keypunching errors. Also as part of this process, approximately 40 cases were selected from each year for coding by a second data coder, producing a sample of 1,651 double-coded cases (approximately 8 percent of the universe of cases). The agreement between coding decisions for each pair of coders was compared for each variable, permitting the calculation of a reliability score. The measure of intercoder reliability was the percentage of values for each variable on which pairs of coders were in agreement. No variable with a reliability score of less than 85 percent was retained in the data file. The average score across all variables was approximately 94 percent.

Geographical data base of domestic assistance awards

The source from which our data on the flow of federal funds to congressional districts have been constructed is the *Federal Assistance Awards Data System* (FAADS), which is maintained by the Bureau of the Census. As described here, we have compiled these data into a geographical data base that reports, for each domestic program and for each congressional district, the number of discrete awards, both new and ongoing, as well as the dollar value of awards. Summary tables and figures for the 1983–90 period for each congressional district are available in Bickers and Stein (1991).

FAADS is compiled by the Office of Management and Budget and maintained by the Bureau of the Census. It was established in 1981, but underwent significant evolution prior to 1983. Most important, FAADS did not identify the congressional district in which awards were made until fiscal year 1983, making it impossible to construct congressional district level figures prior to that year. From its inception, it has been available only in magnetic readable form, consisting of records that each federal agency enters by computer when the agency makes a financial assistance award to a recipient or group of recipients. In most years, the FAADS records exceed a million transactions. FAADS contains extensive information on aid awards, recipients of the aid, and the programs under which awards are made. FAADS includes most of the programs listed in the *Catalog of Federal Domestic Assistance,* and is keyed to the same identification codes that are used in the catalog.

In most cases, FAADS data are presented as action-by-action records of federal spending awards to particular recipients. Accompanying each of these records is information on the recipient's geographical location, including state, congressional district, county, city, standard metropolitan statistical area, and zip code. These data provide the basis for aggregating awards data at different levels of analysis. The coding rules for geographic aggregation of FAADS records reflect our interest in the role of congressional decision making in domestic policy. Consequently, the basic level of analysis in our data base is the congressional district. It is important to note that FAADS reports budgetary obligations and not the actual disbursement of moneys. Budgetary obligations, technically, involve the allotment of a budgeted amount that the recipient is permitted to spend. These obligations are designated for specific periods (e.g., one year). In some instances, recipients fail to exhaust the obligated amount during the designated period. When this occurs, FAADS reports a negative sign before the unused amount. This may mean that the recipient has failed to comply with programmatic conditions for the authorization of outlays. More commonly, a negative sign indicates the recipient has failed to spend up to the full obligation level.

One important limitation of FAADS is the way high-volume programs are treated. For programs that provide transfer payments to individuals and other programs with thousands of transactions each month, FAADS reports aggregate amounts for all recipients in each county area. These county aggregate records pose a coding problem in those situations where counties are represented by more than one member of Congress. The solution adopted here is to apportion outlays to each of these districts based on the proportion of the county's (1980) population that resides in the district. For example, during the 1980s, four congressional districts encompassed portions of Harris County, Texas. In FAADS, expenditures for Social Security, Aid to Families with Dependent Children, and other high-volume programs are not allocated to the four congressional districts representing Harris County, but instead are reported as quarterly aggregates going to the county as a whole. In our data base, such expenditures have been divided among these four districts based on the proportion of the population of Harris County that lives in each of the districts. Consequently, in order to arrive at the total outlays to each district, these expenditures are summed with the outlays going to all of the other counties that are represented, either in whole or in part, by each of the four members of Congress that represent Harris County.

The variables that report the number of new awards and the total number of new and continuing awards represent one of the major innovations included in the U.S. Domestic Assistance Programs Database. It is, therefore, important for users to understand precisely the nature of these variables. A new award is *not* equivalent to a new program. A new award is reported when a recipient is first granted an amount of financial aid for a specified project from a particular program. This recipient may be receiving federal funds for projects under a different program number or, in fact, may be receiving funds for other projects under the same program number. In short, what distinguishes a new award from a continuing award is that the former is reported only at the time a given project commences and immediately follows the announcement of the grant. This initial award is usually a relatively small fraction of the total figure that is budgeted for a project. Continuing awards are reported at regular intervals, usually once per quarter, when the additional increments of the budgeted obligations are provided by the agency to the recipient. The number of continuing awards that will be reported for a project is a function of the length of time required to complete a project and the particular reporting practices of each agency (though most agencies report continuing awards transactions only once per quarter). The total number of new and continuing awards is thus the sum of new transactions and continuing transactions that are made to recipients in each congressional district from a given program.

Also important to note is how FAADS handles the fact that some federal programs allocate moneys to the states to be reallocated to substate recipients. In FAADS, these programs are reported as if the money were allocated entirely to the county or congressional district in which the state capital or state agency that is responsible for the intrastate distribution of funds is located. This poses a difficult problem in determining where the moneys are ultimately allocated, since states employ different criteria for distributing funds. The only fully satisfactory solution would be to incorporate each state's decision rules for reallocating the federal moneys. Though we explored this possibility, we eventually rejected it as infeasible since it would have required contacting each state to discover how it distributed funds under each individual program. Instead, we follow the convention adopted in FAADS, which is to report these moneys as if they were spent in the congressional district or districts that encompass the county containing the state capital. This inflates expenditures to districts that represent state capitals and deflates expenditures to other districts.

A major limitation of FAADS is that the funding amounts reported for insurance, loans, guaranteed loans, and other forms of contingent liabilities do not in all cases represent the actual flow of federal funds. In some cases, the amount reported is the appraised value of the properties or assets that are insured or otherwise guaranteed by the government. This is the liability of the government if it were to reimburse all potential claimants for the full amount of their potential losses simultaneously. For example, FAADS reports the value of all properties that are insured under the flood insurance program, rather than the actual expenditure amounts paid to compensate victims of flood damage, with the result that this program appears to be larger than Social Security. In other cases, the amount reported is an actual outlay to cover a liability for a specific claim. The failure of FAADS to differentiate between these two types of entries can lead to serious misinterpretation of federal funding amounts. For this reason, in our data base, all transactions that involve insurance, direct or guaranteed loans, and other forms of contingent liabilities and intangible or indirect financial assistance have been excluded entirely.

The core information about program-level outlays to recipients in each congressional district is found in a series of eight files, one per year. Each file contains data that is compiled from the FAADS records for each program for each congressional district for the federal fiscal year. The information included in these files includes a variable identifying the state and congressional district in which the program awards have been made; a variable that corresponds to the CFDA program identification number; a variable with the total annual federal obligations from a given program to all recipients located in the congressional district (in current dollars); a variable indicating the number of new awards to recipients located in the congressional district (this field is blank if there were any transactions under the program during the year that involved county aggregate records); and a variable indicating the total number of new and continuing awards to recipients located in the congressional district (this field is also blank if there were any transactions under the program during the year that involved county aggregate records).

Appendix 3. *Programs by agency and policy type*

Department and agency name	Cfdano	Redistrib.	Program name
Agriculture			
Agriculture Research Service	10.001	no	Agricultural Research - Basic and Applied Research
Agricultural Cooperative Service	10.003	no	Morrill - Nelson Funds for Food and Agricultural Higher Education
	10.350	no	Technical Assistance to Cooperatives
Agricultural Marketing Service	10.153	no	Market News
	10.156	no	Marketing Services - Matching Fund Grants
	10.164	no	Wholesale Market Development
Agricultural Stabilization and Conservation Service	10.052	no	Cotton Production Stabilization
	10.053	yes	Dairy Indemnity Payments
	10.054	no	Emergency Conservation Program
	10.055	no	Feed Grain Production Stabilization
	10.058	no	Wheat Production Stabilization
	10.059	no	Shorn Wool and Unshorn Lambs (Pulled Wool) and Mohair Payments
	10.062	no	Water Bank Program
	10.063	no	Agricultural Conservation Program
	10.064	no	Forestry Incentives Program
	10.065	no	Rice Production Stabilization
	10.066	yes	Emergency Livestock Assistance
	10.067	no	Grain Reserve Program
	10.068	no	Rural Clean Water Program
	10.069	no	Conservation Reserve Program
	10.070	no	Colorado River Salinity Control
	10.071	no	Federal - State Cooperation in Warehouse Examination Agreement
Animal and Plant Health Inspection Service	10.025	no	Plant and Animal Disease and Pest Control
	10.028	no	Animal Damage Control
Cooperative State Research Service	10.200	no	Grants for Agricultural Research, Special Research Grants
	10.202	no	Cooperative Forestry Research

Appendix 3. *(cont.)*

Department and agency name	Cfdano	Redistrib.	Program name
	10.203	no	Payments to Agricultural Experiment Stations under Hatch Act
	10.205	no	Payments to 1890 Land-Grant Colleges and Tuskegee Institute
	10.206	no	Grants for Agricultural Research - Competitive Research Grant
	10.207	no	Animal Health and Disease Research
	10.208	no	Alcohol Fuels Research
	10.209	no	1890 Research Facilities
	10.210	no	Food and Agricultural Science National Needs Graduate Fellowship Grants
	10.211	no	Higher Education Strengthening Grants
	10.212	no	Small Business Innovation Research
	10.213	no	Competitive Research Grants for Forest and Rangeland Renewable Resources
	10.214	no	Morrill - Nelson Funds for Food and Agricultural Higher Education
	10.215	no	Low Input Farming Systems - Research and Education
	10.216	no	1890 Institution Capacity Building Grants
	10.217	no	Higher Education Challenge Grants
Economic Research Service	10.250	no	Agricultural and Rural Economic Research
Extension Service	10.500	no	Extension Programs for Community Development
Food and Nutrition Service	10.550	yes	Food Distribution
	10.551	yes	Food Stamps
	10.553	yes	School Breakfast Program
	10.555	yes	National School Lunch Program
	10.556	yes	Special Milk Program for Children
	10.557	yes	Special Supplemental Food Program for Women, Infants, and Children
	10.558	yes	Child and Adult Care Food Program
	10.559	yes	Summer Food Service Program for Children
	10.560	no	State Administrative Expenses for Child Nutrition

162

	10.561	no	State Administrative Matching Grants for Food Stamp Program
	10.564	no	Nutrition Education and Training Program
	10.565	yes	Commodity Supplemental Food Program
	10.567	yes	Food Distribution Program Commodities in Lieu of Food Stamps
	10.568	yes	Temporary Emergency Food Assistance (Administrative Costs)
Food Safety and Inspection Service	10.475	no	Assistance to States for Intrastate Meat and Poultry Inspection
Forest Service	10.652	no	Forestry Research
	10.664	no	Cooperative Forestry Assistance
	10.665	no	Schools and Roads - Grants to States
	10.666	no	Schools and Roads - Grants to Counties
	10.667	no	School Funds - Grants to Arizona (Arizona School Fund)
	10.668	no	Additional Lands - Grants to Minnesota
	10.669	no	Accelerated Cooperative Assistance for Forest Programs on Certain Lands Adjacent to the Boundary Waters Canoe Area
Human Nutrition Information Service	10.375	no	Human Nutrition Information Service
National Agricultural Library	10.700	no	National Agricultural Library
National Agricultural Statistics Service	10.950	no	Agricultural Statistical Reports
Soil Conservation Service	10.900	no	Great Plains Conservation
	10.901	no	Resource Conservation and Development
	10.904	no	Watershed Protection and Flood Prevention
	10.909	no	Resource Appraisal and Program Development
	10.910	no	Rural Abandoned Mine Program
Commerce			
Economic Development Administration	11.300	yes	Economic Development - Grants and Loans for Public Works
	11.301	yes	Economic Development - Business Development Assistance
	11.302	yes	Economic Development - Support for Planning Organizations
	11.303	yes	Economic Development - Technical Assistance
	11.304	yes	Economic Development - Public Works Impact Projects

163

Appendix 3. *(cont.)*

Department and agency name	Cfdano	Redistrib.	Program name
	11.305	yes	Economic Development - State and Local Economic Development
	11.306	yes	Economic Development - Direct Operational Assistance
	11.307	yes	Economic Development - Special Economic Development and Adjustment Assistance Program
International Trade Administration	11.312	no	Research and Evaluation Program
	11.108	no	Export Promotion Services
	11.109	yes	Trade Adjustment Assistance
	11.110	no	Business Assistance, Services, and Information
Minority Business Development Agency	11.800	yes	Minority Business Development - Management and Technical Assistance
	11.801	no	American Indian Program
National Bureau of Standards	11.603	no	National Standard Reference Data System
	11.606	no	Weights and Measures Service
	11.609	no	Measurement and Engineering Research and Standards
National Institute of Standards and Technology	11.613	no	State Technology Extension Program
National Oceanic and Atmospheric Administration	11.400	no	Geodetic Surveys and Services
	11.401	no	Nautical Charts and Related Data
	11.405	no	Anadromous and Great Lakes Fisheries Conservation
	11.407	no	Commercial Fisheries Research and Development
	11.408	yes	Fishermen's Contingency Fund
	11.409	yes	Fishing Vessel and Gear Damage Compensation Fund
	11.417	no	Sea Grant Institutional Support
	11.419	no	Coastal Zone Management Program Administration Grants
	11.420	no	Coastal Zone Management Estuarine Research Reserves
	11.421	yes	Coastal Energy Impact Program - Formula Grants
	11.422	no	Coastal Energy Impact Program - Planning Grants
	11.426	no	Financial Assistance for Marine Pollution Research

164

	11.428	no	Intergovernmental Climate - Demonstration Project
	11.429	no	Marine Sanctuary Program
	11.430	no	Undersea Research
	11.431	no	Climate and Atmospheric Research
	11.432	no	Environmental Research Laboratories Joint Institutes
National Telecommunications and Information Admin.			
	11.550	no	Public Telecommunications Facilities - Construction and Planning
Defense			
National Guard Bureau			
	12.400	no	Military Construction, Army National Guard
Education			
State and Local Programs and Support			
Assistant Secretary for Educational Research and Improvement			
	84.002	no	Adult Education-State-Administered Basic Grant Program
	84.034	yes	Public Library Services
	84.035	no	Interlibrary Cooperation and Resource Sharing
	84.036	yes	Library Career Training
	84.039	no	Library Research and Demonstration
	84.154	yes	Library Services and Construction Act - Construction
	84.163	no	Library Services for Indian Tribes and Hawaiian Natives
	84.167	no	Library Literacy
	84.184	no	National Program for Drug-Free Schools and Communities
	84.197	no	College Library Technology and Cooperation Grants
	84.203	no	Star Schools Program
	84.206	no	Jacob K. Javits Gifted and Talented Students
	84.208	no	Native Hawaiian Model Curriculum Development
	84.209	no	Native Hawaiian Family Based Education Centers
	84.210	no	Native Hawaiian Gifted and Talented
	84.211	no	FIRST Schools and Teachers
	84.212	no	FIRST Family School Partnerships
	84.215	no	Innovation in Education - Secretary's Fund
	84.222	no	National School Volunteer Program
	84.228	no	Educational Partnerships
Assistant Secretary for Special Education and Rehabilitative Services	84.009	no	Program for Education of Handicapped Children in State Operated or Supported Schools

Appendix 3. *(cont.)*

Department and agency name	Cfdano	Redistrib.	Program name
	84.023	no	Handicapped - Innovation and Development
	84.024	no	Handicapped Early Childhood Assistance
	84.025	no	Handicapped Innovative Programs - Deaf - Blind Centers
	84.026	no	Handicapped Media Services and Captioned Films
	84.027	no	Handicapped Preschool and School Programs
	84.028	no	Handicapped Regional Resource Centers
	84.029	no	Training Personnel for the Education of the Handicapped
	84.030	no	Handicapped Teacher Recruitment and Information Dissemination
	84.086	no	Innovative Programs for Severely Handicapped Children
	84.125	no	Clearinghouse on Disability and Rehabilitation Research
	84.128	no	Rehabilitation Services - Special Projects
	84.132	yes	Centers for Independent Living
	84.158	no	Secondary Education and Transitional Services for Handicapped Youth
	84.159	no	Handicapped - Special Studies
	84.160	no	Training Interpreters for Deaf Individuals
	84.161	no	Client Assistance for Handicapped Individuals
	84.169	yes	Comprehensive Services for Independent Living
	84.173	no	Handicapped - Preschool Incentive Grants
	84.175	yes	Rehabilitation Services - Innovation and Expansion (I and E)
	84.176	no	Congressional Teacher Scholarships
	84.177	yes	Rehabilitation Services - Independent Living for Older Blind Individuals
	84.180	no	Technology, Educational Media and Materials for the Handicapped
	84.187	yes	Supported Employment Services for Individuals with Severe Handicaps
	84.221	no	Native Hawaiian Special Education
	84.224	no	State Grants for Technology-Related Assistance to Individuals with Disabilities
	84.231	no	Demonstration and Innovation Projects of National Significance

Assistant Secretary for Vocational and Adult Education		
Vocational Education - Basic Grants to States	84.048	yes
Vocational Education - Consumer and Homemaker Education	84.049	yes
Vocational Education - Program Improvement and Supportive Service	84.050	no
Vocational Education - Program Improvement Projects	84.051	no
Vocational Education - Special Programs for the Disadvantaged	84.052	yes
Vocational Education - State Planning and Evaluation	84.121	no
National Adult Education Discretionary Program	84.191	no
Adult Education for the Homeless	84.192	yes
Workplace Literacy	84.198	no
Vocational Education - Cooperative Demonstration	84.199	yes
English Literacy Program	84.223	no
Technology Education Demonstration	84.230	no
Bilingual Education and Minority Languages		
Bilingual Education	84.003	no
Bilingual Vocational Training	84.077	yes
Bilingual Vocational Instructor Training	84.099	no
Bilingual Vocational Materials, Methods, and Techniques	84.100	yes
Emergency Immigrant Education Assistance	84.162	no
Bilingual Education Support Services	84.194	no
Bilingual Education Training Grants	84.195	no
Compensatory Education Programs		
Educationally Deprived Children - Local Educational Agencies	84.010	yes
Educationally Deprived Children - State Administration	84.012	no
Even Start - Local Education Agencies	84.013	no
Private School - Capital Expenses	84.216	no
State Program Improvement Grants	84.218	no
Deputy Under Secretary for Management		
Federal Real Property Assistance Program	84.145	no
Office of Assistant Secretary for Elementary and Secondary Education		
Civil Rights Technical Assistance and Training	84.004	no
Alcohol and Drug Abuse Education Program	84.008	no
Migrant Education - Basic State Formula Grant Program	84.011	no
Educationally Deprived Children in State Administered Institutions Serving Neglected or Delinquent Children	84.013	no
Follow Through	84.014	yes

Appendix 3. (cont.)

Department and agency name	Cfdano	Redistrib.	Program name
	84.040	yes	Impact Aid - Construction
	84.041	yes	Impact Aid - Maintenance and Operation
	84.060	no	Indian Education - Entitlement Grants to Local Educational Agencies and Tribal Schools
	84.061	no	Indian Education - Special Programs and Projects
	84.062	no	Indian Education - Adult Indian Education
	84.072	yes	Indian Education - Grants to Indian Controlled Schools
	84.083	no	Women's Educational Equity
	84.141	no	Migrant Education - High School Equivalency Program
	84.148	yes	Allen J. Ellender Fellowship Program
	84.152	no	Neglected or Delinquent Transition Services
	84.164	no	Mathematics and Science Education
	84.186	no	Drug-Free Schools and Communities - State Grants
	84.188	no	Drug-Free Schools and Communities - Regional Centers
	84.190	no	Christa McAuliffe Fellowships
	84.196	no	State Activities - Education of Homeless Children and Youth
	84.201	no	School Dropout Demonstration Assistance
	84.207	no	Educational Personnel Training
	84.214	no	Even Start - Migrant Education
	84.227	no	Secondary Schools - Basic Skills Demonstration Assistance
Office of Assistant Secretary for Post Secondary Education	84.007	yes	Supplemental Educational Opportunity Grants
	84.015	yes	National Resource Centers and Fellowships in International Studies
	84.016	no	Undergraduate International Studies and Foreign Language Program
	84.018	no	Fulbright-Hays Seminars Abroad - Special Bilateral Projects
	84.019	no	Fulbright-Hays Training Grants - Faculty Research Abroad
	84.020	no	Fulbright-Hays Training Grants - Foreign Curriculum Consultants
	84.021	no	Fulbright-Hays Training Grants - Group Projects Abroad

Office	Code		Program
	84.022	no	Fulbright-Hays Training Grants - Doctoral Dissertation Research Abroad
	84.032	yes	Guaranteed Student Loans
	84.033	yes	College Work - Study Program
	84.037	no	National Defense/Direct Student Loan Cancellations
	84.038	yes	National Defense/Direct Student Loans
	84.047	yes	Upward Bound
	84.063	yes	Pell Grant Program
	84.064	no	Higher Education - Veterans' Education Outreach Program
	84.066	yes	Educational Opportunity Centers
	84.116	no	Fund for the Improvement of Postsecondary Education
	84.120	no	Minority Institutions Science Improvement Program
	84.135	no	Aid to Land-Grant Colleges
	84.136	yes	Legal Training for the Disadvantaged
	84.153	no	Business and International Education
	84.170	no	National Graduate Fellows
	84.172	no	Construction, Reconstruction, and Renovation of Academic Facilities
	84.185	no	Robert C. Byrd Honors Scholarships
	84.200	no	Graduate Assistance in Areas of National Need
	84.202	no	Grants to Institutions to Encourage Minority Participation in Graduate Education
	84.217	yes	Ronald E. McNair Post-Baccalaureate Achievement
	84.219	yes	Student Literacy Corps
	84.226	yes	Income Contingent Loan Program
	84.229	no	Language Resource Centers
Office of the Secretary	84.122	no	Secretary's Discretionary Program
	84.168	no	National Program for Mathematics and Science Education
Energy			
Office of General Counsel	81.003	no	Granting of Patent Licenses
Conservation and Renewable Energy	81.036	no	Energy-Related Inventions
	81.041	no	State Energy Conservation Program
	81.042	yes	Weatherization Assistance Program for Low Income Persons

Appendix 3. *(cont.)*

Department and agency name	Cfdano	Redistrib.	Program name
	81.048	no	Priorities and Allocations for Energy Programs and Projects
	81.050	no	Energy Extension Service
	81.051	no	Appropriate Energy Technology
	81.052	no	Energy Conservation for Institutional Buildings
	81.078	no	Industrial Energy Conservation
	81.079	no	Biofuels and Municipal Waste Technology and Regional Program
	81.086	no	Conservation Research and Development
	81.087	no	Renewable Energy Research and Development
Office of the Secretary	81.049	no	Basic Energy Sciences, High Energy/Nuclear Physics, Magnetic Fusion Energy, Health and Environmental Research, Program Analysis and Field Operations Management
	81.075	no	Energy Graduate Traineeship Program
Intergovernmental and Public Affairs	81.076	no	Indian Energy Resources
Office of Energy Research	81.022	no	Energy-Related Laboratory Equipment Grants
	81.064	no	DOE Technical Information Center
	81.077	yes	University Research Instrumentation
Office of Fossil Energy	81.056	yes	Coal Loan Guarantees
	81.057	no	University Coal Research
	81.089	no	Fossil Energy Research and Development
Office of Minority Economic Impact	81.082	no	Management and Technical Assistance for Minority Business Enterprises
	81.083	no	Minority Educational Institution Research Travel Fund
	81.085	no	National Minority Energy Information Clearinghouse
	81.091	yes	Socioeconomic and Demographic Research, Data and Other Information
	81.094	no	Minority Educational Institution Assistance
Office of Policy	81.080	no	Energy Policy, Planning and Development

170

Health and Human Services

Food and Drug Administration

Program	Number	
Food and Drug Administration - Research Grants	13.103	no

Administration for Children, Youth and Families

Program	Number	
State Postsecondary Education Commissions Program - Intrastate Planning	13.550	no
Indian Education - Grants to Non-Federal Educational Agencies	13.551	no
Administration for Children, Youth and Families - Adoption Opportunities	13.652	no
Temporary Child Care and Crisis Nurseries	13.656	no
Drug Abuse Prevention and Education for Runaway and Homeless Youth	13.657	no
Foster Care - Title IV - E1	13.658	yes
Adoption Assistance	13.659	yes
Drug Abuse Prevention and Education Relating to Youth Gangs	13.660	no
Comprehensive Child Development Centers	13.666	yes
Child Abuse Challenge Grants	13.672	no
Grants to States for Planning and Development of Dependent Care Programs	13.673	no
Independent Living	13.674	no

Agency for Health Care Policy and Research

Program	Number	
Medical Treatment Effectiveness Research	13.180	no

Alcohol, Drug Abuse and Mental Health Administration

Program	Number	
Mental Health Planning and Demonstration Projects	13.125	no
Small Business Innovation Research	13.126	no
Refugee Assistance - Mental Health	13.128	no
Protection and Advocacy for Mentally Ill Individuals	13.138	no
Drug and Alcohol Abuse - High-Risk Youth Demonstration Grants	13.144	no
Mental Health Services for the Homeless Block Grant	13.150	no
Community Demonstration Grant Projects for Alcohol and Drug Abuse Treatment of Homeless Individuals	13.152	no
Model Projects for Pregnant and Postpartum Women and Their Infants (Substance Abuse)	13.169	yes
Community Youth Activity Demonstration Grants	13.170	yes
Community Youth Activity Program Block Grants	13.171	no
Human Genome Research	13.172	no
Conference Grant (Substance Abuse)	13.174	no
Drug Abuse Treatment Waiting List Reduction Grants	13.175	yes
ADAMHA Small Instrumentation Program Grants	13.176	no

171

Appendix 3. *(cont.)*

Department and agency name	Cfdano	Redistrib.	Program name
	13.179	no	State Data Collection - Uniform Alcohol and Drug Abuse Data
	13.194	no	Community Partnership Demonstration Grant
	13.195	no	Disaster Relief Assistance Grants for Drug Abuse Treatment
	13.196	no	Cooperative Agreements for Drug Abuse Treatment Improvement Projects in Target Cities
	13.242	no	Mental Health Research Grants
	13.244	no	Mental Health Training Grants
	13.271	no	Alcohol Scientist Development Award and Research Scientist Development Award for Clinicians
	13.272	no	Alcohol National Research Service Awards for Research Training
	13.273	no	Alcohol Research Programs
	13.274	no	Alcohol, Clinical or Service-Related Training Programs
	13.277	no	Drug Abuse Research Development Awards
	13.278	no	Drug Abuse National Research Service Awards
	13.279	no	Drug Abuse Research Programs
	13.281	no	Mental Health Research Development Awards
	13.282	no	Mental Health National Research Service Awards
	13.891	no	Alcohol Research Center Grants
	13.901	no	Communications Programs Aimed Toward the Prevention of Alcohol and Other Drug Problems
	13.982	no	Mental Health Disaster Assistance and Emergency Mental Health
	13.992	no	Alcohol and Drug Abuse and Mental Health Services Block Grant
Bureau of Health Care Delivery	13.110	yes	Maternal and Child Health Federal Consolidated Programs
	13.151	no	Project Grants for Health Services to the Homeless
	13.888	yes	Home Health Services Grant Program
Centers for Disease Control	13.116	no	Project Grants and Cooperative Agreements for Tuberculosis
	13.118	no	Acquired Immunodeficiency Syndrome (AIDS) Activity

Organization	Code	Program	
	13.135	Centers for Research and Demonstration for Health Promotion and Disease Prevention	no
	13.136	Research and Demonstration Projects, Injury Prevention Research Centers, and Incentive Grants for Intervention Projects	no
	13.262	Occupational Safety and Health - Research Grants	no
	13.263	Occupational Safety and Health - Training Grants	no
	13.268	Disease Control - Project Grants	no
	13.977	Preventive Health Service - Sexually Transmitted Diseases Control Grants	no
	13.978	Preventive Health Service - Sexually Transmitted Diseases Research	no
	13.987	Health Programs for Refugees	no
	13.988	Cooperative Agreements for State-Based Diabetes Control Programs	no
	13.991	Preventive Health and Health Services Block Grant	no
Family Support Administration	13.780	Family Support Payments to States - Assistance Payments	yes
	13.781	Job Opportunities and Basic Skills Training	yes
	13.789	Low Income Home Energy Assistance	yes
	13.790	Work Incentive Program/WIN Demonstration Program	yes
Health Care Financing Administration	13.714	Medical Assistance Program	yes
	13.766	Health Care Financing Research, Demonstrations and Evaluations	yes
	13.773	Medicare - Hospital Insurance	yes
	13.774	Medicare - Supplementary Medical Insurance	yes
	13.775	State Medicaid Fraud Control Units	no
	13.776	Professional Standards Review Organizations	no
Health Resources and Services Administration	13.117	Grants for Preventive Medicine Residency Training	no
	13.119	Grants for Podiatric Medicine Training	no
	13.124	Nurse Anesthetist Traineeships	no
	13.133	Health Services Delivery to AIDS Victims - Demonstration Grants	no
	13.146	AIDS Drug Reimbursements	yes
	13.153	Pediatric AIDS Health Care Demonstration Program	no
	13.162	National Health Service Corps Loan Repayment	no
	13.224	Health Services Development - Project Grants	no
	13.246	Migrant Health Centers Grants	no

173

Appendix 3. (cont.)

Department and agency name	Cfdano	Redistrib	Program name
	13.288	yes	National Health Service Corps Scholarship Program
	13.297	no	Nursing Research Service Awards
	13.298	no	Nurse Practitioner Training Programs
	13.299	no	Advanced Nurse Training Programs
	13.339	no	Health Professions - Capitation Grants
	13.342	yes	Health Professions - Student Loans
	13.358	no	Professional Nurse Traineeships
	13.359	no	Special Project Grants for Improvement in Nurse Training
	13.361	no	Nursing Research Project Grants
	13.364	yes	Nursing Student Loans
	13.379	no	Grants for Graduate Training in Family Medicine
	13.381	yes	Health Professions - Financial Distress Grants
	13.820	yes	Scholarships for Students of Exceptional Financial Need
	13.822	yes	Health Careers Opportunity Program
	13.824	no	Area Health Education Centers
	13.884	no	Grants for Residency Training in General Internal Medicine and/or General Pediatrics
	13.886	no	Grants for Physician Assistant Training Program
	13.895	no	Grants for Faculty Development in Family Medicine
	13.897	no	Residency Training in the General Practice of Dentistry
	13.900	no	Grants for Faculty Development in General Internal Medicine
	13.962	no	Health Administration Graduate Traineeships
	13.963	no	Graduate Programs in Health Administration
	13.964	no	Traineeships for Students in Schools of Public Health and Other Graduate Public Health Programs
	13.965	no	Coal Miners Respiratory Impairment Treatment Clinics and Services
	13.969	no	Curriculum Development Grants

	Number	Program	
	13.973	Special Grants for Former National Health Service Corps Members	no
	13.984	Grants for Establishment of Departments of Family Medicine	no
Health Standards and Quality Bureau	13.994	Maternal and Child Health Services Block Grant	yes
	13.777	State Health Care Providers Survey Certification	no
Indian Health Service	13.166	Indian Health Service Health Promotion and Disease Prevention Demonstration Projects	no
	13.228	Indian Health Services - Health Management Development Program	no
	13.970	Health Professions Recruitment Program for Indians	no
	13.971	Health Professions Preparatory Scholarship Programs for Indians	no
	13.972	Health Professions Scholarship Program for Indians	no
National Center for Health Services Research	13.226	Health Services Research and Development - Grants and Contracts	no
National Institutes of Health	13.112	Characterization of Environmental Health Hazards	no
	13.113	Biological Response to Environmental Health Hazards	no
	13.114	Applied Toxicological Research and Testing	no
	13.115	Biometry and Risk Estimation - Health Risks from Environment	no
	13.121	Diseases of the Teeth and Supporting Tissues	no
	13.122	Disorders of Craniofacial Structure and Function, and Behavior	no
	13.131	Shared Research Facilities for Heart, Lung, and Blood Diseases	yes
	13.132	Acquired Immunodeficiency Syndrome (AIDS) Research	no
	13.141	Alcohol, Drug Abuse Treatment and Rehabilitation Block Grant	no
	13.142	NIEHS Hazardous Waste Worker Health and Safety Training	no
	13.143	NIEHS Superfund Hazardous Substances - Basic Research and Education	no
	13.167	Research Facilities Improvement	no
	13.306	Laboratory Animal Sciences and Primate Research	no
	13.333	General Clinical Research Centers	no
	13.337	General Research Support Grants	no
	13.371	Biomedical Research Technology	no
	13.375	Minority Schools Biomedical Support	no
	13.389	Research Centers in Minority Institutions	no
	13.390	Academic Research Enhancement Award	no
	13.392	Cancer - Construction	no

Appendix 3. *(cont.)*

Department and agency name	Cfdano	Redistrib.	Program name
	13.393	no	Cancer Cause and Prevention Research
	13.394	no	Cancer Detection and Diagnosis Research
	13.395	no	Cancer Treatment Research
	13.396	no	Cancer Biology Research
	13.397	no	Cancer Centers Support
	13.398	no	Cancer Research Manpower
	13.399	no	Cancer Control Research
	13.821	no	Biophysics and Physiological Sciences
	13.837	no	Heart and Vascular Diseases Research
	13.838	no	Lung Diseases Research
	13.839	no	Blood Diseases and Resources Research
	13.840	no	Caries Research
	13.841	no	Periodontal and Soft Tissue Diseases Research
	13.842	no	Craniofacial Anomalies Research
	13.843	no	Restorative Materials Research
	13.844	no	Pain Control and Behavioral Studies
	13.845	no	Dental Research Institutes - Research in Oral Biology
	13.846	no	Arthritis, Musculoskeletal, and Skin Diseases Research
	13.847	no	Diabetes, Endocrinology and Metabolism Research
	13.848	no	Digestive Diseases and Nutrition Research
	13.849	no	Kidney Diseases, Urology and Hematology Research
	13.853	no	Clinical Research Related to Neurological Disorders
	13.854	no	Biological Basis Research in the Neurosciences
	13.855	no	Allergy, Immunology and Transplantation Research
	13.856	no	Microbiology and Infectious Diseases Research
	13.859	no	Pharmacology - Toxicology Research
	13.862	no	Genetics Research

	13.863	no	Cellular and Molecular Basis of Disease Research
	13.864	no	Population Research
	13.865	no	Research for Mothers and Children
	13.866	no	Aging Research
	13.867	no	Retinal and Choroidal Diseases Research
	13.868	no	Corneal Diseases Research
	13.869	no	Cataract Research
	13.870	no	Glaucoma Research
	13.871	no	Sensory and Motor Disorders of Vision Research
	13.878	no	Soft Tissue Stomatology and Nutrition Research
	13.879	no	Medical Library Assistance
	13.880	no	Minority Access to Research Careers
	13.894	no	Resource and Manpower Development
	13.985	no	Eye Research - Facility Construction
	13.989	no	Senior International Awards Program
Office of Child Support Enforcement	13.679	yes	Child Support Enforcement
	13.783	yes	Child Support Enforcement
	13.811	no	Child Support Enforcement Interstate Grants
Office of Community Services	13.665	yes	Community Services Block Grant
	13.792	yes	Community Services Block Grant
	13.793	yes	Community Services Block Grant - Discretionary Awards
	13.795	yes	Community Services Block Grant Discretionary Awards - Community Food and Nutrition
	13.796	no	Emergency Community Services for the Homeless
Office of Human Development Services	13.600	yes	Child Development - Head Start
	13.608	no	Child Development - Child Welfare Research and Demonstration Grants
	13.612	no	Native American Programs - Financial Assistance Grants
	13.614	yes	Child Development Associate Scholarships
	13.623	no	Runaway Youth
	13.628	no	Child Abuse and Neglect Prevention and Treatment
	13.630	no	Developmental Disabilities - Basic Support and Advocacy Grants

Appendix 3. (cont.)

Department and agency name	Cidano	Redistrib.	Program name
	13.631	no	Developmental Disabilities - Special Projects
	13.632	no	Developmental Disabilities - University Affiliated Programs
	13.633	yes	Special Programs for the Aging - Title III Parts A and B-Grants for Social Services and Centers
	13.635	yes	Special Programs for the Aging - Nutrition Program for the Elderly
	13.641	yes	Special Programs for the Aging - Title III, Part D-In-Home Services for Frail Older Individuals
	13.645	yes	Child Welfare Services - State Grants
	13.646	yes	Work Incentives Program
	13.648	no	Child Welfare Services Training Grants
	13.655	no	Special Programs for the Aging - Title VI - Grants to Indian Tribes
	13.661	no	Native American Programs - Research, Demonstration, and Evaluation
	13.662	no	Native American Programs - Training and Technical Assistance
	13.667	no	Social Services Block Grant
	13.668	no	Special Programs for the Aging - Title IV-Training, Research and Discretionary Projects and Programs
	13.670	no	Administration for Children, Youth and Families - Child Abuse and Neglect Discretionary Activities
	13.671	no	Family Violence Prevention and Services
Office of Refugee Resettlement	13.786	no	State Legalization Impact Assistance Grants
	13.787	no	Refugee and Entrant Assistance - State Administered Programs
	13.788	no	Refugee Assistance - Voluntary Agency Programs
	13.814	no	Refugee Assistance - State Administered Programs
	13.815	no	Refugee Assistance - Voluntary Agency Programs
Office of the Assistant Secretary for Health	13.217	yes	Family Planning Projects
	13.260	no	Family Planning Services - Training Grants and Contracts
	13.974	no	Family Planning Services Delivery Improvement Research Grants

Social Security Administration

National Health Promotion Training Network	13.990	no
Adolescent Family Life Demonstration Projects	13.995	no
Social Security - Disability Insurance	13.802	yes
Social Security - Retirement Insurance	13.803	yes
Social Security - Survivors Insurance	13.805	yes
Special Benefits for Disabled Coal Miners	13.806	no
Supplemental Security Income	13.807	yes
Assistance Payments - Maintenance Assistance (State Aid)	13.808	yes
Assistance Payments - State and Local Training	13.810	no
Public Assistance Research	13.812	no
Refugee Assistance - Cuban and Haitian Entrants	13.817	no
Low Income Home Energy Assistance	13.818	yes

Housing and Urban Development

Housing - Federal Housing Commissioner

Interest Reduction Payments - Rental and Cooperative Housing for Lower Income Families	14.103	yes

Community Planning and Development

Community Development Block Grants/Entitlement Grants	14.218	yes
Community Development Block Grants/Discretionary Grants	14.219	no
Urban Development Action Grants	14.221	yes
Indian Community Development Block Grant Program	14.223	no
Community Development Block Grants/Secretary's Discretionary Fund/Insular Areas	14.225	no
Community Development Block Grants/Secretary's Discretionary Fund	14.227	no
Community Development Block Grants/State's Program	14.228	no
Community Development Block Grants/Secretary's Discretionary Fund	14.229	no
Rental Housing Rehabilitation	14.230	yes
Emergency Shelter Grants Program	14.231	yes
Community Development Block Grant/Secretary's Discretionary Fund/Special Programs	14.232	no

Housing - Federal Housing Commissioner

Low Income Housing - Assistance Program (Public Housing)	14.146	yes
Rent Supplements - Rental Housing for Low Income Families	14.149	yes

179

Appendix 3. *(cont.)*

Department and agency name	Cfdano	Redistrib.	Program name
	14.156	yes	Lower-Income Housing Assistance Program
	14.157	yes	Housing for the Elderly and Handicapped
	14.167	no	Mortgage Insurance - Two Year Operating Loss Loans, Section 22
	14.169	yes	Housing Counseling Assistance Program
	14.174	yes	Housing Development Grants
	14.178	no	Supportive Housing Demonstration Program
Public and Indian Housing	14.850	yes	Public and Indian Housing
	14.851	yes	Low Income Housing - Homeownership Opportunities for Low Income Families
	14.852	yes	Public and Indian Housing - Comprehensive Improvement Assistance
Interior			
Office of Surface Mining Reclamation and Enforcement	15.250	no	Regulation of Surface Coal Mining and Surface Effects of Underground Coal Mining
Bureau of Mines	15.308	no	Grants for Mining and Mineral Resources and Research Institutes
Geological Survey	15.800	no	Geologic and Mineral Resource Surveys and Mapping
	15.801	no	Cartographic Information
	15.803	no	National Mapping, Geography and Surveys
	15.804	no	Water Resources Investigations
	15.805	no	Assistance to State Water Resources Research Institutes
	15.806	no	National Water Resources Research Program
	15.807	no	Earthquake Hazards Reduction Program
	15.808	no	Geological Survey - Research and Data Acquisition
National Park Service	15.904	no	Historic Preservation Grants-in-Aid
	15.914	no	National Register of Historic Places
	15.915	no	Technical Preservation Services

180

Agency / Office	Program	Number	Indicator
	Outdoor Recreation - Acquisition, Development and Planning	15.916	no
	Urban Park and Recreation Recovery Program	15.919	yes
Office of Surface Mining Reclamation and Enforcement	Abandoned Mine Land Reclamation Program	15.252	no
Office of Water Policy	Water Resources Research - Assistance to State Institutes	15.951	no
U.S. Fish and Wildlife Service	Anadromous Fish Conservation	15.600	no
	Fish Restoration	15.605	no
	Migratory Bird Banding and Data Analysis	15.606	no
	Wildlife Restoration	15.611	no
	Rare and Endangered Species Conservation	15.612	no
	Marine Mammal Grant Program	15.613	no
Justice			
National Institute of Corrections	Corrections - Training and Staff Development	16.601	no
	Corrections - Research and Evaluation and Policy Formulation	16.602	no
Office of Juvenile Justice and Delinquency Prevention	Juvenile Justice and Delinquency Prevention - Allocation to States	16.540	no
	Juvenile Justice and Delinquency Prevention - Special Emphasis	16.541	no
	Missing Children's Assistance	16.543	no
Labor			
Employment and Training Administration	Comprehensive Employment and Training Programs	17.232	yes
	Employment and Training Research and Development Projects	17.233	no
	Senior Community Service Employment Program	17.235	yes
	Trade Adjustment Assistance - Workers	17.245	yes
	Migrant and Seasonal Farmworkers	17.247	yes
	Employment and Training Research and Development Projects	17.248	yes
	Job Training Partnership Act	17.250	yes
Occupational Safety and Health Administration	Occupational Safety and Health	17.500	no
Office of the Assistant Secretary for Veterans' Employment and Training	Veterans Employment Program	17.802	yes
Transportation			
Federal Aviation Administration	Loan Guarantees for Purchase of Aircraft and Spare Parts	20.105	yes

181

Department and agency name	Cfdano	Redistrib.	Program name
Federal Highway Administration	20.107	no	Airway Science
	20.218	no	Motor Carrier Safety Assistance Program
	20.308	no	Local Rail Service Assistance
Maritime Administration	20.803	no	Maritime War Risk Insurance
	20.805	no	Ship Sales
	20.811	no	Research and Development Assistance
Research and Special Programs Administration	20.700	no	Gas Pipeline Safety
Urban Mass Transportation	20.500	yes	Urban Mass Transportation Capital Improvement Grants
	20.502	no	Urban Mass Transportation Grants for University Research and Training
	20.503	no	Urban Mass Transportation Managerial Training Grants
	20.504	no	Urban Mass Transportation Research, Development, and Demonstration Grants
	20.506	no	Urban Mass Transportation Demonstration Grants
	20.511	no	Human Resource Programs
	20.512	no	Urban Mass Transportation Technical Assistance
Veterans Affairs			
Veterans' Health Services and Research Administration	64.014	yes	Veterans State Domiciliary Care
	64.015	yes	Veterans State Nursing Home Care
	64.023	no	Health Professional Scholarships - Nursing
Veteran Benefit Administration	64.101	no	Burial Expenses Allowance for Veterans
	64.104	yes	Pension for Nonservice-Connected Disability for Veterans
	64.105	yes	Pension to Veterans' Surviving Spouses, and Children
	64.110	yes	Veterans Dependency and Indemnity Compensation for Service-Connected Death
	64.116	yes	Vocational Rehabilitation for Disabled Veterans
	64.119	yes	Veterans Housing - Mobile Home Loans

	Program	Number	
Action			
Action	Post-Vietnam Era Veterans' Educational Assistance	64.120	no
	Vocational Training for Certain Veterans Receiving VA Pension	64.123	yes
	Foster Grandparent Program	72.001	yes
	Retired Senior Volunteer Program	72.002	yes
	Volunteers in Service to America	72.003	yes
	Mini-Grant Program	72.010	yes
	State Volunteer Services Coordinator Program	72.011	yes
	Special Volunteer Programs	72.012	yes
	Technical Assistance Program	72.013	yes
	Drug Alliance	72.014	no
Appalachian Regional Commission			
Appalachian Regional Commission	Appalachian Development Highway System	23.003	no
	Appalachian Health Programs	23.004	no
	Appalachian Local Access Roads	23.008	no
	Appalachian State Research, Technical Assistance, and Demonstration Projects	23.011	no
	Appalachian Special Transportation Related Planning, Research and Demonstration Projects	23.017	no
Environmental Protection Agency			
Office of Water	Construction Grants for Wastewater Treatment Works	66.418	no
Office of Research and Development	Environmental Protection Comprehensive Research Grants	66.500	no
	Air Pollution Control Research Grants	66.501	no
	Solid Waste Disposal Research Grants	66.504	no
	Water Pollution Control - Research, Development, and Demonstration Grants	66.505	no
	Safe Drinking Water Research and Demonstration Grants	66.506	no
	Toxic Substances Research Grants	66.507	no
	Superfund Innovative Technology Evaluation Program	66.807	no
Office of Solid Waste and Emergency Response	Hazardous Waste Management State Program Support	66.801	no
	Hazardous Waste Management Financial Assistance	66.803	no
	State Underground Storage Tanks Program	66.804	no

Appendix 3. *(cont.)*

Department and agency name	Cfdano	Redistrib.	Program name
	66.804	no	State Underground Storage Tanks Program
	66.805	no	Underground Storage Tank Trust Fund Program
Office of Water	66.425	no	Drinking Water Supply - Technical Assistance
	66.432	no	State Public Water System Supervision Program Grants
	66.433	no	State Underground Water Source Protection - Program Grants
	66.454	no	Water Quality Management Planning
	66.455	no	Construction Grants for Abatement of Combined Sewer Overflow
	66.458	no	Capitalization Grants for State Revolving Funds
	66.460	no	Nonpoint Source Implementation
Federal Emergency Management Agency			
Emergency Management Institute	83.401	no	Emergency Management - Architect/Engineer Student Development
	83.402	no	Radiological Emergency Response - Training Assistance
	83.408	no	Technical Support Services
	83.409	no	Reimbursement for Firefighting on Federal Property
State and Local Programs and Support	83.500	no	General Research, Development, and Demonstration Activity
	83.502	yes	Acquisition of Flood-Damaged Structures
	83.503	no	Civil Defense - State and Local Emergency Management Assistance
	83.504	no	State and Local Maintenance and Services
	83.505	no	State Disaster Preparedness Grants
	83.511	no	Radiological Protection Planning and Development
	83.512	no	State and Local Emergency Operating Centers
	83.513	no	State and Local Warning and Communication Systems
	83.514	no	Population Protection Planning
	83.515	no	Emergency Broadcast System Guidance and Assistance
	83.519	no	Hazard Mitigation Assistance
	83.520	no	Hurricane Preparedness Grants

184

National Emergency Training Center - Training Program	83.406	no
Emergency Management Institute (EMI) - Home Study Program	83.412	no

National Foundation on the Arts and the Humanities
  National Endowment for the Humanities

Promotion of the Humanities - Media Grants	45.104	no
Promotion of the Humanities - Program Development	45.113	no
Promotion of the Humanities - Summer Seminars for College Teachers	45.116	no
Promotion of the Humanities - Centers for Advanced Study	45.122	no
Promotion of the Humanities - Museums and Historical Organizations	45.125	no
Promotion of the Humanities - Elementary and Secondary Education	45.127	no
Promotion of the Humanities - Humanities Studies Program	45.128	no
Promotion of the Humanities - State Programs	45.129	no
Promotion of the Humanities - Science, Technology and Human Values	45.133	no
Promotion of the Humanities - Basic Research/Research Conferences	45.134	no
Promotion of the Humanities - Basic Research/Project Research	45.140	no
Promotion of the Humanities - Fellowships for University Teachers	45.142	no
Promotion of the Humanities - Reference Materials/Tools	45.145	no
Promotion of the Humanities - Research Materials/Editions	45.146	no
Promotion of the Humanities - Basic Research/Intercultural Research	45.148	no
Promotion of the Humanities - Research Resources/Preservation	45.149	no
Promotion of the Humanities - Summer Seminars for Secondary School Teachers	45.151	no
NEH/Reader's Digest Teacher - Scholar Program	45.154	no

National Science Foundation
  National Science Foundation

Mathematical and Physical Sciences and Engineering	47.049	no
Astronomical, Atmospheric, Earth and Ocean Sciences	47.050	no
Two-Year and Four-Year College Research Instrumentation	47.055	no
Visiting Professorships for Women in Science and Engineering	47.059	no
Precollege Science and Mathematics Education	47.063	no
College Science Instrumentation Program	47.064	no
Advanced Scientific Computing Resources	47.065	no
Teacher Preparation and Enhancement	47.066	no

185

Appendix 3. *(cont.)*

Department and agency name	Cídano	Redistrib.	Program name
	47.067	no	Materials Development and Research
	47.068	no	Research, Studies, and Program Assessment
	47.069	no	Research Initiation and Improvement
	47.070	no	Computer and Information Science and Engineering
	47.072	no	Young Scholars
Small Business Administration			
Small Business Administration	59.006	yes	Minority Business Development - Procurement Assistance
	59.011	yes	Small Business Investment Companies
	59.026	yes	Service Corps of Retired Executives Association
	59.031	yes	Small Business Pollution Control Financing Guarantee
	59.033	yes	Minority Small Business and Capital Ownership Development
	59.036	no	Certified Development Company Loans

Agriculture
    Agricultural Stabilization and Conservation Service
    Economic Research Service
    National Agricultural Statistics Service
    Human Nutrition Information Service
    Agricultural Marketing Service
    Animal and Plant Health Inspection Service
    Agricultural Cooperative Service
    Food Safety and Inspection Service
    Forest Service
    Soil Conservation Service
    Agriculture Research Service
    Cooperative State Research Service
    Extension Service
    National Agricultural Library
Commerce
    National Oceanic and Atmospheric Administration
    International Trade Administration
    National Telecommunications and Information Administration
    National Bureau of Standards
Defense
    National Guard Bureau
Education
    Office of the Secretary
    Office of Assistant Secretary for Elementary and Secondary Education
    Compensatory Education Programs
    Office of Assistant Secretary for Post Secondary Education
    Assistant Secretary for Educational Research and Improvement
    Assistant Secretary for Special Education and Rehabilitative Services
    Assistant Secretary for Vocational and Adult Education
    State and Local Programs and Support
Energy
    Office of the Secretary
    Conservation and Renewable Energy
    Assistant Secretary for International Affairs and Energy Emergencies
    Office of Minority Economic Impact
    Office of Energy Research
    Office of Policy
Health and Human Services
    Office of Human Development Services
    Public Health Service
    National Center for Health Services Research
    Centers for Disease Control
    Food and Drug Administration
    Agency for Toxic Substances and Disease Registry
    Alcohol, Drug Abuse and Mental Health Administration
    National Institutes of Health

Indian Health Service
Health Resources and Services Administration
Health Services Administration
Office of Refugee Resettlement
Health Standards and Quality Bureau

Housing and Urban Development
Community Planning and Development

Interior
National Park Service
U.S. Fish and Wildlife Service
Office of Surface Mining Reclamation and Enforcement
Geological Survey
Bureau of Reclamation

Justice
National Institute of Corrections
Law Enforcement Assistance Administration
Office of Juvenile Justice and Delinquency Prevention
Bureau of Justice Statistics
National Institute of Justice

Labor
Occupational Safety and Health Administration
Mine Safety and Health Administration
Office of the Assistant Secretary for Veterans' Employment and Training
Bureau of Labor Statistics

Transportation
Federal Highway Administration
National Highway Traffic Safety Administration
Urban Mass Transportation
Maritime Administration
Research and Special Programs Administration

Treasury
Internal Revenue Service

Environmental Protection Agency
Office of Administration
Office of Solid Waste and Emergency Response
Office of Air and Radiation
Office of Pesticides and Toxic Substances
Office of Research and Development
Office of Water

Federal Emergency Management Agency
Emergency Management Institute
United States Fire Administration
Training and Fire Programs Directorate

Commissions
Appalachian Regional Commission

Equal Employment Opportunity Commission
Nuclear Regulatory Commission

Foundations and Institutes
National Endowment for the Humanities
National Science Foundation
Smithsonian Institute

Note: Distributive policy agencies are identified as those in which fewer than 50 percent of the programs providing direct forms of financial assistance included income level or unemployment status in the eligibility requirements for the selection of program beneficiaries.

Appendix 5. Federal agencies in four cabinet departments: Budgetary changes proposed by the Reagan administration for FY1983

Federal agencies with domestic assistance programs	Actual FY81	Proposed FY83
Department of Agriculture		
Agricultural Cooperative Service	$3,797,645	$3,543,269
Agricultural Marketing Service	$88,451,820	$125,097,115
Agricultural Stabilization and Conservation Service	$661,751,606	$449,503,846
Agriculture Research Service	$468,047,109	$457,157,692
Animal and Plant Health Inspection Service	$323,849,036	$227,975,962
Cooperative State Research Service	$214,102,784	$222,172,115
Economic Research Service[1]	$0	$39,071,154
Extension Service	$326,477,516	$300,957,692
Farmers Home Administration	$18,608,238,758	$13,669,637,500
Food and Nutrition Service	$5,215,910,064	$4,058,382,692
Food Safety and Inspection Service	$401,337,259	$308,264,423
Forest Service	$1,674,935,760	$1,483,097,115
Human Nutrition Information Service[2]	$0	$7,970,192
National Agricultural Library	$9,588,865	$8,669,231
Office of International Cooperation and Development	$17,788,009	$16,129,808
Packers and Stockyards Administration[3]	$0	$8,234,615
Soil Conservation Service	$634,089,936	$475,386,538
Department of Commerce		
Economic Development Administration	$422,165,953	$113,892,308
International Trade Administration	$128,189,507	$131,069,231
Minority Business Development Agency	$53,460,385	$57,391,346

National Bureau of Standards	$183,109,208	$157,165,385
National Oceanic and Atmospheric Administration	$904,457,173	$778,433,654
National Telecommunications and Information Administration	$19,392,934	$11,939,423
Department of Education		
Educational Research and Improvement	$588,276,231	$0
Elementary and Secondary Education	$5,437,694,861	$0
Office of the Secretary	$269,869,379	$0
Post Secondary Education	$7,055,018,201	$0
Special Education and Rehabilitative Services	$2,873,808,351	$0
Vocational and Adult Education	$1,438,684,154	$0
Department of Health and Human Services		
Administration for Children, Youth and Families	$890,871,520	$887,711,538
Alcohol, Drug Abuse and Mental Health Administration	$501,823,340	$116,244,231
Bureau of Health Maintenance Organizations	$28,920,771	$36,902,885
Centers for Disease Control	$393,459,315	$208,838,462
Food and Drug Administration	$80,070,664	$84,855,769
Health Care Financing Administration	$75,083,539,615	$87,161,104,808
Health Services Administration	$1,582,013,919	$1,584,909,615
Indian Health Service	$631,690,578	$589,692,308
National Institute of Mental Health	$705,313,704	$188,252,885
National Institutes for Deafness	$82,683,084	$85,414,423
National Institutes of Health	$4,090,495,717	$3,924,145,192
Office of Child Support Enforcement	$470,421,842	$393,199,038

Appendix 5. (*cont.*)

Federal agencies with domestic assistance programs	Actual FY81	Proposed FY83
Office of Community Services	$0	$108,173,077
Office of Human Development Services	$5,600,889,722	$3,697,520,192
Social Security Administration	$172,376,873,662	$183,653,846,154

Note: Figures reflect the sum of each agency's program activity obligations (costs) and, with the exception of agencies in Education, are from the FY1983 Appendix to the Budget of the United States Government, Executive Office of the President, Office of Management and Budget. Education agency figures for 1981 are estimated obligations from the FY1982 Appendix to the Budget, since the FY1983 Appendix to the Budget proposed the termination or transfer to other agencies of all of the Department of Education program activities. Figures are reported in constant 1982 dollars, using the implicit price deflator for Government Purchases of Goods and Services, table 759, Statistical Abstract of the United States, 1990.

[1] Economic Research Service (not to be confused with the Agriculture Research Service) was to be created, in part, by transfer of one program activity (of three) formerly administered by the Economics and Statistics Service.

[2] Human Nutrition Information Service was to be created, in part, by transfer of functions from the Agriculture Research Service and the National Agricultural Library.

[3] This agency is arguably quite old, rather than newly created. The Reagan administration proposed to reestablish a separate Packers and Stockyard Administration, as had been the case from the New Deal through the Ford administration. During the latter part of the Carter administration, the Packers and Stockyard Administration was placed within the Agricultural Marketing Service.

Appendix 6. *Financial assistance programs by public law bundle*

Public law bundle	Program number	Program name
99-319	13.138	Protection and Advocacy for Mentally Ill Individuals
99-443	10.212	Small Business Innovation Research*
99-443	13.103	Food and Drug Administration - Research*
99-443	13.113	Biological Response to Environmental Health Hazards*
99-443	13.114	Applied Toxicological Research and Testing*
99-443	13.115	Biometry and Risk Estimation - Health Risks from Environ. Exposures*
99-443	13.121	Diseases of the Teeth and Supporting Tissues*
99-443	13.262	Occupational Safety and Health Research Grants*
99-443	13.306	Laboratory Animal Sciences and Primate Research*
99-443	13.333	General Clinical Research Centers*
99-443	13.361	Nursing Research*
99-443	13.371	Biomedical Research Technology*
99-443	13.393	Cancer Cause and Prevention Research*
99-443	13.394	Cancer Detection and Diagnosis Research*
99-443	13.395	Cancer Treatment Research*
99-443	13.396	Cancer Biology Research*
99-443	13.821	Biophysics and Physiological Sciences*
99-443	13.837	Heart and Vascular Diseases Research*
99-443	13.838	Lung Diseases Research*
99-443	13.839	Blood Diseases and Resources Research*
99-443	13.846	Arthritis, Musculoskeletal, and Skin Diseases Research*
99-443	13.847	Diabetes, Endocrinology and Metabolism Research*
99-443	13.848	Digestive Diseases and Nutrition Research*
99-443	13.849	Kidney Diseases, Urology, and Hematology Research*
99-443	13.853	Clinical Research Related to Neurological Disorder*

Appendix 6. *(cont.)*

Public law bundle	Program number	Program name
99-443	13.854	Biological Basis Research in the Neurosciences*
99-443	13.855	Allergy, Immunology and Transplantation Research*
99-443	13.856	Microbiology and Infectious Diseases Research*
99-443	13.859	Pharmacological Sciences*
99-443	13.862	Genetics Research*
99-443	13.863	Cellular and Molecular Basis of Disease Research*
99-443	13.864	Population Research*
99-443	13.865	Research for Mothers and Children*
99-443	13.866	Aging Research*
99-443	13.867	Retinal and Choroidal Diseases Research*
99-443	13.868	Anterior Segment Diseases Research*
99-443	13.871	Strabismus, Amblyopia and Visual Processing*
99-443	47.053	Scientific, Technological, and International Affairs*
99-457	84.023	Handicapped - Innovation and Development*
99-457	84.024	Handicapped Early Childhood Education*
99-457	84.025	Handicapped Education - Deaf-Blind Centers*
99-457	84.026	Handicapped Media Services and Captioned Films*
99-457	84.027	Handicapped - State Grants
99-457	84.028	Handicapped Regional Resource and Federal Centers
99-457	84.029	Handicapped Education - Special Education Personnel*
99-457	84.030	Clearinghouses for the Handicapped Program*
99-457	84.078	Postsecondary Education Programs for Handicapped Persons*
99-457	84.086	Handicapped Education - Severely Handicapped Program*
99-457	84.158	Secondary Education and Transitional Services*
99-457	84.159	Handicapped - Special Studies*

99-499	13.161	Health Program for Toxic Substances and Disease Research
99-499	66.802	Hazardous Substance Response Trust Fund*
99-603	10.551	Food Stamps
100-241	10.551	Food Stamps
100-242	14.156	Lower-Income Housing Assistance Program
100-242	14.169	Housing Counseling Assistance Program
100-242	14.218	Community Development Block Grants/Entitlement Grants
100-4	66.418	Construction Grants for Wastewater Treatment Works*
100-4	66.438	Construction Management Assistance*
100-4	66.454	Water Quality Management Planning
100-4	66.458	Capitalization Grants for State Revolving Funds
100-4	66.459	Nonpoint Source Reservation
100-4	66.600	Environmental Protection Consolidated Grants - Program Support
100-485	13.658	Foster Care - Title IV-E
100-485	13.659	Adoption Assistance
100-485	13.667	Social Services Block Grant
100-485	13.714	Medical Assistance Program
100-485	13.780	Family Support Payments to States - Assistance Payments
100-485	13.783	Child Support Enforcement
100-485	13.803	Social Security - Retirement Insurance
100-485	13.805	Social Security - Survivors Insurance

*Programs providing distributive benefits. Such programs had no income or unemployment eligibility tests imposed on applicants or beneficiaries and more than 50 percent of the transactions were in the form of project grants or cooperative agreements during the Congress in which the public law was passed.

Appendix 7. *PACs whose parent interest groups testified in hearings, grouped by public law and PAC coalition*

Public law	PAC coalition	PAC name
99-443	*	KMS Fusion Inc Political Action Fund
99-499	1	AFL-CIO Committee on Political Education/Political Contributions Committee
99-499	1	Democratic Republican Independent Voter Education Committee
99-499	1	Industrial Union Department AFL-CIO Voluntary Fund
99-499	1	International Association of Firefighters Interested in Registration and Education PAC
99-499	1	Sierra Club Committee on Political Education
99-499	1	UAW - V - CAP (UAW Voluntary Community Action Program)
99-499	1	United Steel Workers of America Political Action Fund
99-499	2	AETNA Life and Casualty Company Political Action Committee
99-499	2	American Insurance Association Political Action Committee
99-499	2	Crum & Forster Voluntary Political Action Committee
99-499	2	Interstate Natural Gas Association of America Political Action Committee
99-499	2	LTV Steel Active Citizenship Campaign
99-499	2	Monsanto Citizenship Fund
99-499	2	Professional Insurance Agents Political Action Committee
99-499	2	The Travelers Corporation Political Action Committee (T-PAC)
99-499	3	American Consulting Engineers Political Action Committee (ACE/PAC)
99-499	3	American Medical Association Political Action Committee
99-499	3	ARCO PAC, Atlantic Richfield Company
99-499	3	Associated General Contractors Political Action Committee
99-499	3	CH2M Hill PAC Inc
99-499	3	Chevron Employees Political Action Committee
99-499	3	Independent Insurance Agents of America Inc Political Action Committee (IINSURPAC)

99-499	3	The Signal Companies, Inc Political Action Committee
99-499	3	Sun Company Inc Political Action Committee
99-499	*	AMAX Inc Concerned Citizens Fund
99-499	*	ASARCO Employees Political Action Committee (ASARCOPAC)
99-499	*	BPA-PAC (The BP America Political Action Committee) (FKA Standard Oil Co PAC)
99-499	*	Crown Central Petroleum Federal Political Action Committee
99-499	*	Ecology and Environment Committee for Responsible Government
99-499	*	Environmental Action's Political Action Committee (ENACT/PAC)
99-499	*	National Association of Metal Finishers Political Action Committee
99-499	*	National Constructors Association Political Action Committee (NCAPAC)
99-499	*	National Solid Wastes Management Association Waste PAC
99-499	*	National Tank Truck Carriers Political Action Committee
99-499	*	Pennsylvania Public Interest Coalition Voters' Alliance
99-499	*	Planning Research Corporation Political Action Committee
99-499	*	Recycling Industry Political Action Committee
99-499	*	Union Carbide Corporation Political Action Committee
99-603	1	Active Ballot Club, A Dept of United Food & Commercial Workers Int'l Union
99-603	1	AFL-CIO Committee on Political Education/Political Contributions Committee
99-603	1	American Federation of Government Employees' Political Action Committee
99-603	2	American Bankers Association BANKPAC
99-603	2	American Health Care Association Political Action Committee (AHCA-PAC)
99-603	2	American Hotel Motel Political Action Committee
99-603	2	American Medical Association Political Action Committee
99-603	2	National Cattlemen's Association Political Action Committee

Appendix 7. (cont.)

Public law	PAC coalition	PAC name
99-603	2	National Restaurant Association Political Action Committee
99-603	2	Political Action Committee of the American Hospital Association
99-603	3	American Express Company Committee for Responsible Government
99-603	3	American Society of Travel Agents PAC
99-603	3	BUSPAC-Political Action Committee of the American Bus Association
99-603	3	California Farm Bureau Federation Political Action Committee (FARM PAC)
99-603	3	National Tour Association Inc Political Action Committee ("TOURPAC")
99-603	3	Pan Am Political Action Committee
99-603	3	Travel Industry Association of America Political Action Committee (Travel PAC)
99-603	3	Western Growers Association Political Action Committee Federal
99-603	3 *	Arizona Cotton Growers Association Political Action Committee
99-603	*	Hospital Association Political Action Committee - Federal (HAPAC-Federal)
99-603	*	Texas Shrimp Association National Political Action Committee
99-603	*	United Fresh Fruit & Vegetable Association Political Action Committee (UNIPAC)
99-603	*	United States Telephone Ass'n PAC (formerly-United States Independent Telephone Ass'n PAC)
99-603	*	Warner Cable Communications Inc Political Action Committee
100-241	*	Bristol Bay Native Corporation Political Action Committee
100-241	*	NRA Political Victory Fund
100-241	*	Sierra Club Committee on Political Education
100-242	1	American Bankers Association BANKPAC
100-242	1	Build Political Action Committee of the National Association of Home Builders
100-242	1	Mortgage Bankers Association of America Political Action Committee
100-242	1	National Association of Independent Insurers Political Action Committee
100-242	1	Realtors Political Action Committee
100-242	2	AFL-CIO Committee on Political Education/Political Contributions Committee
100-242	2	AFL-CIO Cope Political Contributions Committee
100-242	2	National Council of Senior Citizens Political Action Committee

100-242	2	UAW - V - CAP (UAW Voluntary Community Action Program)
100-242	3	Independent Bankers - Political Action Committee
100-242	3	Mortgage Insurance Political Action Committee
100-242	3	National Council of Savings Institutions (THRIFTPAC)
100-242	3	National Multi Housing Council Political Action Committee
100-242	3	U S League-Savings Association Political Elections Committee
100-242	*	Alliance of American Insurers Political Action Committee
100-242	*	Amalgamated Clothing & Textile Workers Union
100-242	*	Amalgamated Clothing & Textile Workers Union Political Action Committee
100-242	*	American Home Builders PAC (FKA Southwest Builders PAC)
100-242	*	American Institute of Architects' Quality Government Fund
100-242	*	Coopers & Lybrand PAC
100-242	*	CRS Group (Federal) Political Action Committee
100-242	*	Leader Federal Savings & Loan Association Political Action Committee
100-242	*	National Association of Mutual Insurance Companies (NAMIC) PAC
100-242	*	National Housing Rehabilitation Association Political Action Committee
100-242	*	Southdown Inc Political Action Committee (FKA Moore McCormack Resources PAC)
100-242	*	Weyerhaeuser Company Political Action Committee
100-4	1	AMAX Inc Concerned Citizens Fund
100-4	1	Associated General Contractors Political Action Committee
100-4	1	Build Political Action Committee of the National Association of Home Builders
100-4	1	Civic Involvement Program/General Motors Corp.
100-4	1	COALPAC - The Political Action Committee of the National Coal Association
100-4	1	Forest Industries Political Action Committee

199

Appendix 7. *(cont.)*

Public law	PAC coalition	PAC name
100-4	1	Monsanto Citizenship Fund
100-4	1	National Cattlemen's Association Political Action Committee
100-4	1	National Society of Professional Engineers - Political Action Committee
100-4	1	Power PAC of The Edison Electric Institute
100-4	2	American Federation of Government Employees' Political Action Committee
100-4	2	Political Educational Fund of the Building and Construction Trades Department
100-4	2	Sierra Club Committee on Political Education
100-4	*	American Consulting Engineers Political Action Committee (ACE/PAC)
100-4	*	Clean Water Action Project
100-4	*	Clean Water Action Project Vote Environment '88
100-4	*	Federal Arthur Young & Company Political Action Committee
100-4	*	MARC-PAC
100-4	*	National Association of Metal Finishers Political Action Committee
100-4	*	National Fisheries Institute Political Action Committee (FISHPAC)
100-4	*	National Utility Contractors Assn Legislation Information & Action Committee
100-4	*	Trinity Improvement Association - PAC
100-485	1	AFL-CIO Committee on Political Education/Political Contributions Committee
100-485	1	AFL-CIO Cope Political Contributions Committee
100-485	1	American Federation of State, County and Municipal Employees, AFL-CIO (D.C.)
100-485	1	American Nurses' Association PAC (ANA-PAC) (FKA N-CAP)
100-485	1	National Association of Social Workers Political Action for Candidate Election
100-485	1	Service Employees Int'l Union Committee on Political Education Political Campaign Committee
100-485	*	American Health Care Association Political Action Committee (AHCA-PAC)
100-485	*	Corporate Citizenship Committee (ITT)
100-485	*	First Bank Political Action Committee
100-485	*	First Bank System Minnesota Good Government Committee

*Indicates PAC contributions are uncorrelated with any underlying factor.

Appendix 8. *Roll call votes in the U.S. House of Representatives on nine public laws*

Public law 99-319

V457   Y=240 N=134

TO ADOPT H RES 360, THE RULE UNDER WHICH HR 4055, A BILL APPROVING AID TO STATES FOR LEGAL ADVOCACY AND PROTECTIVE SERVICES FOR THE MENTALLY ILL, WILL BE CONSIDERED.

V458   Y=280 N=90   LUKEN (D, OH)

TO AMEND HR 4055 TO ELIMINATE LANGUAGE THAT WOULD HAVE DECLARED THOSE STATES WITH ESTABLISHED PROTECTION AND ADVOCACY PROGRAMS FOR THE MENTALLY ILL INELIGIBLE TO RECEIVE NEW AID FOR SUCH PROGRAMS.

V459   Y=290 N=84

TO PASS HR 4055, A BILL TO PROVIDE $33 MILLION IN AID TO STATES FOR LEGAL ADVOCACY AND PROTECTIVE SERVICES FOR THE MENTALLY ILL IN FISCAL YEARS 1986-8.

V560   Y=383 N=21

TO ACCEPT THE CONFERENCE REPORT ON S 974, A MEASURE PROVIDING FUNDS FOR 1986-8 TO AGENCIES THAT OFFER PROTECTION AND ADVOCACY SERVICES FOR THE MENTALLY ILL.

Public law 99-443

V755   Y=421 N=1   MAVROULES (D, MA)

TO SUSPEND THE RULES AND PASS HR 4260, A BILL TO PROVIDE THE SMALL BUSINESS ADMINISTRATION CONTINUING AUTHORITY TO ADMINISTER A PROGRAM FOR SMALL INNOVATIVE FIRMS. (MOTION PASSED; TWO-THIRDS OF THOSE PRESENT VOTING IN FAVOR.)

Public law 99-457

V550   Y=401 N=0   WILLIAMS (D, MT)

TO SUSPEND THE RULES AND ADOPT HR 4021, A BILL TO EXTEND FEDERAL AID FOR VOCATIONAL REHABILITATION OF THE HANDICAPPED THROUGH 1991. (MOTION PASSED; TWO-THIRDS OF THOSE PRESENT VOTING IN FAVOR.)

Appendix 8. (cont.)

Public law 99-499

V404   Y=376 N=33   PEPPER (D, FL)

TO APPROVE H RES 331 WHICH CONSIDERS HR 2817 SUPERFUND REAUTHORIZATION, A BILL THAT PROVIDES $10 BILLION TO FUND EFFORTS TO CLEAN THE NATION'S WORST ABANDONED HAZARDOUS WASTE SITES OVER THE NEXT FIVE YEARS.

V405   Y=62 N=330   DAUB (R, NE)

AN AMENDMENT TO HR 2817 SUPERFUND REAUTHORIZATION THAT EXEMPTS PERSONS FROM LIABILITY FOR THE COSTS OF CLEANING UP AN AREA WITH HAZARDOUS WASTES IF THEY CAN PROVE THAT THEY ARE NOT RESPONSIBLE FOR THE LEAKAGE OF THE WASTES.

V406   Y=183 N=166   EDGAR (D, PA)

AN AMENDMENT TO HR 2817 THAT REQUIRES COMPANIES TO MAKE AVAILABLE A LIST OF THEIR EMISSIONS OF CHEMICALS THAT ARE KNOWN TO CAUSE OR SUSPECTED OF CAUSING BIRTH DEFECTS, HERITABLE GENETIC MUTATIONS, OR OTHER CHRONIC HEALTH PROBLEMS.

V408   Y=142 N=256   MCKERNAN (R, ME)

AN AMENDMENT TO HR 2817 SUPERFUND REAUTHORIZATION THAT ALLOWS EIGHT STATES TO CONTINUE TO MAINTAIN THEIR OWN FUNDS THAT PAY FOR REMOVING OIL SLICKS.

V415   Y=74 N=349   DUNCAN (R, TN)

AN AMENDMENT TO HR 2817, THE SUPERFUND REAUTHORIZATION BILL FOR FISCAL 1986-90, WHICH MODIFIES THAT BILL TO DISPENSE WITH THE VALUE-ADDED TAX; TO AUTHORIZE TAX INCREASES ON CHEMICAL FEEDSTOCKS, CRUDE OIL, HAZARDOUS WASTE, GASOLINE, AND CHEMICAL DERIVATIVES; AND TO CREATE A TRIGGER MECHANISM FOR IMPOSING AN ENVIRONMENTAL SURCHARGE TAX ON CORPORATIONS AFTER A 3-YEAR PERIOD UNDER CERTAIN CONDITIONS. (MOTION FAILED)

V416   Y=220 N=206   DOWNEY (D, NY)

AN AMENDMENT TO HR 2817, THE SUPERFUND REAUTHORIZATION BILL FOR FISCAL 1986-90, WHICH ALTERS THAT BILL TO ELIMINATE PROVISION FOR THE VALUE-ADDED TAX AND TO INCREASE $10 BILLION OVER FIVE YEARS FOR THE HAZARDOUS WASTE CLEANUP PROGRAM THROUGH INCREASED TAXES ON CHEMICAL FEEDSTOCKS, OIL, AND HAZARDOUS WASTES AND INCREASED GENERAL REVENUES. (MOTION PASSED)

V417   Y=162 N=261 FRANK (D, MA)

AN AMENDMENT TO HR 2817 THAT ALLOWS PERSONS HARMED BY THE RELEASE OF TOXIC SUBSTANCES TO BRING LAWSUITS AGAINST THE RESPONSIBLE PARTIES IN FEDERAL COURT. (MOTION FAILED)

V418   Y=212 N=211 EDGAR (D, PA)

AN AMENDMENT TO HR 2817 WHICH ORDERS THAT COMPANIES PROVIDE TO THE PUBLIC AN INVENTORY OF CHEMICAL EMISSIONS THAT ARE KNOWN OR SUSPECTED CAUSES OF CANCER, BIRTH DEFECTS, OR OTHER CHRONIC DISEASES. (MOTION PASSED)

V419   Y=391 N=33

TO PASS HR 2817, THE SUPERFUND REAUTHORIZATION BILL FOR FISCAL 1986-90, WHICH AMENDS AND REAUTHORIZES THE "SUPERFUND" HAZARDOUS-WASTE CLEANUP PROGRAM UNDER THE COMPREHENSIVE ENVIRONMENTAL RESPONSE, COMPENSATION AND LIABILITY ACT OF 1980 AT A COST OF $10 BILLION. (MOTION PASSED)

V854   Y=311 N=104 DERRICK (D, SC)

TO AGREE TO ORDER THE PREVIOUS QUESTION, THEREBY ENDING DEBATE AND FURTHER AMENDMENT TO H RES 577, THE RULE FOR HR 2005.

V855   Y=339 N=74

TO ADOPT H RES 577, THE RULE WAIVING CERTAIN POINTS OF ORDER AGAINST THE CONFERENCE REPORT TO HR 2005, A BILL TO REAUTHORIZE THE SUPERFUND HAZARDOUS WASTE CLEANUP PROGRAM.

V857   Y=386 N=27

TO ACCEPT THE CONFERENCE REPORT ON HR 2005, THE SUPERFUND HAZARDOUS WASTE CLEANUP PROGRAM, CLEARING THE MEASURE FOR THE PRESIDENT.

Public law 99-603

V155   Y=104 N=307 SENSENBRENNER (R, WI)

TO AMEND HR 1452, A BILL AMENDING THE IMMIGRATION AND NATIONALITY ACT TO EXTEND FOR TWO YEARS THE AUTHORIZATION OF APPROPRIATIONS FOR REFUGEE ASSISTANCE. THE SENSENBRENNER AMENDMENT STRIKES THE $50 MILLION AUTHORIZATION AND LANGUAGE FOR TARGETED ASSISTANCE PROJECT GRANTS FOR EACH OF FISCAL YEARS 1986 AND 1987. (MOTION FAILED)

Appendix 8. *(cont.)*

V156   Y=278 N=112   PURSELL (R,MI)

TO AMEND HR 1452, A BILL AMENDING THE IMMIGRATION AND NATIONALITY ACT TO EXTEND FOR TWO YEARS THE AUTHORIZATION OF APPROPRIATIONS FOR REFUGEE ASSISTANCE. (MOTION PASSED)

V834   Y=180 N=202

TO ADCPT H RES 559, THE RULE PROVIDING FOR THE CONSIDERATION OF HR 3810, A BILL TO AMEND THE IMMIGRATION AND NATIONALITY ACT TO REVISE AND REFORM THE IMMIGRATION LAWS.

V835   Y=81 N=308   MAZZOLI (D, KY)

TO SUSPEND THE RULES AND PASS HR 5559, A BILL TO AMEND THE IMMIGRATION AND NATIONALITY ACT TO IMPROVE THE ADMINISTRATION OF THE IMMIGRATION AND NATIONALITY LAWS. (MOTION FAILED; TWO-THIRDS OF THOSE PRESENT NOT VOTING IN FAVOR.)

V861   Y=299 N=103   BEILENSON (D, CA)

TO AGREE TO ORDER THE PREVIOUS QUESTION, THEREBY ENDING DEBATE AND FURTHER AMENDMENT TO H RES 580, THE RULE FOR HR 3810.

V862   Y=278 N=129

TO ADOPT H RES 580, THE RULE UNDER WHICH HR 3810, AN IMMIGRATION AND NATIONALITY BILL, WILL BE CONSIDERED.

V863   Y=55 N=342   FORD (D, MI)

TO AMEND HR 3810 TO STRIKE PROVISIONS EXEMPTING EMPLOYERS FROM PENALTIES IN CASES WHERE AN EMPLOYEE IS REFERRED FOR EMPLOYMENT BY A STATE EMPLOYMENT AGENCY.

V864   Y=137 N=264   BARTLETT (R, TX)

TO AMEND HR 3810 TO PROVIDE FOR CIVIL RATHER THAN CRIMINAL PENALTIES FOR EMPLOYERS WHO ENGAGE IN A PATTERN OF HIRING ILLEGAL ALIENS.

V865   Y=140 N=260   SENSENBRENNER (R,WI)

TO AMEND HR 3810 TO STRIKE THE PROVISIONS PROHIBITING EMPLOYMENT DISCRIMINATION BASED ON NATIONAL ORIGIN OR CITIZENSHIP STATUS.

204

V866   Y=221 N=170 DE LA GARZA (D, TX)
TO AMEND HR 3810, TO PROHIBIT INS OFFICIALS FROM ENTERING A FARM OR AGRICULTURAL OPERATION WITHOUT A SEARCH WARRANT OR PERMISSION FROM THE OWNER IN ORDER TO QUESTION A PERSON BELIEVED TO BE AN ILLEGAL ALIEN.

V867   Y=73 N=310 GONZALEZ (D, TX)
TO AMEND HR 3810, TO PROVIDE THAT A FAMILY CONTAINING ONE PERSON ELIGIBLE FOR HOUSING ASSISTANCE MAY RECEIVE FEDERAL HOUSING ASSISTANCE WITHOUT REGARD TO THE IMMIGRATION STATUS OF OTHER FAMILY MEMBERS.

V868   Y=192 N=199 MCCOLLUM (R, FL)
TO AMEND HR 3810, TO STRIKE THE LEGALIZATION PROGRAM PROVISIONS.

V869   Y=197 N=199 FISH (R, NY)
TO AMEND HR 3810, TO STRIKE PROVISIONS PROVIDING FOR THE INVESTIGATION, REVIEW, AND TEMPORARY LIMITATION ON DEPORTATION OF DISPLACED SALVADORANS AND NICARAGUANS.

V870   Y=230 N=166
TO PASS HR 3810, A BILL TO AMEND THE IMMIGRATION AND NATIONALITY ACT TO REVISE AND REFORM THE IMMIGRATION LAWS.

Public law 100-241

V493   Y=397 N=9 UDALL (D, AZ)
TO SUSPEND THE RULES AND AGREE WITH AN AMENDMENT TO THE SENATE AMENDMENT TO HR 278, ALASKA NATIVE CLAIMS SETTLEMENT ACT.

Public law 100-242

V173   Y=179 N=246 WYLIE (R, OH)
TO AMEND IN THE NATURE OF A SUBSTITUTE HR 4, HOUSING AND COMMUNITY DEVELOPMENT, TO REDUCE TOTAL AUTHORIZATION FOR THE HOUSING/COMMUNITY DEVELOPMENT BILL BY $1.7 BILLION TO $14.2 BILLION.

V174   Y=176 N=249 BARTLETT (D, TX)
TO AMEND HR 4, HOUSING AND COMMUNITY DEVELOPMENT, TO STRIKE LANGUAGE REQUIRING CORPORATE PUBLIC HOUSING MANAGERS TO ABIDE BY COLLECTIVE BARGAINING AGREEMENTS WITH EMPLOYEES OF THE CORPORATION.

Appendix 8. (cont.)

V175   Y=284 N=137 GRAY (D, IL)
TO AMEND HR 4, HOUSING AND COMMUNITY DEVELOPMENT, TO REDUCE RENTAL PAYMENTS FROM 30 PERCENT TO 25 PERCENT FOR ELDERLY FAMILIES.

V176   Y=258 N=161 MORRISON (D, CT)
TO AMEND IN THE NATURE OF A SUBSTITUTE THE KEMP (R, NY) AMENDMENT TO HR 4, HOUSING AND COMMUNITY DEVELOPMENT, TO PROVIDE LOW INCOME FAMILIES WITH THE OPPORTUNITY TO PURCHASE LIVING UNITS IN PUBLIC HOUSING PROJECTS.

V177   Y=129 N=282 HEFLEY (R, CO)
TO AMEND HR 4, HOUSING AND COMMUNITY DEVELOPMENT, TO STRIKE LANGUAGE REQUIRING THE DEVELOPMENT OF AN ALTERNATE SYSTEM FOR THE IMPLEMENTATION OF VOLUNTARY PREEMPTIVE NATIONAL CODES FOR MODULAR HOUSING.

V178   Y=163 N=245 HILER (R, IN)
TO AMEND HR 4, HOUSING AND COMMUNITY DEVELOPMENT, TO FAVOR THE REHABILITATION OR RENOVATION OF VACANT INDUSTRIAL BUILDINGS IN GIVING OUT URBAN DEVELOPMENT ACTION GRANTS.

V179   Y=242 N=166 GONZALEZ (D, TX)
TO AMEND HR 4, HOUSING AND COMMUNITY DEVELOPMENT, AS AMENDED BY THE HILER (R, IN) AMENDMENT TO REQUIRE THAT AUTHORIZATION LEVELS IN THE BILL NOT EXCEED THE LIMIT SET BY A BUDGET RESOLUTION FOR FISCAL 1988.

V180   Y=162 N=243 WYLIE (R, OH)
TO RECOMMIT HR 4, HOUSING AND COMMUNITY DEVELOPMENT, TO THE COMMITTEE ON BANKING, FINANCE AND URBAN AFFAIRS WITH INSTRUCTIONS TO ALLOW RESIDENTS TO PURCHASE UNITS AT 25 PERCENT OF THE FAIR MARKET VALUE.

V181   Y=285 N=120
TO PASS HR 4, HOUSING AND COMMUNITY DEVELOPMENT, A BILL TO AUTHORIZE $15.9 BILLION FOR HOUSING AND COMMUNITY DEVELOPMENT IN FISCAL 1988.

Public law 100-4

V16   Y=286 N=124 MOAKLEY (D, MA)
TO ORDER THE PREVIOUS QUESTION ON H RES 27, THE RULE TO PROVIDE FOR HOUSE FLOOR CONSIDERATION OF HR 1, THE CLEAN AIR ACT, A BILL TO AMEND AND REAUTHORIZE THE CLEAN WATER ACT OF 1972.

V17 Y=406 N=8
TO PASS HR 1, THE CLEAN AIR ACT, A BILL TO AMEND AND REAUTHORIZE THE CLEAN WATER ACT OF 1972 TO PROVIDE FOR THE RENEWAL OF THE QUALITY OF THE NATION'S WATER.

V23 Y=401 N=26
TO PASS, OVER PRESIDENT REAGAN'S VETO, HR 1, THE CLEAN WATER ACT, A BILL TO AMEND AND REAUTHORIZE THE CLEAN WATER ACT OF 1972. (VETO OVERRIDDEN; TWO-THIRDS OF THOSE PRESENT VOTING IN FAVOR.)

Public law 100-485
V470 Y=213 N=206
TO ADOPT THE RULE H RES 331 TO PROVIDE FOR HOUSE FLOOR CONSIDERATION OF HR 1720, FAMILY WELFARE REFORM, A BILL TO CHANGE THE AID TO FAMILIES WITH DEPENDENT CHILDREN PROGRAM.

V473 Y=336 N=87 ANDREWS (D, TX)
TO AMEND HR 1720, FAMILY WELFARE REFORM, TO REDUCE COSTS OF THE BILL BY TEN PERCENT OVER FIVE YEARS AND REQUIRING STATES TO IMPLEMENT IMMEDIATE WAGE WITHHOLDING FOR CHILD SUPPORT PAYMENTS.

V474 Y=173 N=251 MICHEL (R, IL)
TO AMEND IN THE NATURE OF A SUBSTITUTE HR 1720, FAMILY WELFARE REFORM, AND REPLACE IT WITH HR 3200.

V475 Y=230 N=194
TO PASS HR 1720, FAMILY WELFARE REFORM, A BILL TO CHANGE THE AID TO FAMILIES WITH DEPENDENT CHILDREN PROGRAM TO A FAMILY SUPPORT PROGRAM.

V710 Y=227 N=168 BROWN (R, CO)
TO INSTRUCT THE HOUSE CONFEREES ON HR 1720, FAMILY WELFARE REFORM, TO ALLOCATE NO MORE THAN $2.8 BILLION AND ALLOW NO IMPEDIMENTS TO EMPLOYMENT FOR WELFARE RECIPIENTS.

V812 Y=249 N=130 BROWN (R, CO)
TO INSTRUCT THE HOUSE CONFEREES ON HR 1720, WELFARE REFORM, TO KEEP COSTS LESS THAN OR EQUAL TO THE $2.8 MILLION IN THE SENATE AMENDMENT TO THE BILL.

V858 Y=347 N=53
TO ADOPT THE CONFERENCE REPORT ON HR 1720, WELFARE REFORM, TO CREATE THE FAMILY SUPPORT PROGRAM (SUPERCEDES AFDC), TO STRESS CHILD SUPPORT AND FAMILY SUPPORT FOR ATTEMPTS TO FIND AND KEEP JOBS AND TO SET UP PROGRAMS TO HELP AVOID LONG-TERM WELFARE DEPENDENCY.

Appendix 9. Probit results for House roll call votes on nine public laws

Pub. law category	Conc. costs/ benefits	Public law	Vote	Intercept	Party	Committee member	Election margin	Part. benefits	PAC1	PAC2	PAC3	Pseudo R square	Number voting	Proportion voting yes
Consensual Narrow	No	100-241	V493	4.96	-3.11	3.07	-0.003		-0.39 0.00	2.59 0.00	0.36 0.00	0.05	406	0.98
Consensual Narrow	No	100-485	V470	0.59**	-5.61	0.52*	-0.003		0.73** 0.20			0.74	419	0.51
Consensual Narrow	No	100-485	V473	1.11**	1.48**	-0.27	-0.003		-0.55** -0.17			0.20	423	0.79
Consensual Narrow	No	100-485	V474	-1.88**	3.91**	0.29	-0.002		-0.82** -0.02			0.93	424	0.41
Consensual Narrow	No	100-485	V475	0.40*	-2.21**	0.29	0.001		0.87** 0.24			0.66	424	0.54
Consensual Narrow	Yes	100-485	V710	0.18	2.23**	-0.25	-0.001		-0.80** -0.30			0.52	395	0.57
Consensual Narrow	Yes	100-485	V812	0.52**	2.02**	-0.32*	-0.001		-0.71** -0.28			0.39	379	0.66
Consensual Narrow	No	100-485	V858	1.77**	-0.24	-0.14	-0.007**		-0.35 -0.05			0.02	400	0.87
Consensual Narrow	No	99-319	V457	1.94**	-2.57**	-0.42	-0.003					0.60	374	0.64
Consensual Narrow	Yes	99-319	V458	2.49**	-2.07**	0.06	-0.013*					0.32	370	0.76
Consensual Narrow	No	99-319	V459	1.95**	-1.50**	-0.35*	-0.007**					0.22	374	0.78
Consensual Narrow	No	99-319	V560	5.17	-3.70	-0.58*	-0.005					0.10	404	0.95
Consensual Broad	No	99-443	V755									1.00	422	1.00
Consensual Broad	No	99-457	V550									1.00	401	1.00

Conflictual Narrow	No	100-242	V173	-1.63**	2.86**	-0.27	0.007**		0.15 / 0.02	-0.81** / -0.06	0.31 / 0.05	0.79	425	0.42
Conflictual Narrow	Yes	100-242	V174	-1.19**	2.22**	-0.33	0.006*		0.13 / 0.03	-1.39** / -0.14	0.41 / 0.12	0.74	425	0.41
Conflictual Narrow	Yes	100-242	V175	1.09**	-1.38**	0.19	-0.003		0.47* / 0.09	0.14 / 0.03	-0.55** / -0.17	0.28	421	0.67
Conflictual Narrow	No	100-242	V176	1.32**	-3.25**	0.59**	-0.004		0.71* / 0.08	0.45 / 0.06	-0.34 / -0.08	0.80	419	0.62
Conflictual Narrow	Yes	100-242	V177	-1.02**	1.55**	-0.43**	-0.001		0.05 / 0.01	-1.11** / -0.14	0.38* / 0.11	0.53	411	0.31
Conflictual Narrow	Yes	100-242	V178	-0.96**	3.00**	-0.35*	-0.002		-0.59 / -0.10	0.25 / 0.07	-0.05 / -0.01	0.70	408	0.40
Conflictual Narrow	No	100-242	V179	1.19**	-2.71**	0.35	-0.002		0.04 / 0.01	0.76** / 0.10	-0.16 / -0.04	0.79	408	0.59
Conflictual Narrow	No	100-242	V180	-1.66**	3.37**	-0.17	0.002		-0.26 / -0.02	-0.54 / -0.04	0.38 / 0.06	0.87	405	0.40
Conflictual Narrow	No	100-242	V181	2.15**	-2.63**	0.45**	-0.009		0.36 / 0.02	0.24 / 0.01	-0.40** / -0.04	0.57	405	0.70
Conflictual Narrow	No	99-499	V404	4.32	-3.64	0.17	0.003	-0.30	0.44 / 0.00	0.18 / 0.00	-0.28 / 0.00	0.14	409	0.92
Conflictual Narrow	Yes	99-499	V405	-2.37**	1.78**	-0.05	0.003	-0.62*	-0.68** / -0.01	0.48 / 0.02	0.06 / 0.00	0.30	392	0.16
Conflictual Narrow	Yes	99-499	V406	0.67**	-1.03**	0.09	-0.004	-0.25	1.12** / 0.24	-0.44* / -0.16	-0.52* / -0.19	0.38	349	0.52
Conflictual Narrow	Yes	99-499	V408	-0.50**	0.40**	-0.03	0.000	-0.09	-0.32* / -0.10	-0.36* / -0.11	0.52** / 0.20	0.06	398	0.36
Conflictual Narrow	Yes	99-499	V415	-2.62**	2.11**	0.06	0.007**	-0.44	-0.29 / 0.00	0.04 / 0.00	0.07 / 0.00	0.31	423	0.17

Appendix 9. (cont.)

Pub. law category	Conc. costs/benefits	Public law	Vote	Intercept	Party	Committee member	Election margin	Part. benefits	PAC1	PAC2	PAC3	Pseudo R square	Number voting	Proportion voting yes
Conflictual Narrow	Yes	99-499	V416	0.78**	-0.11	-0.29**	-0.004*	-0.26	0.63**	-0.47*	-0.35	0.12	426	0.52
									0.15	-0.17	-0.12			
Conflictual Narrow	Yes	99-499	V417	0.42*	-0.82**	-0.15	0.000	-0.09	1.59**	-0.65**	-1.15**	0.36	423	0.38
									0.31	-0.25	-0.43			
Conflictual Narrow	Yes	99-499	V418	0.54**	-0.94**	0.00	-0.003	0.05	1.24**	-0.22	-0.77**	0.37	423	0.50
									0.27	-0.08	-0.30			
Conflictual Narrow	No	99-499	V419	1.82**	-0.61**	0.02	-0.002	0.14	1.04**	0.06	-0.42	0.10	424	0.92
									0.04	0.00	-0.05			
Conflictual Narrow	No	99-499	V854	0.99**	-1.11**	0.12	0.001	-0.35	0.53**	-0.20	0.08	0.26	415	0.75
									0.09	-0.05	0.02			
Conflictual Narrow	No	99-499	V855	1.83**	-1.18**	0.04	-0.006*	-0.47*	0.56**	-0.40	0.13	0.22	413	0.82
									0.03	-0.05	0.01			
Conflictual Narrow	No	99-499	V857	1.99**	-1.20**	0.26	0.000	-0.55*	0.45	-0.03	0.06	0.09	413	0.93
									0.02	0.00	0.00			
Conflictual Narrow	Yes	99-603	V155	-1.21**	0.73**	-0.13	0.002		-1.22**	0.63**	0.12	0.29	411	0.25
									-0.12	0.17	0.03			
Conflictual Narrow	No	99-603	V156	0.42*	0.56**	-0.04	-0.009**		-0.61**	0.88**	-0.81**	0.21	390	0.71
									-0.24	0.28	-0.31			
Conflictual Narrow	No	99-603	V834	0.09	-1.51**	0.21	0.002		0.95**	-0.38	-0.05	0.49	382	0.47
									0.31	-0.15	-0.02			
Conflictual Narrow	No	99-603	V835	-1.10**	-1.23**	0.41**	0.005**		0.77**	-0.46*	0.06	0.21	389	0.21
									0.26	-0.09	0.02			
Conflictual Narrow	No	99-603	V861	0.80**	-0.89**	0.06	-0.002		0.29	0.17	0.75**	0.18	402	0.74
									0.08	0.05	0.16			
Conflictual Narrow	No	99-603	V862	0.58**	-0.68**	-0.07	0.000		0.16	0.13	0.39	0.10	407	0.68
									0.05	0.04	0.11			
Conflictual Narrow	Yes	99-603	V863	-1.55**	-1.25**	0.29	0.004		0.90**	-0.25	-0.45	0.16	397	0.14
									0.22	-0.03	-0.05			
Conflictual Narrow	Yes	99-603	V864	-1.03**	0.41**	0.08	0.002		0.04	0.37*	-0.37	0.04	401	0.34
									0.01	0.11	-0.08			
Conflictual Narrow	Yes	99-603	V865	-1.20**	1.13**	-0.12	0.000		-1.02**	0.79**	0.12	0.42	400	0.35

210

Type	Sample	Congress	Variable										N	R²
Conflictual Narrow	Yes	99-603	V866	0.11	-0.20	0.22*	-0.002		-0.02	0.08	0.27	0.02	391	0.57
									-0.01	0.03	0.11			
Conflictual Narrow	Yes	99-603	V867	-1.37**	-0.52*	0.09	0.005*		1.41**	-0.64**	-0.15	0.21	383	0.19
									0.46	-0.08	-0.03			
Conflictual Narrow	No	99-603	V868	0.20	0.44**	-0.23	0.001		-1.23**	0.36	-0.24	0.31	391	0.49
									-0.43	0.13	-0.09			
Conflictual Narrow	No	99-603	V869	-0.41	1.00**	-0.16	0.004		-1.62**	0.88**	0.08	0.54	396	0.50
									-0.35	0.34	0.03			
Conflictual Narrow	No	99-603	V870	0.16	-0.54**	-0.07	-0.003		0.62**	0.10	0.53**	0.17	396	0.58
									0.22	0.04	0.20			
Conflictual Broad	No	100-4	V16	1.26**	-3.26**	0.57**	0.004	0.57	0.30	0.89**		0.68	410	0.70
									0.04	0.08				
Conflictual Broad	No	100-4	V17	4.79	-3.78	3.78	-0.008	0.58	0.23	3.13		0.13	414	0.98
									0.00	0.00				
Conflictual Broad	No	100-4	V23	3.74	-3.66	0.63**	0.000	0.73**	0.09	1.00		0.18	427	0.94
									0.00	0.00				

Note: Values below PAC coefficients represent the change in probability of voting yes for a "typical" legislator that received a contribution from any PAC in the PAC coalition compared to an identical "typical" legislator that did not. The typical legislator was a Democrat, not sitting on a committee that held hearings on the public law, winning the last election by the average margin over his or her major party opponent, and receiving no particularized benefits from any programs reauthorized by the public law. Party is coded Dem = 0, Rep = 1.

$*p < 0.10$, two-tailed $**p < 0.05$, two-tailed

Appendix 10. *Concepts and measures*

Concept	Measure and source	Variable coding and frequencies	Valid obs.
Awareness of new projects in district	"Do you happen to remember anything special representative (Name) has done for the people in (His/Her) district while (he/she) has been in Congress?" (NES, ref. no. 792, 1988)	1 = Respondent remembers (16%) 0 = Respondent does not remember (84%)	1705
Information about politics and government	"I think that I am better informed about politics and government than most people?" (NES, ref. no. 943, 1988)	1 = Agree strongly or somewhat (27%) 0 = Disagree strongly, disagree somewhat, or neither agree nor disagree (73%)	1705
Group affiliation	"Do you belong to any organizations or take part in any activities that represent the interests and viewpoints of group (name)?" (NES, ref. no. 1113, 1988)	1 = Yes (29%) 0 = No (71%)	1705
Voter support for incumbent	"I am going to read a list of candidates for the major races in your district. In the election for the House of Representatives the ballot listed: Who did you vote for?" (NES, ref. nos. 792)	1 = Voted for the incumbent (81%) 0 = Voted for candidate other than incumbent (19%)	987
Party affiliation of incumbent, 1988	(Makinson, 1992)	1 = Republican (29.9%) 0 = Democrat (71.1%)	396 districts
Incumbent campaign spending, 1985-86	Incumbent campaign spending as a percent of total campaign spending during two year election cycle (Makinson, 1992)	Mean = 91% Standard Deviation = 13%	396 districts

Variable	Description	Coding / Statistics	N
Incumbent campaign spending, 1987-8	Incumbent campaign spending as a percent of total campaign spending during two year election cycle (Makinson, 1992)	Mean = 91% Standard deviation = 13%	396 districts
Electoral margin for House incumbent, 1986	Percent of vote for incumbent House member in 1986 general election (Makinson, 1992)	Mean = 70% Standard deviation = 12.9	396 districts
Electoral margin for House incumbent, 1988	Percent of vote for incumbent House member in 1988 general election (Makinson, 1992)	Mean = 70% Standard deviation = 12.9	396 districts
Party congruence, 1988	Congruence between respondent party identification and incumbent party affiliation	1 = Same party (41.1%) 0 = Respondent is independent (36.5%) -1 = Opposite parties (22.4%)	1705
Incumbent tenure	Number of congressional terms served by incumbent through 100th Congress.	Mean = 4.7 Standard deviation = 3.5	396 districts
Specific likes about incumbent	"Was there anything in particular that you liked about the Democratic/Republican candidate for the U.S. House of Representatives?" (NES, ref nos. 674, 686, 1988)	1 = Mentioned a like (54%) 0 = Mentioned no likes (46%)	1705
Specific dislikes about incumbent	"Was there anything in particular that you disliked about the Democratic/Republican candidate for the U.S. House of Representatives?" (NES, ref nos. 680, 692, 1988)	1 = Mentioned a dislike (15%) 0 = Mentioned no dislikes (85%)	1705
Feeling thermometer about incumbent	(NES, ref. nos. 601, 602, 1988)	Mean = 66.6 Standard deviation = 21.1	1429

Notes

Chapter 1

1 Personal communication (ca. November 1992) between Robert M. Stein and Congressman Michael Andrews.
2 Undated letter (ca. September 1993) from Phil Boyer, president, Aircraft Owners and Pilots Association Political Action Committee, to Kenneth N. Bickers.

Chapter 2

1 Typically those who have studied growth in the public sector have focused on dollars. Indeed research on the correlates and causes of government growth has constituted something of a cottage industry in recent years (cf. reviews by Lybeck, 1988; Larkey, Stolp, and Winer, 1981; Borcherding, 1977; and Tarschys, 1975). Research has focused on the empirical utility of factors that have been proposed as potential sources of government growth (e.g., Berry and Lowery, 1987; Cameron, 1978). Research also has focused on methodological debates about how to measure and compare the scope of the public sector over time and cross-nationally (e.g., Klein, 1985; Lewis-Beck and Rice, 1985; Beck, 1976). Our argument is that focusing on the size of government in the aggregate (however measured) tends to mask the issue of what aspects of the government's responsibilities are increasing or decreasing in size and importance.
2 Appropriations for the Health Care Finance Administration (HCFA) as well the Federal Highway Administration understate appropriations for these agencies because a substantial amount of spending for these agencies comes from trust funds and not directly from congressional appropriations.
3 The Social Security Administration lost several programs as a result of the creation of the HCFA, which will be discussed in the context of agencies with predominately distributive program portfolios.

Chapter 3

1 For aid transactions that involve federal insurance, direct loans, or guaranteed loans, FAADS does not differentiate between the value of the subsidy that is

215

provided and the face value of the insurance policy or loan, making it impossible to estimate the actual financial subsidy to a recipient. Consequently, the data reported in this chapter exclude all such transactions. This may understate the true level of benefits going to some districts, but means that benefits measured here represent only direct financial assistance outlays.

2 In the case of programs that have undergone administrative reorganizations (e.g., a program shifted to a new agency, split into multiple programs, or consolidated from other programs), the year of creation is calculated in terms of the most recent reorganization, on the assumption that such programs are best treated as new entities.

Chapter 5

1 For example, a program for the treatment of deaf children would be coded in the National Institute for Deafness, which is part of National Institutes of Health, which in turn is the responsibility of the assistant secretary for health, which is one part of the Department of Health and Human Services.

2 The twelve recipient categories are (1) state governments and state higher educational institutions, (2) regional commissions or authorities, (3) counties, (4) towns and cities, (5) special districts, (6) private institutions of higher education, (7) independent school districts, (8) nonprofit agencies, (9) for-profit organizations, (10) small businesses, (11) Indian tribes, and (12) individuals and families.

Chapter 6

1 Sorauf (1992:16) reports, "What was a 1.5 to 1 advantage over their challengers in receipts in 1978 became a 3.7 to 1 spread in 1990."

2 The public law that was dropped dealt with copyright restrictions, but was shown in the catalog as authorizing the nuclear waste disposal siting program. After checking to ensure that the two were not linked by a rider to a different bill, we concluded that the catalog was in error and dropped the case.

3 Common factor analysis was employed in this analysis, where the communality estimate was the squared multiple correlation of each variable with all other variables. An eigenvalue of 1.0 or more was used to extract the number of common factors in each analysis. Orthogonal rotation was employed using the Varimax method, although the Equimax rotation method produced essentially the same results.

4 PACs were assigned to a PAC cluster on the basis of their correlation with the underlying factor. Correlations of .3 and above were used to determine an acceptably high correlation with a factor. If a member received a campaign contribution from any of the PACs correlated with the underlying factor at the .3 level or above, then the member is scored as receiving a benefit from the PAC cluster. Otherwise the member is scored as not receiving a benefit.

Chapter 7

1 This of course does not preclude the possibility that members seek district level benefits for reasons other than their reelection, for example, the policy needs of their district.

2 The major welfare entitlement programs (i.e., Medicaid, food stamps, and AFDC) represent nearly 40 percent of total domestic outlays (U.S. Bureau of the Census, 1989).

3 One exception to this generalization involves highly visible projects that already exist in a district and that are threatened with elimination, as in a proposed closure of a military base. In such situations, legislators may derive high levels of publicity from their efforts to retain the existing federal benefits. Such a retentive strategy is likely to be more prevalent in periods of budgetary retrenchment than in periods of growth.

4 Our measure of an individual's awareness of new grant awards in the district asked whether "you happen to remember anything special [their representative's name] has done for the people in [his/her] district while [he/she] has been in Congress?" Although this wording is somewhat more inclusive than the procurement of grant projects for the district, it certainly encompasses new grant projects. Other researchers (Cain, Ferejohn, and Fiorina, 1987;175–6; Fiorina, 1981a:562) have used this wording to measure a respondent's awareness of new grant projects in the district. These authors have obtained results similar to those reported in Tables 7.4 and 7.5.

5 An alternative model was estimated where the percent change in total grant dollars allocated to a district was substituted for the change in the proportion of new to total grant awards. As expected, the estimate for a dollar measure of district-level benefits was statistically insignificant (t-value $= -.903$). The estimates for other independent regressors in this equation were substantially unchanged from those reported in Table 7.2.

6 Because it is plausible to think that the marginal impact of electoral vulnerability on the flow of new awards may decline as vulnerability decreases, we visually inspected the residuals from the regression in Table 7.3. The plot of the residuals of the dependent variable and vulnerability suggested that the relationship between the two variables might be curvilinear, with the flow of new awards decreasing as members become less vulnerable and increasing again among the safest members. A regression fitting this quadratic curvilinear relationship confirmed that there was a U-shaped relationship with a strong left branch and weak right branch. In a model with the same variables as Table 7.3 but which included a quadratic term for the vulnerability measure, both the quadratic and linear terms attained significance at the 0.05 level, but the improvement in fit over the simple linear relationship was only a one point increase in the R square. Our conclusion was that the simple linear model describes reasonably well the relationship between vulnerability and the flow of new awards over most of the range of electoral vulnerability, but that, for reasons about which we can only speculate, the relationship reverses at very high levels of electoral safety. Our suspicion is that some members with extreme safeness may pursue aggressively new awards in order to mount races for higher offices or (given the particular year in which these data are measured) to fend off attempts to redistrict them into substantially new districts. This is a question that bears further research.

7 For the three continuous independent variables (i.e., incumbent share of campaign spending, incumbent tenure, and the change in the proportion of new to total grant awards), we have calculated the change in the probabilities for each dependent variable when the independent variable is set to one standard deviation above and below the mean values for these measures. For each of the dichotomous independent variables, the effect of each variable is evaluated at the 0 and 1 values.

217

Chapter 8

1 The Social Security program is actually comprised of three subparts: Disability Insurance (13.802), Retirement Insurance (13.803), and Survivors Insurance (13.805). Medicare is comprised of Hospital Insurance (13.773) and Supplemental Medical Insurance (13.774). Medicaid is technically the Medical Assistance program (13.714).

2 See White and Wildavsky, 1989; Wildavsky, 1980.

3 It is worth noting that subsystems are less likely to develop around public policies that are "funded" through cost shifting. In policy areas that are directly implemented by government agencies, the agencies provide a daily opportunity for subsystem actors to shape the implementation of policies. Funding through cost shifting often removes federal agencies from direct participation in policy implementation. Also, funding through cost shifting removes periodic congressional reauthorization of the mandate or an appropriation that covers the full cost involved in the implementation of the policy. In directly funded policy areas, committee hearings, markup sessions, floor debate, and conference reports are setting in which interest groups and other subsystem actors can mobilize their resources to influence policy. In essence, cost shifting bypasses the decision-making loop where subsystems thrive.

Bibliography

Aldrich, John, and Charles Cnudde. 1977. "Probing the Bounds of Conventional Wisdom: A Comparison of Regression, Probit and Discriminant Function Analysis." *American Journal of Political Science* 34:578–608.

Anagnoson, Theodore. 1982. "Federal Grant Agencies and Congressional Election Campaigns." *American Journal of Political Science* 26:547–61.

Anagnoson, J. Theodore. 1983. "Bureaucratic Reactions to Political Pressures: Can a Grant Agency 'Manage' Its Political Environment?" *Administration and Society* 15 (May):97–118.

Anton, Thomas. 1983. "The Regional Distribution of Federal Expenditures, 1970–1980." *National Tax Journal* 36:429–42.

Anton, Thomas J. 1989. *American Federalism and Public Policy: How the System Works*. New York: Random House, pp. 82–99.

Anton, Thomas J., J. P. Cawley, and K. L. Kramer. 1980. *Moving Money*. Cambridge, MA: Oelgeschlager, Gunn & Hain.

Arnold, R. Douglas. 1979. *Congress and the Bureaucracy: A Theory of Influence*. New Haven, CT: Yale University Press.

Arnold, R. Douglas. 1990. *The Logic of Congressional Action*. New Haven, CT: Yale University Press.

Baron, David P. 1989. "Bargaining in Legislatures." *American Journal of Political Science* 83:1181–1206.

Barry, Brian. 1965. *Political Argument*. New York: Humanities Press.

Baumgartner, Frank A., and Bryan D. Jones. 1993. *Agendas and Instability in American Politics*. Chicago: University of Chicago Press.

Beck, M. 1976. "The Expanding Public Sector: Some Contrary Evidence." *National Tax Journal* 57:15–26.

Berry, Jeffrey. 1989. "Subgovernments, Issue Networks and Political Conflict." In *Remaking American Politics*, ed. R. Harris and S. Milkis, pp. 239–260. Boulder, CO: Westview.

Berry, W. D., and D. Lowery. 1987. *Understanding United States Government Growth: An Empirical Analysis of the Postwar Era*. New York: Praeger.

Bickers, Kenneth. 1991. "The Programmatic Expansion of the U.S. Government." *Western Political Quarterly* 45:891–914.

Bickers, Kenneth, and Robert Stein. 1991. *Federal Domestic Outlays, 1983–1990: Data Book*. Armonk, NY: M. E. Sharpe.

Borcherding, T. E. 1977. "The Sources of Growth of Public Expenditures in the United States, 1902–70." In *Budgets and Bureaucrats: The Sources of Govern-*

219

ment Growth, ed. T. E. Borcherding, pp. 45–70. Durham, NC: Duke University Press.

Brady, David. 1988. *Critical Elections and Congressional Policymaking.* Stanford, CA: Stanford University Press.

Brady, David, Joseph Cooper, and Patricia Hurley. 1979. "The Decline of Party in the U.S. House of Representatives, 1887–1968." *Legislative Studies Quarterly* 4:381–407.

Browning, Robert X. 1986. *Politics and Social Welfare Policy in the United States.* Knoxville: University of Tennessee Press.

Buchanan, J. M., and G. Tullock. 1962. *The Calculus of Consent.* Ann Arbor: University of Michigan Press.

Bullock, Charles S., III, and Burdett Loomis. 1985. "The Changing Congressional Career." In *Congress Reconsidered,* 3d ed., ed. L. Dodd and B. Oppenheimer, pp. 65–86. Washington, DC: Congressional Quarterly Press.

Cain, Bruce, John Ferejohn, and Morris Fiorina. 1987. *The Personal Vote: Constituency Service and Electoral Independence.* Cambridge, MA: Harvard University Press.

Cameron, David R. 1978. "The Expansion of the Public Economy: A Comparative Analysis." *American Political Science Review* 72:1243–61.

Carlton, Ralph, Timothy Russell, and Richard Winters. 1980. "Distributive Benefits, Congressional Support, and Agency Growth: The Cases of the National Endowments for the Arts and Humanities." In *Political Benefits,* ed. Barry Rundquist, pp. 93–116. Lexington, MA: Lexington Books.

Cater, Douglas. 1964. *Power in Washington.* New York: Vintage Press.

Center for Political Studies. 1988. *National Election Study.* Ann Arbor, Mich.: Interuniversity Consortium for Political and Social Research.

Chappell, Henry. 1982. "Campaign Contributions and Congressional Voting: A Simultaneous Probit-Tobit Model." *Review of Economics and Statistics* 62:77–83.

Chubb, John, and P. Peterson. 1985. *New Directions in American Politics.* Washington, DC: Brookings Institution.

Clubb, Jerome, and Santa A. Traugott. 1988. "Partisan Cleavage and Cohesion in the House of Representatives, 1861–1974." *Journal of Interdisciplinary History* 8 (Winter):375–401.

Cohen, Jeffrey. 1986. "Political Control of the Independent Regulatory Commissions: A Comparative Perspective." Paper presented at the annual meeting of the American Political Science Association, Washington, DC.

Collie, Melissa P. 1988a. "The Legislative and Distributive Policy Making in Formal Perspective." *Legislative Studies Quarterly* 13:427–58.

Collie, Melissa P. 1988b. "Universalism and the Parties in the U.S. House of Representatives." *American Journal of Political Science* 32:865–83.

Conlan, Timothy. 1988. *New Federalism: Intergovernmental Reform from Nixon to Reagan.* Washington, DC: Brookings Institution.

Cooper, Joseph, and David Brady. 1981. "Institutional Context and Leadership Style: The House from Cannon to Rayburn." *American Political Science Review* 75:411–25.

Cronin, Thomas E. 1975. *The State of the Presidency.* Boston: Little, Brown.

Deering, Christopher, and Steven Smith. 1985. "Subcommittees in Congress." In *Congress Reconsidered,* 3d ed., ed. L. Dodd and B. Oppenheimer, pp. 189–210. Washington, DC: Congressional Quarterly Press.

Denzau, Arthur T., and Michael C. Munger. 1986. "Legislators and Interest

Groups: How Unorganized Interests Get Represented." *American Political Science Review* 80:89–107.

Dodd, Lawrence C., and Richard L. Schott. 1979. *Congress and the Administrative State.* New York: John Wiley and Sons.

Ellwood, J. W., ed. 1982. *Reductions in U.S. Domestic Spending.* New Brunswick, NJ: Transaction.

Erikson, Robert S. 1976. "Is There Such a Thing as a Safe Seat?" *Polity* 8:623–32.

Evans, Diana. 1986. "PAC Contributions and Roll-Call Voting: Conditional Power." In *Interest Group Politics,* 2d ed., ed. Allan J. Cigler and Burdett A. Loomis, pp. 114–32. Washington, DC: Congressional Quarterly Press.

Executive Office of the President, Office of Management and Budget. *Appendix to the Budget of the United States Government.* Various years.

Feldman, Paul, and James Jondrow. 1984. "Congressional Elections and Local Federal Spending." *American Journal of Political Science* 28:147–64.

Fenno, Richard F., Jr. 1973. *Congressmen in Committees.* Boston: Little, Brown.

Ferejohn, John A. 1974. *Pork Barrel Politics: Rivers and Harbors Legislation, 1947–1968.* Stanford, CA: Stanford University Press.

Ferejohn, John A. 1977. "On the Decline of Competition in Congressional Elections." *American Political Science Review* 71:166–76.

Ferejohn, John A., Morris P. Fiorina, and Richard D. McKelvey. 1987. "Sophisticated Voting and Agenda Independence in the Distributive Politics Setting." *American Journal of Political Science* 31:169–93.

Fiorina, Morris P. 1977. *Congress: Keystone of the Washington Establishment.* New Haven, CT: Yale University Press.

Fiorina, Morris P. 1978. "Economic Retrospective Voting in American National Elections." *American Journal of Political Science* 22:426–43.

Fiorina, Morris P. 1981a. "Some Problems in Studying the Effects of Resource Allocation in Congressional Elections." *American Journal of Political Science* 25:543–68.

Fiorina, Morris P. 1981b. "Universalism, Reciprocity, and Distributive Policymaking in Majority Rule Institutions." In *Research in Public Policy Analysis and Management,* vol. 1, ed. John Crecine, pp. 35–59. Greenwich, CT: JAI Press.

Fiorina, Morris P. 1989. *Congress: Keystone of the Washington Establishment.* 2d ed. New Haven, CT: Yale University Press.

Freeman, J. Lieper. 1965. *The Political Process.* New York: Random House.

Frendreis, John, and Richard Waterman. 1985. "PAC Contributions and Legislative Behavior: Senate Voting on Trucking Deregulation." *Social Science Quarterly* 66 (June):401–12.

Froman, Lewis. 1968. "The Categorization of Policy Contents." In *Political Science and Public Policy,* ed. A. Ranney, pp. 12–37. Chicago: Markham.

Goodsell, Charles. 1983. *The Case for Bureaucracy.* Chatham, NJ: Chatham House.

Goss, Carol. 1972. "Military Committee Membership and Defense Related Benefits in the House of Representatives." *Western Political Quarterly* 25:215–33.

Gramlich, Edward. 1977. "Intergovernmental Grants: A Review of the Empirical Literature." In *The Political Economy of Fiscal Federalism,* ed. Wallace Oates, pp. 219–41. Lexington, MA: D. C. Heath.

Grenzke, Janet M. 1988. "Comparing Contributions to U.S. House Members from Outside Their Districts." *Legislative Studies Quarterly* 13:83–103.

Grenzke, Janet M. 1989a. "Shopping in the Congressional Supermarket: The Currency Is Complex." *American Journal of Political Science* 33:1–24.

Bibliography

Grenzke, Janet M. 1989b. "Candidate Attributes and PAC Contributions." *Western Political Quarterly* 42:245–64.

Hall, Richard, and Frank Wayman. 1990. "Buying Time: Moneyed Interests and the Mobilization of Bias in Congressional Committees." *American Political Science Review* 84:797–820.

Hamm, Keith E. 1983. "Patterns of Influence among Committees, Agencies, and Interest Groups." *Legislative Studies Quarterly* 8:379–426.

Hamman, John A. 1993. "Universalism, Program Development, and the Distribution of Federal Assistance." *Legislative Studies Quarterly* 17:553–68.

Hammond, Susan Webb. 1991. "Congressional Caucuses and Party Leaders in the House of Representatives." *Political Science Quarterly* 106:277–94.

Hayes, M. T. 1978. "The Semi-Sovereign Pressure Groups: A Critique of Current Theory and an Alternative Typology." *Journal of Politics* 40:134–61.

Heclo, Hugh. 1978. "Issue Networks and the Executive Establishment." In *The New American Political System*, ed. Anthony King, pp. 87–124. Washington, DC: American Enterprise Institute.

Hird, John. 1990. "Superfund Expenditures and Cleanup Priorities: Distributive Politics or the Public Interest?" *Journal of Policy Analysis and Management* 9:455–83.

Huntington, Samuel P. 1952. "The Marasmus of the ICC." *Yale Law Journal* 61 (April):467–509.

Jacobson, Gary C. 1978. "The Effects of Campaign Spending in Congressional Elections." *American Political Science Review* 72:469–91.

Jacobson, Gary C. 1980. *Money in Congressional Elections*. New Haven, CT: Yale University Press.

Jenkins-Smith, Hank, Gilbert St. Clair, and Brian Woods. 1991. "Explaining Change in Policy Subsystems: Analysis of Coalition Stability and Defection over Time." *American Journal of Political Science* 35:851–80.

Johannes, John R. 1984. *To Serve the People: Congress and Constituency Service*. Lincoln: University of Nebraska Press.

Johannes, John R., and John C. McAdams. 1981. "The Congressional Incumbency Effect: Is It Casework, Policy Compatibility, or Something Else?" *American Journal of Political Science* 25:512–42.

Jones, Charles O. 1981. "House Leadership in an Age of Reform." In *Understanding Congress*, ed. F. H. Mackaman, pp. 11–27. Washington, DC: Congressional Quarterly Press.

Kau, James B., and Paul H. Rubin. 1982. *Congressmen, Constituents, and Contributors: Determinants of Roll Call Voting in the House of Representatives*. Boston: Martinus Nijhoff.

Kelman, Steven. 1987. *Making Public Policy: A Hopeful View of American Government*. New York: Basic Books.

Kinder, Donald R., and D. Roderick Kiewiet. 1979. "Economic Discontent and Political Behavior: The Role of Personal Grievances and Collective Economic Judgements in Congressional Voting." *American Journal of Political Science* 23:495–527.

Kingdon, John W. 1984. *Agendas, Alternatives, and Public Policies*. Boston. Little, Brown.

Klein, Rudolf. 1985. "Public Expenditures in an Inflationary World." In *The Politics of Inflation and Economic Stagnation*, ed. L. N. Lindberg and C. S. Maier, pp. 196–223. Washington, DC: Brookings Institution.

Bibliography

Krehbiel, Keith. 1991. *Information and Legislative Organization.* Ann Arbor: University of Michigan Press.

Larkey, P. D., C. Stolp, and M. Winer. 1981. "Theorizing about the Growth of Government: A Research Assessment." *Journal of Public Policy* 1:157–220.

Lewis-Beck, M. S., and T. W. Rice. 1985. "Government Growth in the United States." *Journal of Politics* 47:2–30.

Lindblom, Charles E. "Still Muddling, Not Yet Through." *Public Administration Review* 40(1979):517–26.

Lowi, Theodore J. 1964. "American Business, Public Policy, Case Studies, and Political Theory." *World Politics* 15:677–715.

Lowi, Theodore J. 1969. *The End of Liberalism: Ideology, Policy, and the Crisis of Public Authority.* New York: Norton.

Lowi, Theodore J. 1972. "Four Systems of Policy, Politics and Choice." *Public Administration Review* 32:298–310.

Lowi, Theodore J. 1979. *The End of Liberalism: The Second Republic of the United States.* 2d ed. New York: Norton.

Lybeck, Johan A. 1988. "Comparing Government Growth Rates: The Non-Institutional vs. the Institutional Approach." In *Explaining the Growth of Government,* ed. J. A. Lybeck and M. Henrekson, pp. 29–47. Amsterdam: North-Holland.

Lynn, Laurence E., Jr. 1984. "The Reagan Administration and the Renitent Bureaucracy." In *The Reagan Presidency and the Governing of America,* ed. Lester M. Salamon and Michael S. Lund, pp. 339–70. Washington, DC: Urban Institute Press.

Maass, Arthur. 1951. *Muddy Waters: The Army Engineers and the Nation's Rivers.* Cambridge, MA: Harvard University Press.

Makinson, Larry. 1992. *Open Secrets: The Encyclopedia of Congressional Money and Politics.* Washington, DC: Congressional Quarterly Press.

Manley, John F. 1970. *The Politics of Finance: The House Committee on Ways and Means.* Boston: Little, Brown.

Mann, Thomas E., and Norman Ornstein. 1992. *Renewing Congress.* Washington, DC: American Enterprise Institute for Public Policy Research and Brookings Institution.

Mayhew, David. 1974. *Congress: The Electoral Connection.* New Haven, CT: Yale University Press.

McConnell, Grant. 1966. *Private Power and American Democracy.* New York: Alfred Knopf.

McCool, Daniel. 1990. "Subgovernments as Determinants of Political Viability." *Political Science Quarterly* 105:269–93.

Meier, Kenneth J. 1985. *Regulation: Politics, Bureaucracy, and Economics.* New York: St. Martin's Press.

Miller, Warren E. 1988. "American National Election Study, 1988: Pre- and Post-Election Survey." 9196 National Science Foundation.

Miller, Warren E., Donald R. Kinder, Steven J. Rosenstone, and the National Election Studies. 1990. "American National Election Study, 1990: Post-Election Survey." 09548 National Science Foundation.

Moneypenny, Phillip. 1958. *The Impact of Federal Grants in Illinois.* Urbana: University of Illinois.

Moneypenny, Phillip. 1960. "Federal Grants-in-Aid to State Governments: A Political Analysis." *National Tax Journal* 13:1–16.

Nathan, Richard, and Fred Doolittle. 1987. *Reagan and the States*. Princeton, NJ: Princeton University Press.

Niou, Emerson, and Peter Ordeshook. 1985. "Universalism in Congress." *American Journal of Political Science* 29:246–90.

Niskanen, W. A. 1971. *Bureaucracy and Representative Government*. Chicago: Aldine and Atherton.

Office of the President. 1980. *U.S. Government Manual*. Washington, DC: U.S. Government Printing Office.

Olson, Mancur. 1965. *The Logic of Collective Action*. Cambridge, MA: Harvard University Press.

Owens, John R., and Larry L. Wade. 1984. "Federal Spending in Congressional Districts." *Western Political Quarterly* 37:404–23.

Palmer, John L., and Isabell V. Sawhill, eds. 1984. *The Reagan Record*. Cambridge, MA: Ballinger Press.

Parker, Glenn. 1986. *Homeward School: Explaining Changes in Congressional Behavior*. Pittsburgh: University of Pittsburgh Press.

Pertschuk, Michael. 1982. *Revolt against Regulation*. Berkeley: University of California Press.

Plott, Charles. 1968. "Some Organizational Influences on Urban Renewal Decisions." *American Economic Review* 58:306–11.

Ray, Bruce. 1980. "Congressional Losers in the U.S. Federal Spending Process." *Legislative Studies Quarterly* 3:359–72.

Rich, Michael. 1989. "Distributive Politics and the Allocation of Federal Grants." *American Political Science Review* 83:193–213.

Ripley, Randall B. 1987. *Policy Implementation and Bureaucracy*. Chicago: Dorsey Press.

Ripley, Randall B., and Grace A. Franklin. 1976. *Congress, the Bureaucracy, and Public Policy*. Homewood, IL: Dorsey Press.

Ripley, Randall B., and Grace A. Franklin. 1984. *Congress, the Bureaucracy, and Public Policy*. 3d ed. Pacific Grove, CA: Brooks Cole.

Ripley, Randall B., and Grace A. Franklin. 1991. *Congress, the Bureaucracy, and Public Policy*. 5th ed. Pacific Grove, CA: Brooks Cole.

Ritt, Leonard. 1976. "Committee Position, Seniority and the Distribution of Government Expenditures." *Public Policy* 24:463–89.

Rose, Richard. 1984. "The Programme Approach to the Growth of Government." *British Journal of Political Science* 15:1–28.

Rubin, Irene S. 1985. *Shrinking the Federal Government: The Effect of Cutbacks on Five Federal Agencies*. New York: Longman Press.

Rundquist, Barry. 1973. "Congressional Influences on the Distribution of Prime Military Contracts." Ph.D. dissertation, Stanford University.

Runquist, Barry, and David Griffith. 1976. "An Interrupted Time-Series Test of the Distributive Theory of Military Policy-Making." *Western Politial Quarterly* 24:620–6.

Sabatier, Paul, and Neil Pelkey. 1987. "Incorporating Multiple Actors and Guidance Instruments into Models of Regulatory Policymaking: An Advocacy Coalition Framework." *Administration and Society* 19(August):236–63.

Sabato, Larry J. 1985. *PAC Power: Inside the World of Political Action Committees*. New York: Norton.

Salisbury, Robert. 1968. "The Analysis of Public Policy: A Search for Theories and Roles." In *Political Science and Public Policy*, ed. A. Ranney, pp. 11–37. Chicago: Markham.

Bibliography

Salisbury, Robert, John P. Heinz, Edward O. Laumann, and Robert L. Nelson. 1987. "Who Works with Whom: Interest Group Alliances and Opposition." *American Political Science Review* 81:1217–34.

Schattschneider, E. E. 1935. *Politics, Pressure and the Tariff.* Englewood Cliffs, NJ: Prentice-Hall.

Schattschneider, E. E. 1960. *The Semisovereign People: A Realist's View of Democracy in America.* Hinsdale, IL: Dryden Press.

Schlozman, Kay Lehman, and John T. Tierney. 1986. *Organized Interests and American Democracy.* New York: Harper and Row.

Schwarz, John E. 1988. *America's Hidden Success: A Reassessment of Public Policy from Kennedy to Reagan.* New York: Norton.

Shepsle, Kenneth A. 1979. "Institutional Arrangements and Equilibrium in Multidimensional Voting Models." *American Journal of Political Science* 23:27–59.

Shepsle, Kenneth A., and Barry Weingast. 1981. "Political Preferences for the Pork Barrel: A Generalization." *American Journal of Political Science* 25:96–111.

Silberman, Jonathan, and Garey C. Durden. 1976. "Determining Legislative Preferences on the Minimum Wage: An Economic Approach." *Journal of Political Economy* 84:317–29.

Sinclair, Barbara. 1981. "The Speaker's Task Force in the Post-Reform House of Representatives." *American Political Science Review* 68:667–81.

Skowronek, Stephen. 1982. *Building a New American State: The Expansion of National Administrative Capacities, 1877–1920.* Cambridge: Cambridge University Press.

Sorauf, Frank J. 1992. *Inside Campaign Finance: Myths and Realities.* New Haven: Yale University Press.

Sorauf, Frank J. 1985. "Who's in Charge? Accountability in Political Action Committees." *Political Science Quarterly* 99:591–614.

Stein, Robert M. 1979. "Federal Categorical Aid: Equalization and the Application Process." *Western Political Quarterly* 32:396–409.

Stein, Robert M. 1981. "The Allocation of Federal Aid Monies: The Synthesis of a Demand-Side and Supply-Side Explanations." *American Political Science Review* 75:334–43.

Stein, Robert M. 1982. "Municipal Public Employment: An Intergovernmental Perspective." *American Journal of Political Science* 26:637–57.

Stein, Robert M. 1984. "Structural Characteristics of Federal Aid." *Research in Urban Economics* (fall)167–86.

Stein, Robert M., and Kenneth N. Bickers. 1994. "Universalism and the Electoral Connection: A Test and Some Doubts." *Political Research Quarterly* 47:295–317.

Stockman, David A. 1986. *The Triumph of Politics: How the Reagan Revolution Failed.* New York: Harper and Row.

Tarschys, Daniel. 1975. "The Growth of Public Expenditures: Nine Modes of Explanation." *Scandinavian Political Studies* 10:9–31.

Truman, David. 1951. *The Governmental Process.* New York: Alfred Knopf.

U.S. Bureau of the Census. Various years. *Statistical Abstract of the United States.* Washington, DC: U.S. Government Printing Office.

U.S. Department of Commerce, Bureau of the Census. Dated Years. *Federal Assistance Awards Data System* (machine readable data tape). Washington, DC.

U.S. General Accounting Office. "Line Item Veto: Estimating Potential Savings." Report to the Congressional Committees. 1992.

U.S. General Services Administration. Dated Years. *Catalog of Federal Domestic Assistance*. Washington, DC: U.S. Government Printing Office.

Watson, Richard. 1993. *Presidential Vetos and Public Policy*. Lawrence: University of Kansas Press.

Wayman, Frank W. 1985. "Arms Control and Strategic Arms Voting in the U.S. Senate: Patterns of Change, 1967–1983." *Journal of Conflict Resolution* 29:225–51.

Weingast, Barry. 1979. "A Rational Choice Perspective on Congressional Norms." *American Journal of Political Science* 23:245–63.

Weingast, Barry, Kenneth Shepsle, and Christopher Johnsen. 1981. "The Political Economy of Benefits and Costs: A Neoclassical Approach to Distributive Politics." *Journal of Political Economy* 89:642–64.

Welch, William P. 1982. "Campaign Contributions and Legislative Voting: Milk Money and Dairy Price Supports." *Western Political Quarterly* 35:267–76.

White, Joseph, and Aaron Wildavsky. 1989. *The Deficit and the Public Interest: The Search for Responsible Budgeting in the 1980s*. Berkeley: University of California Press.

Wildavsky, Aaron. 1980. *How to Limit Government Spending: Or How a Constitutional Amendment Tying Public Spending to Economic Growth Will Decrease Taxes and Lessen Inflation*. Berkeley: University of California Press.

Will, George F. 1992. *Restoration: Congress, Term Limits and the Recovery of Deliberative Democracy*. New York: Free Press.

Wilson, Rick K. 1986. "An Empirical Test of Preferences for the Political Pork Barrel: District Level Appropriations for River and Harbor Legislation, 1899–1913." *American Journal of Political Science* 30:621–49.

Witte, John F. 1985. *The Politics and Development of the Federal Income Tax*. Madison: University of Wisconsin Press.

Wright, Deil. 1988. *Understanding Intergovernmental Relations*. 3d ed. Monterey, CA: Brooks Cole.

Wright, John R. 1985. "PACs, Contributions, and Roll Calls: An Organizational Perspective." *American Political Science Review* 79:400–14.

Wright, John R. 1989. "PAC Contributions, Lobbying and Representation." *Journal of Politics* 51:813–29.

Wright, John R. 1990. "Contributions, Lobbying and Committee Voting in the U.S. House of Representatives." *American Political Science Review* 84:417–37.

Index

accountability
  line-item veto proposal related to, 147
  of policy subsystems, 142–3
  term limits to increase legislator, 147–8
actors
  in agencies with threats to funding, 72–89
  around program portfolios, 4–5
  in policy subsystems, 5–10, 22, 51–61, 142
  in policy subsystems with campaign reform, 149
  trade-off strategies, 59–61
agencies
  as actors in policy subsystems, 5–7, 48–50
  discretion in entitlement programs, 122
  with distributive program portfolios, 16, 24–9, 187–9
  in four federal cabinet departments, 190–2
  with redistributive program portfolios, 16, 24–7
  resistance to Reagan program cuts, 75
  responsibility for programs, 25, 27–8
  role in shaping homogeneous recipient population, 53–5
  specialization of programs within, 28
  strategies with threats to funding, 72–89
  threatened and nonthreatened early in Reagan administration, 78–9
Aircraft Owners' and Pilots Association, 3–4
Alaska Native Claims Settlement Act (1987–8), 100, 106
Anagnoson, Theodore, 33, 52, 119, 121, 122, 123
Andrews, Mike, 3
Anton, Thomas, 59
appropriations allocation, 25–6

Arnold, R. Douglas, 5, 33, 98, 119, 123
awards, discretionary assistance, 122
  See also benefit distribution
  in analysis of electoral vulnerability, 129–36
  volume and dollar size of, 127–8
awards, entitlement, 124

balanced budget amendment, 144
Baron, David P., 30
Barry, Brian, 8
Baumgartner, Frank A., 5
beneficiaries. See recipients, program
benefit distribution
  See also cost–benefit distribution issues
  broad and narrow conflictual, 102t, 112–13, 116
  broad and narrow consensual, 102t, 112–13, 116
  increasing, 61
benefits
  See also recurrence of benefits
  from bundling nonrecurring programs, 59
  with narrow and recurring program coverage, 57–8
  from nonrecurring district coverage, 58–9
  PAC coalition strategies with broad or narrow distribution, 96–8
  PAC compensation for narrow distributive programs, 95–6
Berry, Jeffrey, 5, 47, 48
Bickers, Kenneth, 18, 34, 36, 52, 70, 122, 140, 157
Boyer, Phil, 3
Brady, David, 34
Browning, Robert X., 154
Buchanan, James M., 7–8
Buckley v. Valeo (1976), 91

budget deficit reform proposal, 144–6
Bullock, Charles S. III, 34
bundling, program
　analysis of, 63
　to make program portfolios, 4
　strategy, 34–5, 58–9
Bush administration, 20

campaign contributions, 91
　See also PAC contributions
campaign finance reform, 148–9
Carlton, Ralph, 35
Catalog of Federal Domestic Assistance
　(CFDA), 18, 20, 36, 62, 76, 153–6
Cater, Douglas, 5, 47
Cawley, J. P., 59
Chappell, Henry, 93
Chubb, John, 70
Clean Water Reauthorization Act (1987–
　8), 100, 111, 112–13
Clinton, Bill
　budgetary proposal, 3–4
　health care proposal, 146
Clubb, Jerome, 34
coalitions
　See also interest group coalitions
　formation of legislative, 30–1
　policy subsystem strategies to build, 51–
　61
　universalization of legislative, 33
Cohen, Jeffrey, 47
collective action
　circumstances for reduction of prob-
　lems, 61
　costs of, 55
　interest groups' problems of, 51
　policy subsystem strategy for problems
　of, 52–5
　relation to district coverage, 65
Collie, Melissa P., 31
committees, congressional
　jurisdiction for policy subsystems, 24
conflict over programs, 95
Congress
　influence over awards distribution, 122
　influence over executive branch agen-
　cies, 142
　proposal to enhance efficiency and effec-
　tiveness, 149–50
　symbiotic relationship with agencies, 49
congressional districts
　receiving outlays from distributive pro-
　gram portfolios (1983–90), 40–2
　receiving outlays from distributive pro-
　grams (1983–90), 37–9
Conlan, Timothy, 20, 70
consensus

See also benefit distribution
　building, 5
　policy, 95–6
constituents
　awareness and actions in analysis of
　awards on electoral vulnerability,
　131–6
　awareness of district-level awards and
　benefits, 124–5
　lobbying by, 58–9
　as recipients of entitlements, 146–7
　contributions. *See* campaign contributions;
　PAC contributions
Cooper, Joseph, 34
cooperation
　of actors across subsystems, 61
　between legislators and interest groups,
　32
cost–benefit distribution issues, 98
cost shifting, 146
Cronin, Thomas E., 142

data sources
　See also Federal Assistance Awards Data
　System; *National Election Study*
　analysis of formation of legislative coali-
　tions, 36
　Catalog of Federal Domestic Assistance
　(CFDA), 18, 20, 36, 62, 153–6
　for electoral connection analysis, 127,
　129
　policy subsystem model, 62–4
　for policy subsystem response analysis,
　76–7
Deering, Christopher, 34
defense spending, 145–6
Del Balzo, Joseph, 4
Denzau, Arthur T., 50
departments, executive
　and distributive policy agencies, 187–9
　federal agencies in four, 190–2
discretionary programs
　growth of financial assistance programs,
　139–40
　outlays as proportion of total budget,
　145
distributive programs
　See also redistributive programs
　with broad and narrow benefits, 100
　broad and recurring district coverage,
　57f, 58
　congressional districts receiving outlays
　(1983–90), 37–9
　cuts during 1980s, 16
　elimination during Republican admin-
　istrations, 20–1
　growth of, 10, 16, 20–1, 30

limits on universal distribution, 33
narrow and broad nonrecurring
  coverage, 58–9
opportunities for political advantage, 16
provision of narrow benefits, 34
role of, 15–16
spending (1971–90), 18–20, 22
with and without agency discretion, 22–
  3
district coverage
differing levels of, 64–9
in maximization of political support, 61
recurring, 63
Dodd, Lawrence C., 142
Doolittle, Fred, 70
Durden, Garey C., 93

efficacy of interest groups, 7
electoral connection
between benefits and votes, 43
electoral margins, 129–30
Ellwood, J. W., 70
entitlement programs
  See also redistributive programs
awards to individuals under, 124
congressional allocation formula for,
  122
proposals to cut, 145
as source of spending growth, 139–40
Erikson, Robert S., 120
Evans, Diana, 93

Family Welfare Reform Act (1987–8),
  100, 106–7, 114
Federal Assistance Awards Data System
  (FAADS), 36, 62, 76, 127, 157–60
Federal Assistance Programs Retrieval Sys-
  tems (FAPRS), 49
Federal Aviation Administration, 3–4
Federal Election Campaign Act amend-
  ments (1974), 91
Feldman, Paul, 120
Fenno, Richard F., Jr., 120
Ferejohn, John A., 5, 17, 34, 120, 123
Fiorina, Morris P., 8, 48, 118, 119, 120,
  121
Franklin, Grace A., 17, 18, 34
Freeman, J. Lieper, 5, 47
Frendreis, John, 93
Froman, Lewis, 18

General Revenue Sharing, 58
Goodsell, Charles, 8
Goss, Carol, 123
Gramlich, Edward, 34, 52
Gramm–Rudman deficit reduction agree-
  ment, 70

Grenzke, Janet M., 92
Griffith, David, 119, 120, 123

Hall, Richard, 50, 91, 94
Hamm, Keith E., 47, 48
Hamman, John A., 52, 66
Hammond, Susan Webb, 34
Hayes, M. T., 18
Heclo, Hugh, 5, 47, 48
Hird, John, 123
homogeneity, recipient
at different levels of district coverage,
  65–6
within programs, 53–5, 62
Housing and Community Development
  Reauthorization Act (1987–8), 100,
  110–11
Huntington, Samuel P., 47
Hurley, Patrick, 34

Immigration and Nationality Extension
  and Reauthorization Act (1986–7),
  100, 109–10
incentives
of agencies in policy subsystems, 50
of legislator to support policy subsystems, 149
policy subsystem, 55–6
for program bundling, 58
incumbents
advantages with policy subsystems,
  143–4
in analysis of effect of awards on electoral vulnerability, 130–6
campaign contributions to, 91
vulnerable, 147–8
institutional reform proposals, 149–50
interest group coalitions
around distributive policy issues, 93–4
expected strategies, 96–8
interest groups
as actors in policy subsystems, 5–7, 48,
  50–1
mobilization by policy subsystems, 53–
  61
relationship to agencies in policy subsystem, 49–51
response to demands of, 28
role in aggregation of constituent preferences, 32
strategy for allocation of campaign resources, 92
iron triangles, 5, 47

Jacobson, Gary C., 19, 148
Jenkins-Smith, Hank, 47
Johannes, John R., 48

Johnsen, Christopher, 30, 35
Jondrow, James, 120
Jones, Bryan D., 5
Jones, Charles O., 34

Kau, James B., 93
Kelman, Steven, 8–9
Kiewiet, D. Roderick, 121
Kinder, Donald R., 121
Kingdon, John W., 47
Kramer, K. L., 59
Krehbiel, Keith, 150

Legal Advocacy and Protective Services for
    the Mentally Ill Act (1986–7), 100,
    105–6
legislation
    interest group support, 94–5
legislators
    See also incumbents
    as actors in policy subsystems, 5–7, 48–
    9
    conditions for dependence on PACs,
    147–8
    influence on program benefit distribu-
    tion, 123
    local-level political support, 124
    relations with interest groups, 32, 48–
    51, 90
    response to narrow interest goups, 98
    term limit proposal to increase account-
    ability, 147–8
Lindblom, Charles, 142–3
line-item veto, 146–7
logrolls, legislative
    test of organization by program port-
    folios, 37–40
Loomis, Burdett, 34
Lowi, Theodore J., 5, 9, 18, 47, 54
Lynn, Laurence E., Jr., 75

Maass, Arthur, 34
McConnell, Grant, 5, 47
McCool, Daniel, 47
Madison, Dolly McKenna, 3
Makinson, Larry, 129, 212–13
Manley, John F., 35
Mann, Thomas E., 149
Mayhew, David, 5, 8, 30, 35, 118
Meier, Kenneth J., 47
mobilization
    by interest groups at local level, 50
    of interest group support by policy sub-
    systems, 52–5
Munger, Michael C., 50

Nathan, Richard, 70

National Election Study, 129, 212–13
Niou, Emerson, 30
Nixon administration, 20

Olson, Mancur, 51
Ordeshook, Peter, 30
Ornstein, Norman, 149
outlays
    discretionary programs proportion of,
    145
    from distributive programs to congres-
    sional districts, 37–43
    of threatened and nonthreatened agen-
    cies, 83, 85
Owens, John R., 34, 120, 121

PAC contributions
    analysis of influence on legislator voting
    behavior, 104t, 112–17
    broad and narrow conflictual programs,
    102t, 108–11
    broad and narrow consensual programs,
    102t, 105–8
    patterns, 96–8
    relation to legislator vote choices, 102–5
    variation in influence of, 116–17
PACs
    action variation by type of program
    portfolio, 98–9
    conditions for legislator dependence on,
    147–8
    contribution levels and distribution, 91–
    2
    effect of proposed campaign finance re-
    form on, 148–9
    interest group contributions to, 51
    parent interest groups testifying, 195–
    200
Palmer, John L., 70
Parker, Glenn, 48
Pelkey, Neil, 47
permeability of policy subsystems, 5, 48
Pertschuk, Michael, 37
Peterson, P., 70
Plott, Charles, 35, 123
policy process
    in consensual environment, 113
    focus of balanced budget amendment
    proposal on, 144–6
    interest group pursuit of goals in, 50–1
    models of, 6–10
policy subsystems
    actors in, 5–7, 16, 22
    boundaries of, 24
    definition, components, and function, 4,
    6, 48
    development around new program port-
    folios, 28–9

influence on American politics, 141–4
as iron triangles, 5, 47
levels of growth, 10
maximizing political support, 55–9
myths about, 139–41
as permeable issue networks, 5, 48
program portfolio influence on, 23
with proposed congressional reforms,
   149–50
response to attack, 144–5
shaping of homogeneous recipient population, 53–5
strategies, 51–61
strategies with threats to funding, 72–89
political advantage opportunities, 16
politics
   around distributive programs, 16
   of program portfolios, 72
portfolio diversity index, 77
preferences
   diversity of constituent, 33–4
   interest group aggregation of constitu-
      ent, 32
   legislators' reelection, 48
president
   line-item veto power, 147
price support program bundling, 58
program diversity index, average, 77
program portfolios
   absence of universalized, 69
   actors in, 5
   in analysis of PAC contributions, 99
   appropriation distribution across, 25–6
   bundling, 34–5, 58–9
   circumstances for restructuring, 6
   congressional districts receiving outlays
      from distributive (1983–90), 40–2
   distributive agencies, 25–8
   for distributive and redistributive agen-
      cies, 24–7
   district coverage of, 68–9
   in domestic policy subsystems during
      1980s, 16
   estimates for change in number with
      proposed budget changes, 78, 80–1
   function of, 4
   influence on operation of policy sub-
      systems, 23
   interest group mobilization to support,
      52–3
   methodology for analysis of cutback
      threat response, 77–8
   protection of, 27
   redistributive agencies, 25–8
programs
   See also distributive programs; entitle-
      ment programs; program portfolios;

recipients, program; redistributive
   programs
   by agency and policy type, 161–86
   bundled into portfolios, 34–5, 58–9
   delegation to new agencies, 28
   distributive and redistributive U.S.
      (1971–90), 22–3
   distributive benefits, 99
   financial assistance, 193–5
   narrow and recurring district coverage,
      56–8
   in policy subsystems, 4

Ray, Bruce, 119, 120, 123
Reagan administration, 18, 20
   analysis of policy subsystem responses,
      74–6
   favored program portfolio budget
      changes, 75
   proposed budgetary changes (FY1983),
      190–2
   spending curtailment, 70
   threatened and nonthreatened agencies
      early in, 78–9
recipients, program
   See also interest groups
   change related to district coverage and
      program portfolio, 67
   creating homogeneous population, 53–
      4, 62
   in discretionary, distributive programs,
      122–3
   effect of agency administration on, 49–
      50
   of entitlements, 146–7
   measure of diversity, 63–4
   subsidies from distributive programs, 17
recurrence of benefits
   relation to program functional specific-
      ity, 66
   as variable in maximizing political sup-
      port, 61–2
   as variable in political support analysis,
      63
redistributive programs
   See also entitlement programs
   eliminated during Republican admin-
      istrations, 20–1
   function of, 17
   spending (1971–90), 18–20, 22
   spending and growth, 10, 15–16
   spending during 1980s, 16
reelection goals, 90–1
Republican administrations, 20–1
Rich, Michael, 121, 122, 123
Ripley, Randall B., 17, 18, 34
Ritt, Leonard, 123

roll call votes
   on public laws with distributive benefits,
      101, 103–4, 201–11
   showing influence of PAC contributions
      on voting behavior, 112–17
Rose, Richard, 16
Rubin, Irene S., 70, 71
Rubin, Paul H., 93
Rundquist, Barry, 35, 119, 120, 123
Russell, Timothy, 35

Sabatier, Paul, 47
Sabato, Larry J., 50, 51, 92
St. Clair, Gilbert, 47
Salisbury, Robert, 18, 93, 101
Sawhill, Isabel V., 70
Schattschneider, E. E., 34, 95
Schlozman, Kay Lehman, 92, 93, 101
Schott, Richard L., 142
Schwarz, John E., 20
Shepsle, Kenneth A., 8, 17, 30, 33, 35,
      143
Silberman, Jonathan, 93
Sinclair, Barbara, 34
Skowronek, Stephen, 142
Small Business Innovation and Research
      Act (1986–7), 100, 107–8, 112
Smith, Steven, 34
Social Security
   Administration, 25, 78
   expenditures, 139, 158
   Reagan administration threat to, 145
Sorauf, Frank, 91, 92
specificity, functional
   effect of changing, 61–2, 66
   of programs in portfolio, 52, 56–7
spending, government
   curtailment, 70
   distributive and redistributive (1971–
      90), 18–22
   for entitlement programs, 139–40
   growth in domestic, 28
   line-item veto proposal to cut, 146–7
spending, legislators, 148
states
   as intermediate agents to implement
      programs, 55
Stein, Robert M., 33, 36, 52, 58, 121,
      122, 157
Stockman, David, 74
Superfund Reauthorization Act (1986–7),
      100, 108–9

taxation, new, 146
term limits proposal, 147–8
Tierney, John T., 92, 93, 101
timing

of awards to discretionary programs,
      122
Traugott, Santa A., 34
Truman, David, 5, 47
Tullock, Gordon, 7–8

U.S. General Accounting Office (GAO),
      147
U.S. House of Representatives
   probit analysis: roll call votes on nine
      public laws, 208–11
   roll call votes on nine public laws, 201–
      7
universalism thesis
   effect of, 143
   motivation for legislators in, 43
   oversimplification by, 43
   presumed advantages of, 30–1
   tests of, 33–4, 37–43
   as unrealistic assumption, 32
universalization
   See also specificity, functional
   achieving program, 55–6
   constraints on program portfolio with,
      56–7
   of PAC contributions, 95
   of programs, 60

Vocational Rehabilitation of the Handi-
      capped Act (1986–7), 100, 108, 112
voter choice, 143–4
votes
   cast for cost–benefit distribution issues,
      98
   cast for other than cost–benefit distribu-
      tion issues, 98
voting behavior, legislative
   on broad and narrow conflictual pro-
      grams, 102t, 112–13, 116
   on broad and narrow consensual pro-
      grams, 102t, 112–13, 116
   effect of PAC contributions on, 92–4
   universalism thesis, 30–2
vulnerability, incumbent, 147–9

Wade, Larry L., 34, 120, 121
Waterman, Richard, 93
Wayman, Frank, 50, 91, 92, 94
Weingast, Barry, 8, 17, 30, 33, 35, 143
Welch, William P., 92
Will, George F., 147
Wilson, Rick K., 35
Winters, Richard, 35
Witte, John F., 35
Woods, Brian, 47
Wright, Deil, 58
Wright, John R., 92, 94